# Manufacturing at Warp Speed

## Optimizing Supply Chain Financial Performance

Includes Simplified Drum-Buffer-Rope

# The St. Lucie Press/APICS Series on Constraints Management

## Series Advisors

| Dr. James F. Cox, III | Thomas B. McMullen, Jr. |
|---|---|
| *University of Georgia* | *McMullen Associates* |
| *Athens, Georgia* | *Weston, Massachusetts* |

## Titles in the Series

**Introduction to the Theory of Constraints (TOC) Management System**
*by Thomas B. McMullen, Jr.*

**Securing the Future:**
**Strategies for Exponential Growth Using the Theory of Constraints**
*by Gerald I. Kendall*

**Project Management in the Fast Lane:**
**Applying the Theory of Constraints**
*by Robert C. Newbold*

**The Constraints Management Handbook**
*by James F. Cox, III and Michael S. Spencer*

**Thinking for a Change:**
**Putting the TOC Thinking Processes to Work**
*by Lisa J. Scheinkopf*

**Management Dilemmas:**
**The Theory of Constraints Approach to**
**Problem Identification and Solutions**
*by Eli Schragenheim*

**Manufacturing at Warp Speed:**
**Optimizing Supply Chain Financial Performance**
*by Eli Schragenheim and H. William Dettmer*

**The Measurement Nightmare:**
**How The Theory of Constraints Can Resolve**
**Conflicting Strategies, Policies, and Measures**
*by Debra Smith*

# Manufacturing at Warp Speed

## Optimizing Supply Chain Financial Performance

Includes Simplified Drum-Buffer-Rope

Eli Schragenheim

H. William Dettmer

The St. Lucie Press/APICS Series on Constraints Management

S$^t$L

**St. Lucie Press**
Boca Raton • London
New York • Washington, D.C.

**APICS**®

**THE EDUCATIONAL SOCIETY
FOR RESOURCE MANAGEMENT**
Alexandria, Virginia

## LIMITED WARRANTY

CRC Press LLC warrants the physical disk(s) enclosed herein to be free of defects in materials and workmanship for a period of thirty days from the date of purchase. If within the warranty period CRC Press LLC receives written notification of defects in materials or workmanship, and such notification is determined by CRC Press LLC to be correct, CRC Press LLC will replace the defective disk(s).

The entire and exclusive liability and remedy for breach of this Limited Warranty shall be limited to replacement of defective disk(s) and shall not include or extend to any claim for or right to cover any other damages, including but not limited to, loss of profit, data, or use of the software, or special, incidental, or consequential damages or other similar claims, even if CRC Press LLC has been specifically advised of the possibility of such damages. In no event will the liability of CRC Press LLC for any damages to you or any other person ever exceed the lower suggested list price or actual price paid for the software, regardless of any form of the claim.

CRC Press LLC specifically disclaims all other warranties, express or implied, including but not limited to, any implied warranty of merchantability or fitness for a particular purpose. Specifically, CRC Press LLC makes no representation or warranty that the software is fit for any particular purpose and any implied warranty of merchantability is limited to the thirty-day duration of the Limited Warranty covering the physical disk(s) only (and not the software) and is otherwise expressly and specifically disclaimed.

Since some states do not allow the exclusion of incidental or consequential damages, or the limitation on how long an implied warranty lasts, some of the above may not apply to you.

**DISCLAIMER OF WARRANTY AND LIMITS OF LIABILITY:** The author(s) of this book have used their best efforts in preparing this material. These efforts include the development, research, and testing of the theories and programs to determine their effectiveness. Neither the author(s) nor the publisher make warranties of any kind, express or implied, with regard to these programs or the documentation contained in this book, including without limitation warranties of merchantability or fitness for a particular purpose. No liability is accepted in any event for any damages, including incidental or consequential damages, lost profits, costs of lost data or program material, or otherwise in connection with or arising out of the furnishing, performance, or use of the programs in this book.

## Library of Congress Cataloging-in-Publication Data

Schragenheim, Eli.
    Manufacturing at warp speed : optimizing supply chain financial performance / by Eli Schragenheim, H. William Dettmer.
        p.  cm. — (APICS constraints management series)
    Includes bibliographical references and index.
    ISBN 1-57444-293-7
    1. Manufacturing costs. 2. Production management. I. Dettmer, H. William. II. Title.
  III. St. Lucie Press/APICS series on constraints management
  TS167 .S36 2000
  658.5—dc21

                                    00-055295
                                      CIP

### Visit our website at www.crcpress.com.

© 2001 by E. Schragenheim and H.W. Dettmer
St. Lucie Press is an imprint of CRC Press LLC

No claim to original U.S. Government works
International Standard Book Number 1-57444-293-7
Library of Congress Card Number 00-055295
Printed in the United States of America    2 3 4 5 6 7 8 9 0
Printed on acid-free paper

# Dedication

To Eliyahu M. Goldratt, profound thinker and educator.

It is better to light a candle than to curse the darkness.

To teach is to learn twice.
— **Joseph Joubert**

Learning usually passes through three stages. In the beginning you learn the right answers. In the second stage you learn the right questions. In the third and final stage you learn which questions are worth asking.

# Contents

## PART II Traditional Drum-Buffer-Rope

## PART III Simplified Drum-Buffer-Rope

## PART IV Optimizing Decisions

# List of Figures

## List of Figures: Appendices

# Preface

What?! *Another* book on production management? Aren't there enough of them in existence already? The volumes that have been written about this topic, properly stacked, could hold back Mississippi River flood waters. Why another? Like most authors, we believe we have something new to say on the subject — and we think that what we have to say is an improvement on the state of the art. But only you can be the judge of that.

This book emphasizes the role of managers in the realm of production management. From our perspective, management is about assuming responsibility for improving the performance of the organization as a whole. This improvement objective is the focus of this book, and the term "improvement" has meaning only in the context of the entire organization. Consequently, we write about how to make manufacturing production faster and more responsive to the needs of the company, which generally means satisfying the market better. But this can't happen in isolation. Companies are whole systems made up of interdependent parts. Besides production, there are marketing and sales, engineering, purchasing, accounting and finance, human resources, safety, quality, and a whole host of other functions that we haven't touched on here. These functions all have one thing in common: They're in the same boat, and they all sink or sail based on how well they work together and support each other. In other words, success in system integration is what separates the winners from the losers. This means that each function in a company must have a holistic view of its part in the entire organization, and a way to manage holistically.

This book offers such a management approach. Its foundation is systems thinking, which sounds very philosophical yet can be so practical. It recognizes the dependent relationships among the functions mentioned above.

Most of the concepts embodied in this management approach have the theory of constraints (TOC) at their roots, a body of knowledge conceived by Eliyahu M. Goldratt over the past 20 years with contributions from others. As you read this book, you'll find some prescriptions that seem to fly in the face of tradition. Telling an emperor he's not wearing any clothes is a dicey proposition. But progress is an exercise in challenging existing paradigms, many of which are founded on cherished assumptions. If we always do what we've always done, we'll always get what we've always gotten. But the authors don't think that should be necessary. And neither do others who have applied the holistic principles of the theory of constraints.

Yet, in spite of the connotation of the term "theory" to practical people, such as the vast majority of the managers in operations, what we offer here has both feet firmly on the ground. Our reasoning is based on common sense. We don't ask you to "believe" or "trust" what we tell you. We challenge existing methods, but there are valid reasons for doing so. We offer a new paradigm and methods substantiated by logic, followed by an opportunity to test those methods on a wide-scope computer simulation. While this simulation isn't an exact replica of a real shop floor, it's close enough to validate that what doesn't work in the simulation won't work in reality. And an argument (though not a proof) can be made that what works within the simulation may work in reality as well. We do our best to exercise care and good common sense in showing why one method works and another does not.

Consider the possibilities. A recent survey of published results by manufacturing and service companies that have applied constraint management methods effectively shows:*

- A mean reduction in lead times of 70%
- A mean reduction in manufacturing cycle times of 65%
- A mean improvement in due-date performance of 44%
- Mean inventory reductions of 49 percent
- A mean combined financial improvement (revenue, throughput, profit) of 76%

The first four indicators pertain strictly to manufacturing. A skeptical reader might claim that these indicators are not much more than *opportunities* to improve the organization as a whole — that those changes aren't enough alone to produce increases in bottom line performance. And this

---

* *Source*: Mabin, Victoria J. and Steven J. Balderstone, *The World of the Theory of Constraints: A Review of the International Literature*, St. Lucie Press, Boca Raton, FL, 2000.

would be absolutely right! Only the last indicator shows us that in many cases these opportunities converted to better organizational performance.

Remember the definition of "mean." Many individual results were even better than those cited above. And these data come only from those companies that have elected to publish their results.

What kinds of opportunities are there in challenging old paradigms and creating new ones? You hold in your hands one example. The two authors of this book are not close neighbors — unless you consider 8000 miles "close." Writing a book completely in 5 months with the close collaboration this one required is possible only because we challenged the assumption that says face-to-face collaboration between the authors is necessary. This collaboration is, of course, just one out of many new opportunities the Internet age has opened up, but it demonstrates the point of challenging old paradigms.

So, if you'd like to gain a competitive advantage — to "turbocharge" your operations — this book is for you. We invite you to read it and challenge your own paradigms.

Eli Schragenheim  
Ra'anana, Israel  
elyakim@netvision.net.il  
July 2000  

H. William Dettmer  
Port Angeles, Washington, U.S.  
gsi@goalsys.com  
July 2000

# Acknowledgments

We're indebted to many people for their invaluable assistance in the publication of this book. While it isn't possible to acknowledge everyone, these colleagues deserve special mention.

Joseph H. Katz provided the impetus for this book in 1999. Without Joe's determination to have the best possible training in drum-buffer-rope available for his company, Lucent Technologies, the core of this book would never have been structured. Joe's review and editorial comments on the manuscript were likewise meticulous and thorough.

J. Wayne Patterson, professor of business management at Clemson University, provided the all-important peer review, checking our work for validity and integrity to the theory of constraints. In addition, Wayne's incisive suggestions for improving sentence structure and syntax verify, once and for all, that "rednecks" really *are* literate!

Margot V. Tsakonas, director of the office of total quality at Weyerhaeuser, provided invaluable inputs in two areas: readability and verification of the complementary nature of constraint theory and total quality management.

Melvin J. Anderson, adjunct professor at the University of Colorado (Colorado Springs), applied his "eagle eye" to the manuscript to ensure that it was as free of typographical errors as possible, grammatically correct, and didn't diverge in any significant way from essential constraint theory.

Bill Dettmer would particularly like to thank Van D. Gray, professor at the Hankamer Business School, Baylor University, for expanding his horizons in the subjects of constraint theory and production management. Van proved that it really *is* possible to teach an old B-52 pilot new tricks.

We would be remiss if we failed to recognize the professionalism of the CRC Press staff. Drew Gierman's tireless efforts turned the idea for this book into reality. Pat Roberson and Mimi Williams made sure that the book you hold in your hand is a work of which we can be proud.

Last, but most certainly not least, both authors must acknowledge the influence of Eliyahu M. Goldratt, the man who created the theory of constraints, drum-buffer-rope production control, critical chain project scheduling and control, and the logical thinking process. Besides his contributions in systems thinking to the world of business, Eli Goldratt has changed the lives of both of us, most assuredly for the better.

# The Authors

**Elyakim (Eli) M. Schragenheim** is president of Elyakim Management Systems, Ltd. (Israel) and an associate of Goal Systems International (U.S.). He is the author of *Management Dilemmas: The Theory of Constraints Approach to Problem Identification and Solutions* (1998), and co-author (with Carol Ptak) of *ERP: Tools, Techniques and Applications for Integrating the Supply Chain* (1999). His papers have been published in academic and practitioner journals, including the *Production and Inventory Management Journal, The International Journal of Production Research, APICS: The Performance Advantage,* and the *Journal of the Institute of System Improvement.*

Eli is a former partner of the Avraham Y. Goldratt Institute and is currently collaborating with Eliyahu M. Goldratt, creator of the Theory of Constraints and author of *The Goal, The Race, The Haystack Syndrome, It's Not Luck,* and *Critical Chain,* on a new book concerning Enterprise Resource Planning. He is an experienced consultant, trainer, and facilitator in system improvement for Fortune 500 companies in the U.S., including Ford Motor Company Product Development, Technology Systems Corporation, General Motors, Procter & Gamble, General Foods, ABC Technology, Lucent Technologies, and Weyerhaeuser. His clients in Europe and Israel include ADC/Teledata, Comverse, Ltd., Elite Foods, Mezerplas, Motorola, Nilit Ltd., TAAS (Israeli defense industry), Rafale, Ltd., and the Israeli Defense Force/Army (intelligence, logistics, shipyards, headquarters).

Eli is a developer of a line of large-scope simulators used as educational tools for management, including a line of MS-DOS-based tools known as The AGI Simulators. Since 1992, his software creations include the *Management Interactive Case Study Simulator,* included with this book, and the *Project Management Simulator.* He is a featured speaker at international conferences in the U.S., U.K., and Israel on topics concerning the Theory of Constraints, learning from experience, and information systems in operations.

**H. William (Bill) Dettmer** is a senior partner at Goal Systems International. He is author of *Goldratt's Theory of Constraints* (1996) and *Breaking the Constraints to World-Class Performance* (1998). He has published articles in *Quality Progress*, the proceedings of The APICS Constraints Management Symposium, and the proceedings of the American Society for Quality's Quality Management Division annual conference.

Bill has consulted and trained on established applications of constraint management tools in both manufacturing and services with Fortune 500 and other companies, including Lucent Technologies (both in Europe and the U.S.), Tellabs, Western Digital Corporation, NEC America, Kauffman Products, Inc., Kendall Healthcare Products, Ericsson Cellular, Weyerhaeuser, Boeing, Compania de Envases and ICI/Inca Corporations (South America), and Qualiplus, S.A. (Brazil). He has developed new applications for the constraint theory, principles, and tools, including preparation of legal cases for negotiated settlements or courtroom litigation, and the acquisition and turnaround of distressed businesses.

His experience includes logistics, project planning and execution, and contracting/procurement and direct responsibilities for project management, logistics planning, government contracting, system design, financial management, productivity improvement, idea generation, team building, strategic planning, and customer–supplier relations. For 8 years he taught masters level courses in project management; systems analysis and problem solving; systems integration; management control systems; managerial economics; human factors in systems; organizational behavior and development; decision analysis; and management of research, development, test, and evaluation (RDT&E) for the University of Southern California's Institute of Safety and Systems Management.

# About APICS

APICS, The Educational Society for Resource Management, is an international, not-for-profit organization offering a full range of programs and materials focusing on individual and organizational education, standards of excellence, and integrated resource management topics. These resources, developed under the direction of integrated resource management experts, are available at local, regional, and national levels. Since 1957, hundreds of thousands of professionals have relied on APICS as a source for educational products and services.

- **APICS Certification Programs**—APICS offers two internationally recognized certification programs, Certified in Production and Inventory Management (CPIM) and Certified in Integrated Resource Management (CIRM), known around the world as standards of professional competence in business and manufacturing.
- *APICS Educational Materials Catalog*—This catalog contains books, courseware, proceedings, reprints, training materials, and videos developed by industry experts and available to members at a discount.
- *APICS—The Performance Advantage*—This monthly, four-color magazine addresses the educational and resource management needs of manufacturing professionals.
- *APICS Business Outlook Index*—Designed to take economic analysis a step beyond current surveys, the index is a monthly manufacturing-based survey report based on confidential production, sales, and inventory data from APICS-related companies.
- **Chapters**—APICS' more than 270 chapters provide leadership, learning, and networking opportunities at the local level.

- **Educational Opportunities**—Held around the country, APICS' International Conference and Exhibition, workshops, and symposia offer you numerous opportunities to learn from your peers and management experts.
- **Employment Referral Program**—A cost-effective way to reach a targeted network of resource management professionals, this program pairs qualified job candidates with interested companies.
- **SIGs**—These member groups develop specialized educational programs and resources for seven specific industry and interest areas.
- **Web Site**—The APICS Web site at http://www.apics.org enables you to explore the wide range of information available on APICS' membership, certification, and educational offerings.
- **Member Services**—Members enjoy a dedicated inquiry service, insurance, a retirement plan, and more.

For more information on APICS programs, services, or membership, call APICS Customer Service at (800) 444-2742 or (703) 237-8344 or visit http://www.apics.org on the World Wide Web.

# Introduction

Welcome to *Manufacturing at Warp Speed*. In this book, we explore ways that you can be more successful in realizing your objectives today and better meet the demands of the future. It's important that we establish our expectations of what you'll be able to do when you finish reading this book. You're reading this to determine whether there might be some benefit to you or your organization from what follows.

In addition to your expectations, we have some expectations, too. We expect that by the time you finish reading this book, you'll have:

1. A thorough understanding of constraint theory and how it applies to manufacturing operations in general.
2. A clear picture of how constraint theory applies to your operations in particular.
3. A well-defined sense of what must be done in your operations to realize the benefits that constraint management can provide.
4. An understanding of the steps that must be taken, and the obstacles that must be overcome, to manage constraints effectively.

We intend to accomplish this through examples, case studies, and the computer simulation software included with this book. To give you some idea of where we're going, let's take a look at a case study right now. This is a letter from the chief executive of a manufacturing company to the president of his most prominent customer.

# Case Study - Reliable Manufacturing, Inc.

Mr. Philip Sheridan, President - Consumer Products Division
Cryogenic Industries, Inc.
P.O. Box 300125
Chicago, IL 60666

*Dear Phil,*

*Your division's business is very important to us. I promise you that the troubles you've complained about are going to stop. I appreciate your suggestions, but I believe the underlying problem has nothing to do with wrong priorities. Nobody at the Reliable Components Division deliberately favors any other internal customer over you — even though recent events might give this impression. The source of our problem lies elsewhere, and we are working on it now. In less than a month from now all of this will be over.*

*It all started about 3 months ago, when Tony Moreno, our production manager, was notified of the death of his brother in an accident in Milan. Tony returned to Italy to join his family in their grief and a week later faxed his resignation because of his obligation to take over his brother's business and support his family.*

*I see now that I've always underestimated Tony. He seemed to me to be constantly worried and too focused on small details. It always aggravated me that Tony never sat a whole hour in his office, but kept wandering throughout the shop floor. I could never reach him directly when I needed to. However, this kind of behavior also characterizes Arthur Holst, our new production manager, though the similarity between the two stops there.*

*In his resignation letter Tony advised me not to promote Perry, his assistant production manager. He recommended Arthur as a very experienced production manager, living in the area and available for such a job. I ignored his recommendation, to my everlasting regret. It took me only a month to realize that Tony was right. Perry is not right for the job. He has a difficult time processing large amounts of data in his head. But by that time the damage was done.*

*So, I called Arthur Holst. I was surprised to find that Arthur is 68 years old. He retired a few months ago from Broadhurst Industries, a manufacturer of small electrical devices — very different from the kind of complex and fully customized electrical devices and job-shop environment we are. This may have contributed to my reluctance to consider Arthur in the first place. Anyway, Arthur was willing to take the job, and because of my concern that we had let down loyal clients like you, I thought we had to give him a try.*

*Now, Arthur is certainly a professional. You should have seen the care he took in examining the output of our MRP system and asking the computer guys very tough questions about the parameters of the system and the various reports they regularly generate. It is also evident that Arthur has very different views about how production should be handled. He tries to define the key process points of fairly common and routine parts, where intermediate inventory can be maintained. He has also required the redefinition of the bills of materials for most of our products.*

*In short, we're undergoing a major change while doing our best to cope with the current demand. Arthur is confident that within a month the system will be stabilized again. He even contends that we will be able to liberate more capacity from the system through better utilization of our resources and by strategically maintaining stock within the system.*

*Phil, we supported you two years ago when you and your division were threatened by divestiture. I'm asking you to stick with us just a little longer. I've instructed Arthur to expedite your work orders. I'm confident the storm will be over in just few weeks.*

*Sincerely yours,*

*Harold Fairweather, President*
*Reliable Component Division - Cryogenic Industries, Inc.*

While you digest what you've just read, reflect on the following questions.

1. Why would a sudden departure of the production manager cause such disorder, prompting a CEO to apologize to certain large clients?
2. Why do production managers tend to be on the shop floor most of the time?
3. How could two good professional production managers have different views on how to run the system? Is one necessarily wrong and the other right?
4. Should a good production manager have to be able to comprehend huge amounts of data?
5. Is maintaining intermediate inventories clearly good or bad?
6. Why does it take months for an experienced production manager to stabilize the system?
7. Is it important for a new production manager to be experienced in a very similar environment to be quickly effective as a manager?

8. Is it really possible to expose hidden capacity from a production system by changing some operational methods?

9. How can the CEO be sure the new production manager knows what he is doing?

10. Based on the above questions, is production management a science, meaning any decision can be based on well-defined rules, or an art where one relies on intuition?

    Do well-defined rules apply?
    Is it all "intuition"?

11. How is this case DIFFERENT from your situation? How is it SIMILAR?

If manufacturing companies were simple organizations, managing them would not be a difficult task. But several factors combine to make managing a manufacturing operation a complex undertaking. One is the number and types of variables. Some of these the manager controls, others can only be influenced, and still others may not be controllable at all. What's more, many of these variables have some interdependence or effect on others when they are changed. Another complicating factor is the degree of synchronization required to make the manufacturing process function effectively. Some parts of the process are less dependent on previous steps than others. Other parts may be closely tied to preceding steps.

Finally, a manufacturing system is subject to a high degree of uncertainty. Market demand and taste can vary widely, and often without much notice. Suppliers come and go. Some might be unreliable or provide less-than-desirable delivery performance or quality. Internal operations are subject to variability. This is sometimes referred to as the "Murphy" effect ("Anything that *CAN* go wrong *WILL* go wrong").

Figure I.1a and b is a logic tree that illustrates the cause-and-effect common in many manufacturing organizations. As you read through this tree, decide for yourself how well it characterizes manufacturing companies you've seen.*

How closely does this tree reflect YOUR experience with manufacturing systems? The main point of this tree is that if we don't understand the cause-and-effect relationships at work within our systems — and between our

---

* Read the tree in the direction of the arrows (from bottom to top), applying the word "If..." before the cause (the numbered block at the tail of an arrow) and the word "...then..." before the effect (at the head of the same arrow). Ellipses indicate dependent causes. All causes with an ellipse enclosing their arrows are read with "...and..." between them.

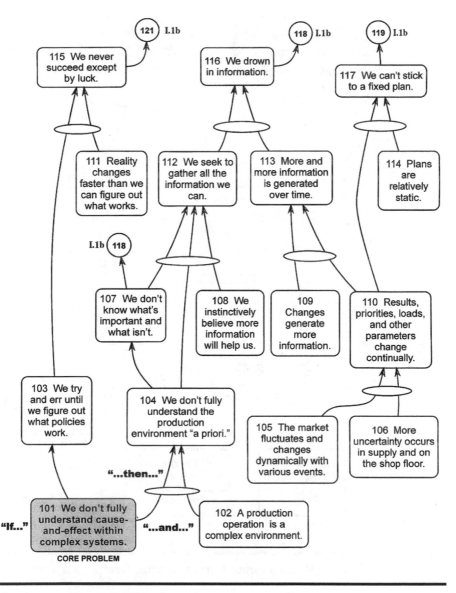

**Figure I.1a    Generic Manufacturing Current Reality Tree**

systems and the external environment — we're likely to succeed only by chance. If surviving by chance isn't good enough for you, we'll show you a better way in this book.

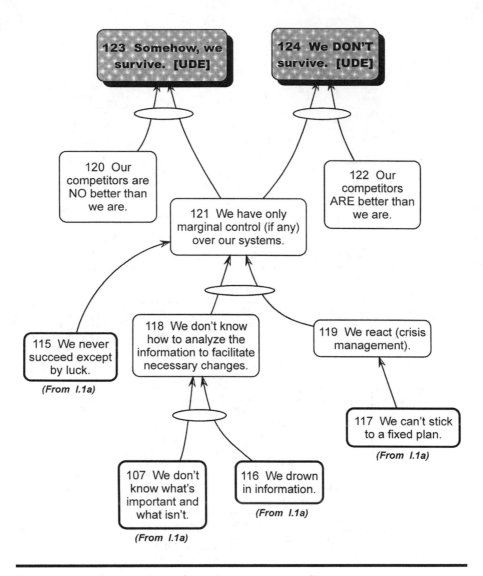

**Figure I.1b  Generic Manufacturing Current Reality Tree**

## What Are Our Requirements for a Solution?

Let's assume for a moment that the Generic Manufacturing Current Reality Tree (Figure I.1) is valid for most organizations, possibly even yours. You're awash in data, you don't really understand why things happen the way they do, and you're managing crises all the time. Sometimes you're lucky — you succeed — and sometimes you're not. Let's assume, too, that you're not happy about that state of affairs; you'd like to change it.

If we were to create an ideal method for managing manufacturing in most production environments, what would it look like? One of the characteristics might be *simplicity*. It should be relatively uncomplicated to use. Another might be that it could be easily supported by a computerized information system. Ideally, it should be supportable by an *existing* information system, so that we would not be faced with significant additional financial investment.

We'd also like our manufacturing solution to give us some specific benefits. Robust planning would be one. It would be nice if our production plans were completed *as planned* most of the time. We'd also like not to have to deviate from the plan very often. In other words, we'd like the plan to accommodate *most* of the unexpected situations we might run into without collapsing.

We'd certainly want the manufacturing solution to give us maximum *flexibility* to respond to any deviations that might actually be required — problems that the plan couldn't foresee or accommodate. And wouldn't it be nice if we could actually get MORE productivity from our entire system than we do now? In other words, we'd like the potential to produce maybe 20 to 50% more than we currently do in the same amount of time.

We'd also like to be able to produce much faster than we do now — a shorter time from the initiation of an order to delivery of that order. And, we'd want the entire system to be more efficient — to know that we were utilizing our resources to the maximum degree possible for the maximum effectiveness of the *whole* system, not just individual parts.

Finally, we'd like to be able to do all of this with less of an investment in inventory. We'd want less work-in-process in the system at any one time, and we'd like to be able to deliver to our customers while maintaining significantly less stocks of finished inventory.

Let's look at manufacturing in a different way — one that provides all of the characteristics and benefits described above. We'll demonstrate that succeeding in the ways that matter depends on looking at production from a systems perspective rather than in isolation. We'll also examine the effects of variability and uncertainty on operations and offer a way to deal with them.

We'll use a combination of case studies, a table-top exercise, and a state-of-the-art computer simulation of a business to learn how to achieve better performance (and control) for the whole system while improving delivery reliability. The table-top exercise is described in Appendix A. The computer simulation, called Management Interactive Case Study Simulator (MICSS), is included on a compact disk accompanying this book. Appendix B describes the MICSS program in detail — a kind of guided tour. Appendices C and D provide detailed information on the two manufacturing scenarios that are included in the MICSS software.

To use the software, you must first register it online. Instructions for doing so are contained on the compact disk. You should register and load your copy of the software before you get to Chapter 6.

## Four Parts

This book is divided into four main parts. The first part describes the principles and concepts behind the theory of constraints (TOC). Some of you who are well read in constraint theory already will undoubtedly see things in this part that you've seen before. But we would also guess that you'll see some things you haven't seen — at the very least, you'll see some familiar things in a new way. We'll also examine the different types of production workflows, referred to as "A," "V," "T," and "I." And we'll talk about different manufacturing approaches: make-to-stock/forecast, make-to-order, and assemble-to-order.

The second part describes the differences between traditional production practices to those prescribed by the theory of constraints. Those of you who use the simulation software will have the opportunity to see this difference in a fairly controllable environment, using a "virtual company" provided by the MICSS. Then we'll examine in detail the principles and procedures of "Drum-Buffer-Rope," or "DBR" — the original TOC method for managing production. We'll also see how existing MRP systems can be used to support a Drum-Buffer-Rope production schedule.

In the third part, we'll see a newer, more simplified version of Drum-Buffer-Rope. If we are able to make no other contribution to your knowledge of TOC, this simplified version, which we'll refer to as S-DBR, is one of the most important concepts you can learn from this book. The world does not stand still. Every paradigm is a candidate for either improvement or obsolescence. Goldratt's creation of traditional Drum-Buffer-Rope in the 1980s constituted a quantum leap forward in the management of production and inventory.

S-DBR builds on that solid foundation with the first substantive refinements to the state-of-the-art in 10 years. You'll find out how to use constraint management to balance — actually to manipulate — what seems to be a less controllable, more uncertain external demand for your products. You'll be able to optimize your manufacturing system with S-DBR. We'll also talk about ways to capitalize on the excess capacity that DBR usually reveals in a production system.

In the fourth part, we'll discuss in more detail the concept of Throughput-Based Decision Support — the "safest" way to make operational decisions in an uncertain, complex environment. Finally, you'll see how TOC fits in with Enterprise Resource Planning (ERP) and Supply Chain Management (SCM). We'll also reinforce the importance of synchronizing production with marketing and sales.

## Learning Outcomes

By the time we're done, you'll understand constraint theory and how it's applied to manufacturing operations. You'll be able to distinguish between what's really important to pay attention to, and what is not. You'll have a clear idea of what it will take to improve your delivery due-date reliability, shorten your production lead time, reduce your inventory, and help make more money for the company. And, you'll have an effective "road map" for applying constraint theory in your organization.

# MANAGING SYSTEM CONSTRAINTS

1

# 1 Systems Thinking: The Foundation

**B**efore we can talk about the application of constraint management to manufacturing, we need to introduce some of the underlying theory. As Deming once observed, effective action is well grounded in theory.[1]

The theory of constraints (TOC) is a body of knowledge about systems and the interaction of their component parts. It was evolved over approximately a 10-year period by an Israeli physicist named Eliyahu M. Goldratt. And the theory is still evolving today. TOC is composed of a collection of principles, a set of generic tools, and the specific applications of those tools. The principles explain systemic interactions and guide management action. The tools are specific methods and procedures for applying the principles in discrete situations. The applications are specific instances where the tools have been successfully applied often enough to qualify as a generic solution.

## System vs. Process

Because the theory of constraints is a *systems* philosophy, our examination of the theory must necessarily begin with a brief discussion of the systems concept. Organizations of any kind — manufacturing, service, government agency, for-profit, not-for-profit, education, charitable, social, or even family — function as *systems,* not as a collection of separate *processes.*

For our purposes, we'll consider a system to be a group of related elements, enclosed by some arbitrary boundary that differentiates "inside" the system from "outside" — an external environment[2] (see Figure 1.1). The

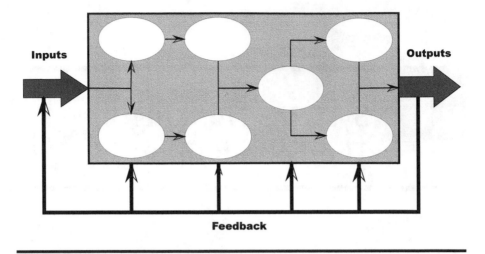

**Figure 1.1   Generic System**

components of the system interact cooperatively in a way that advances progress toward a *goal* common to all the parts of the system. Systems usually take inputs from the outside, *act* on them in some way inside the system, and produce outputs back outside the system. Normally, these outputs have greater value — however that might be defined — to the outside world than the inputs.

Most systems have some means of self-assessment — a feedback mechanism — that evaluates the quality or timeliness of the outputs and points toward adjustment of the system's components, the inputs, or both, if the output is not exactly as desired. Because of the *interdependent* nature of system components, any efforts to improve a system's output must consider the effects of these efforts on the whole system. Consequently, the *system* must be *optimized*, not individual *processes*.

## Work Flow vs. the Organization Chart

One of the biggest challenges we experience in getting the best performance out of our systems is the dichotomy between how we *manage* our organizations and how work *actually flows* through them. Work typically flows *across functions* as it works its way through the organization — the different system components — but we traditionally organize and manage the components individually, by the organization chart (Figure 1.2).

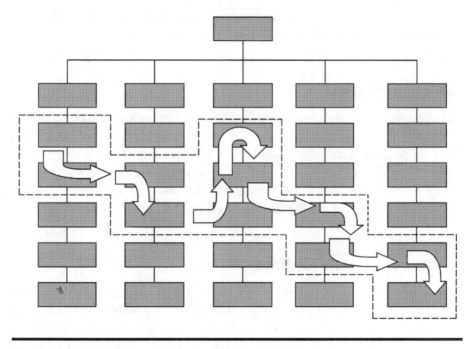

**Figure 1.2   Work Flow vs. the Organization Chart**

Now ordinarily this might not be a problem, except for one thing: The separation of our organizations into functional departments, or "silos," creates invisible barriers or boundaries between functions such as sales and marketing, engineering, production, warehouse, distribution, accounting and finance, and the support staff. And as Deming noted, these invisible barriers inhibit the communication essential to good coordination between these isolated departments.[1]

Each of these different functions "works" on turning the system inputs into outputs of greater value. Sales and marketing strive to create as much demand for products or services as they possibly can. Engineering tries to design as robust a product as it possibly can. Production tries to manufacture a quality product as quickly as possible. Inventory and purchasing managers strive to ensure that all required raw materials are always available and finished stock is ready to send to customers. Distribution, whether internal or external, attempts to ship finished goods to customers as quickly as possible. And the financial department acts as an "efficiency watchdog" for everyone, making sure that all activities are performed at the least cost.

The preceding description paints a picture of a complex organization. It's extremely difficult for one person to monitor and coordinate the efforts of such diverse functions. So we tend to manage our departments in isolation from one another, which typically results in *suboptimization.*

## Suboptimization

Suboptimization is no more than the enhancement of one part of a system at the expense of other parts, or of the system as a whole. How many of us have heard people say something like, "It's not our problem if *they sink,* as long as *we swim*"? This is the essence of suboptimization — people (managers) tend to worry about the success of the areas *they* are responsible for without much regard for the success of other areas of the system.

## Local vs. System Optima

If a system was truly a collection of independent, isolated parts, this would be an acceptable way to manage. But the system as a whole can't succeed if one part enriches its own performance at the expense of another. Organizations live or die as complete systems, not as a collection of isolated parts. However, management typically operates as if the maximum performance of the system was the simple sum of all the local performances.

If this was a valid approach, managing would be as simple as making sure that every department performed to the maximum, as measured against a set of criteria that pertained to that department alone. In fact, this is what we normally do in most organizations — but it's *not* the right way to manage! That's because the system optimum is not the sum of the local (department) optima — it's actually less!

Why is this so? There are two related reasons. First, the components of a system usually perform their tasks in some kind of dependent sequence, meaning that any one part of the system normally depends on the performance of a preceding part to do its own job. Second, statistical variation (fluctuation) affects each part of the system independently. But from the perspective of the whole system, this variation is *compounded* by the dependent nature of the parts (or events taking place) within the system. In any kind of sequential process, all the variations of each component accumulate at the last step of the process.

In a parallel process, such as an assembly operation where two or more parts are combined, the accumulated fluctuation is intensified, because the part requiring the longest time to complete actually determines the earliest time for the assembly operation. Resource dependencies also intensify the impact of fluctuations on the downstream operations. The combination of dependencies and statistical fluctuations generates a situation where any attempt to do the most locally might easily harm the system as a whole.

So when people say that a whole system is more than just the sum of its parts (the definition of synergy), what they really mean is that the interdependency inherent in the system permits the whole system to achieve much more than just a part of it alone can achieve. But you don't realize that synergy by maximizing each system component in isolation. Rather, it's achieved by coordinating and synchronizing the efforts of all parts of the system. This means that some parts of the system might have to operate at less than full throttle for the whole system to benefit the most.

Deming made some of the most perceptive comments ever on the issue of system optimization[3] (see Figure 1.3). In essence, Deming is saying, "it's okay for some parts of the system not to be fully efficient. In fact, some may have to be *not* efficient themselves in order for the system to succeed." The importance of this concept will become clearer as we go on. This whole concept can be summarized as follows:

*The system optimum is NOT the sum of the local optima.*

If the performance of component parts of a system is maximized in isolation from the rest of the system, the performance of the system as a whole will be degraded.

## Systems as Chains

Another way to look at a system — a more realistic way — is to liken it to a *chain,* or network of chains. Like a chain, a system is only as strong as its weakest link. Goldratt has suggested calling that weakest link the *system constraint.*[4] It's the factor that limits, or constrains, the system from achieving its goal.

An interesting phenomenon about chains is that strengthening *any link except* the weakest one does nothing to improve the strength of the whole chain. Strengthening the *weakest link* produces an immediate increase in the strength of the whole chain — but only up to the level of the *next weakest link.*

Similarly, in business systems, it is usually the capacity of one element that determines the overall performance of the business, and striving to improve any aspect of the system other than that constraint won't do anything

**"Optimization is the process of orchestrating the efforts of all components toward achievement of the stated aim. Optimization is management's job.  Everybody wins with optimization."**

**"Anything less than optimization of the system will bring eventual loss to every component in the system.  Any group should have as its aim optimization of the larger system that the group operates in."**

**"The obligation of any component is to contribute its best to the system, not to maximize its own production, profit, or sales, nor any other competitive measure.  Some components may operate at a loss themselves in order to optimize the whole system, including the components that take a loss."**

---

**Figure 1.3    Deming on System Optimization**

beneficial for the system as a whole. Consider total quality management, for example. That philosophy strives to involve everyone in the organization to improve quality and performance everywhere. But if the concept of a system constraint is valid, how much of that effort actually delivers an immediate, measurable improvement in overall system performance? Probably only the effort applied to whatever part of the business is the constraint of the moment to improved performance. The rest is — for the moment — superfluous.

## The Manufacturing Chain

Let's translate the chain concept to a manufacturing system. Here's one (see Figure 1.4). There are seven links in this chain. Each might constitute a resource (a person–machine combination, or a department). Each successive link depends on the preceding link for the work it does. Each of these links has a different capacity, or strength. The first and last links have twice as many physical resources as the rest, and each of the resources in the chain can work at different individual maximum rates.

The percentage numbers below each link represent the degree to which this manufacturing chain was utilized last month. Based on what you can see here, which of these links is likely to be the weakest? In other words, as the load on this chain is increased, which link is likely to limit how much

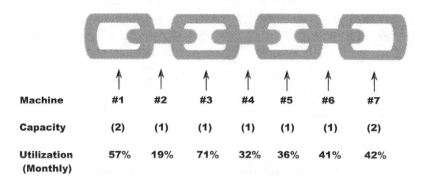

| Machine | #1 | #2 | #3 | #4 | #5 | #6 | #7 |
|---|---|---|---|---|---|---|---|
| Capacity | (2) | (1) | (1) | (1) | (1) | (1) | (2) |
| Utilization (Monthly) | 57% | 19% | 71% | 32% | 36% | 41% | 42% |

**Which is likely to be the weakest link (system limitation)?**

**Figure 1.4   The Manufacturing Chain**

more work the system can take? If you chose the third link (at 71% utilization), you're right. This is the part of the manufacturing system that is most likely to reach its maximum capacity first. And when it does, it will not matter that all the rest of system components have more capacity to spare. Because of the dependent sequence of these manufacturing events, the whole system is limited to the output of the most restricted resource.

Please note that in this particular example, none of these resources is currently loaded to its full capacity. So while link number 3 is likely to become a system constraint someday, it's not the constraint now.

## The Expanded Manufacturing Chain

If we expand our horizons a little, we can see that our chain really extends to the front of, and beyond the end of, the manufacturing process (see Figure 1.5) It includes other non-manufacturing functions, such as sales and marketing, order processing, engineering, planning and scheduling, our external suppliers, warehousing and distribution, and our customer, whose demand for the product keeps us in business in the first place!

At the instant this "snapshot" was taken, the system constraint in this chain is probably in one of these areas, because if it was not, we would find our manufacturing process more fully loaded than it is. In actuality, the current constraint for our manufacturing system is likely to be the fact that we don't have enough customer orders to keep us busy — low market demand

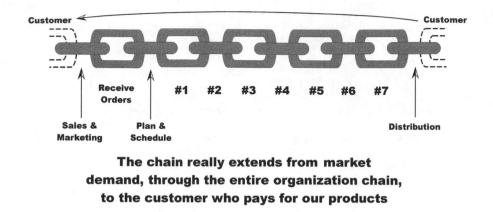

**The chain really extends from market demand, through the entire organization chain, to the customer who pays for our products**

**Figure 1.5    The Expanded Manufacturing Chain**

is limiting the financial success of our business. That's why none of the links in the manufacturing process is used more than 71% of the time. But if that market constraint is overcome, perhaps with an aggressive sales campaign, it should be clear that link number 3 would very likely become the next system constraint.

The "manufacturing system as a chain" analogy, while very enlightening, may seem somewhat simplistic, though it's the one used most often. Perhaps a better analogy for a wider selection of production floors is a network, where materials flow through several directions, ending up as many different end products. Nevertheless, the same principle applies: Only very few variables, possibly only one, limit the whole system from achieving its goal.

## The Eternal Constraint

This brings us to an important concept in constraint theory: Constraints never really disappear — they just migrate to some other place, either within the system or in the surrounding environment.

It's important to note, however, that each time a constraint is broken by improvement efforts, as the constraint shifts from one location to another, system performance usually experiences a quantum improvement. In the preceding example, the next candidate for system constraint is link number 3. But for it to happen, the performance of the whole system will have to rise by nearly 30%! So when it does happen, we can conclude that the system's overall performance has probably improved by that amount — and should be verifiable by measurement.

Thus, we can safely say that constraints never really disappear. Some other factor — either external or internal — becomes the system constraint

## The Importance of Knowing What the System Constraint Is

Why is it so important to know where our system constraint lies? Steven Covey has observed that "anything less than a conscious commitment to the important is an unconscious commitment to the unimportant."[5] This can be likened to the Roman emperor Nero "fiddling while Rome burned," or "rearranging the deck chairs on the Titanic" after striking the iceberg. Grave consequences can result when managers are distracted from the factors most critical to system success.

Covey's statement naturally leads us to one of the most important principles in constraint theory: Only very few variables in any system — maybe only one — are important for us to watch and manage at any given time. While the identity of these factors may change from time to time, their number will always remain small.

## References

1. Deming, W. Edwards, *Out of the Crisis*, MIT Center for Advanced Engineering Study, Cambridge, MA, 1986.
2. Athey, Thomas H., *The Systematic Systems Approach*, Prentice-Hall, Englewood Cliffs, NJ, 1982.
3. Deming, W. Edwards, *The New Economics for Industry, Government and Education*, MIT Center for Advanced Engineering Study, Cambridge, MA, 1993.
4. Goldratt, Eliyahu M., *The Haystack Syndrome: Sifting Information from the Data Ocean*, The North River Press, Croton-on-Hudson, NY, 1990.
5. Covey, Steven, *Daily Reflections for Highly Effective People: Living the Seven Habits*, Simon and Schuster, New York, 1994, 32.

# Principles and Tools of the Theory of Constraints

Earlier we saw that the foundation of the theory of constraints is a set of principles and concepts that points us toward optimizing our systems. Among the most basic of these principles are three key assumptions about constraint management, five focusing steps to guide our system improvement efforts, and three unique measures by which to assess whether the actions we take at the local level are producing the results desired at the global level (Throughput, Investment, and Operating Expense).

These principles play a significant role in constraint management. After we understand the principles of constraint theory, we'll be ready to examine in more detail the tools it provides to optimize our systems. These tools are classified as logistical or policy. The logistical tools include *Drum-Buffer-Rope* (DBR) to schedule and allocate resources in production operations and *Critical Chain* to manage the scheduling and allocation of resources in projects. The policy tools include a logical Thinking Process and specific situational guidelines based on the five focusing steps.

We should note that *policy* is a broad term. It encompasses the policies used to manage production, as well as the policies used to operate the organization as a whole. In a larger sense, policy can be defined as a "mind set" — a way of looking at the world. Have you ever heard either of the following statements?

"That's NOT the way we do things around here." Or,

"THIS is the way we do things around here."

If you've heard either of these, you've heard the verbal expression of a policy constraint of some kind. The policy might be a written procedure or rule, or it could be no more than tradition. Whether they're formal or informal, policies at some point limit what we can or can't do, or what we will or won't do. To the extent that the limitation imposed by a policy inhibits a system from achieving better performance in pursuit of its goal, the policy itself becomes a system constraint. And it is policy analysis tools such as the Thinking Process created by Goldratt that facilitate the identification and elimination of policy constraints.*

The policy tools have application in both the production and project environments. Although we're not going to address the Thinking Process right now, as you get further into this book, you'll see how it is used. For now, let's look at the three key assumptions behind the theory of constraints.

## Constraint Management Assumption #1

The first assumption holds that every system has a goal and a set of necessary conditions that must be satisfied to achieve that goal. The philosopher Friedrich Nietzsche once observed, "by losing your goal, you have lost your way." Or another way of putting it: if you don't know what the destination is, then any path will do.

While this assumption is undoubtedly valid in most cases, there are obviously some organizations that have not expended the time or effort to clearly and unequivocally define what their goal is. And even if they have defined a goal, most have not gone the extra step to define the minimum necessary conditions, or critical success factors, for achieving that goal.

For example, most for-profit companies have something financial as their goal. Goldratt has put it more simply than just about anyone else. The goal of for-profit companies is to "make more money, now and in the future." Another way of saying it is *profitability*. This, of course, would not be an appropriate goal for a government agency, such as the Department of Defense or Department of Education, but it works quite well for most companies engaged in manufacturing.

---

* This book will not address the Thinking Process in any detail, although various logic trees will be used where appropriate. There are several other sources of information on Goldratt's logical Thinking Process. Three suggested references include *Goldratt's Theory of Constraints: A Systems Approach to Continuous Improvement* (Dettmer, 1996); *Breaking the Constraints to World-Class Performance* (Dettmer, 1998); and *Thinking for a Change* (Scheinkopf, 1999). Complete citations are included in the bibliography.

However, having profitability as a goal isn't enough. For any organization to be profitable, and for those profits to consistently increase, there is a discrete set of necessary conditions it must satisfy. Some of these will be unique to the industry that the company is in, others will be generic to all for-profit companies. But one thing that all organizations will have in common: There will be very few of these necessary conditions, maybe fewer than five.

Necessary conditions fall into one of three general types. The first type is a code of ethics. For instance, a company might decide that it is not going to sell to, or buy from, countries that violate basic human rights. The second type defines how much risk the company might take in the pursuit of its goal. Certainly some shareholders might want to preclude the CEO from taking a risk that could endanger the company's existence, even though the odds are very remote. The third type includes critical conditions that are actually necessary to achieve the goal. For instance, employee satisfaction may be considered necessary for achieving the goal. Including such a necessary condition as part of the goal hierarchy gives it credibility, identifying it as something that is not just temporary but must be satisfied throughout the lifetime of the organization.

A necessary condition differs from the goal. While the goal itself has no limit — it's never fully realized — necessary conditions should be more finite. Necessary conditions might be characterized as a "zero-or-one" circumstance; it's either there or it isn't, a "yes-or-no" state. For example, a for-profit organization might want to make as much money as it can — no limits. But employee satisfaction, as a necessary condition, should be established at a well-defined minimum level. A for-profit company's goal isn't to satisfy its employees without limit, but the organization should recognize the need to achieve a certain level of employee satisfaction as one minimum requirement for achieving the goal.

## Constraint Management Assumption #2

The second assumption is that any system is more than just the sum of its parts. In this case, "more" doesn't mean mathematically more. It means that the mathematical sum of the parts alone does not represent the success of the system. We discussed this in Chapter 1 when we said that the sum of the local optima (or local efficiencies) does not produce the system optimum (or best system-wide efficiency).

This is an especially critical assumption, because almost every organization in the world operates as if the sum of the local optima will produce the global system optimum. As we'll see later, the sum of the local efficiencies does not produce the best outcome for the system as a whole.

The theory of constraints suggests that the linkages are as important, if not more so, than the links. In other words, a system's most serious problems occur at the interfaces between components, not necessarily within the components themselves. The whole case for system optimization is wrapped up in the notion of assumption #2.

## Constraint Management Assumption #3

The final assumption is that very few variables — maybe only one — limit the performance of a system at any given time. And we refer to these few critical limiting variables as "constraints."

The rationale behind this assumption is that it isn't possible to manage an organization effectively (or easily) unless only a very few variables constrain its performance. Almost all organizations produce value through the efforts and detailed synchronization of many resources, the individual capacities of which vary. Is it possible to plan the output of the organization so that many of the resources are used to their limits? If this were the case, then any small change to the plan would have a devastating impact on the output.

Is this the way systems typically behave? Does your organization lose profit whenever an employee is late because of a traffic jam? If not, it means that the vast majority of variables don't limit its output. Small changes to plans shouldn't affect the value generated by the organization.

As the complexity of the organization increases, it's inconceivable that any manager can really plan so that output is maximized and many variable resources are fully utilized. When you also add the significant amount of uncertainty inherent in any organizational environment, we hope to use only one or two variables to their limit. All the rest will invariably have excess capacity and capability. The flexibility provided by having only one, or very few, constraints allows us to manage and control organizations with stable behavior where we and our customers know fairly well what products will be delivered tomorrow. If this is an invalid assumption, we would have no hope of controlling our systems. You can't control a system with many independent variables, especially if the system exists in a complex, uncertain environment.

# The Airplane Analogy

As an example, consider the challenge of flying an airplane. A plane can move in three directions: along a vertical axis, and in two horizontal axes (fore-and-aft, and side-to-side). A pilot who wants to fly straight-and-level between two defined points must control the airplane's movement in these three axes. Airplanes usually have "control" instruments to tell the pilot how he or she is doing at this task: an altimeter to provide feedback on the vertical axis, an airspeed indicator to show forward velocity, and a compass and attitude indicator to show lateral variance. Each of these instruments displays the results of control inputs (pilot actions on the control stick, rudder pedals, and throttles).

Because of the interdependencies in the aircraft system, a change (or control input) in one of the axes produces a variance in one or more of the others. If the pilot pushes the nose of the airplane downward to change altitude, airspeed will also increase without any change in the throttle position. If the pilot banks the airplane to the left or right to change the heading, a throttle adjustment will usually be necessary to maintain airspeed.

As uncertainty and variation increase (turbulence, bad weather, changes of heading and altitude directed by air traffic control), the pilot must contend with variance in three interdependent dimensions simultaneously. This can be a very challenging tracking task for the pilot, who now has three variables to pay attention to and try to control: heading, altitude, and airspeed. Complicating the task is the certain knowledge that each has fatal limits — at some point, exceeding the limits of any one of them will kill the pilot (and whoever else might be on board).

Now let's make flight management a little easier on the pilot. We'll give him only one variable to deal with: airspeed. How do we do this? We engage the autopilot, which controls altitude and heading (the vertical axis and one of the horizontal axes). Now all the pilot has to do is glance at the heading and altitude occasionally to make sure the autopilot is doing its job, and pay close attention to the airspeed, correcting it with throttle movements as required.

A situation with only one variable to worry about is *much* easier to manage than a situation with two or more. One cause of aircraft fatalities is sensory overload, or stated another way, "too much to pay attention to at once." The same is true of complex organizational systems. The fewer the variables that need to be watched, the easier a complex system is to manage. The more variables, the greater the odds are that the system will go out of control.

## The "Nero Effect"

Most organizational systems have a lot of variables, so the complexity of managing becomes almost impossible to deal with … unless only a very few variables (maybe only one) really determine the system's success at any given time. Remember the Roman emperor, Nero, who reputedly fiddled while Rome burned? There were a lot of variables in the "operation" of Rome. Fire prevention, or firefighting, was obviously critical to survival. Music appreciation wasn't. If we're overwhelmed by variables in our organizational systems, the "Nero effect" can work both for and against us. It works for us when our system is reasonably stable and in control, and we "fiddle" with variables that have no significant effect on system success. But it works against us when we have problems with a critical variable, but spend too much time and attention fiddling with the ones that aren't very important. This is one reason why some companies are said to succeed in spite of themselves, rather than because of what they do.

We live and work in complex systems. Get used to it — there isn't much we can do about the complexity itself. But to the extent that we can understand the real "drivers" of system success — our constraints — we can often deal quite effectively with that complexity. Since very few variables are usually crucial at any one time, identifying and managing *them* can simplify our jobs tremendously. And if we find that our system really does have a large number of critical variables, it would be well worth our efforts to reduce that number to just a few.

## Implications of Assumption #3

What does assumption #3 mean in a manufacturing environment? Take a look at Figure 2.1. It shows a simple manufacturing process — only five sequential steps, with work progressing from left to right. Notice that each resource has a different capacity for speed or volume of work. This is not unlike the real world. Notice, too, that as demand increases from low to high, the maximum capacity of the second resource (from the left) is reached first. Regardless of how much additional capacity the other resources have, it is this one resource that will govern the maximum performance of the whole system.

Even if we were to add to the capacity of the second resource, making it equal to the first one, the whole system would not be able to produce more than the next least capable resource, which in this example would be the

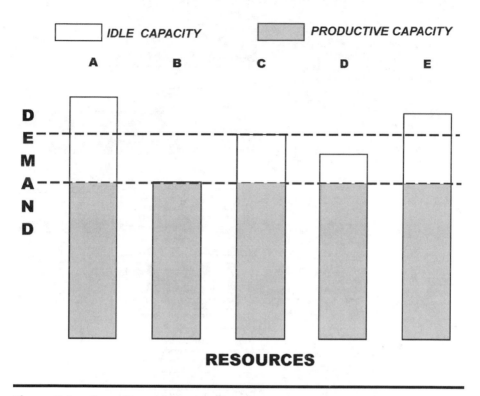

**Figure 2.1 Capacity and Demand**

fourth from the left. Notice, too, the unused capacity in this system. Even if we increased the capacity of the second resource, there would still be unused capacity in the system. The only way to eliminate that unused capacity would be to *balance* the system — to make every resource equally capable. Besides being expensive to do, this is also extremely difficult to achieve, and even a completely balanced system won't stay that way for very long. Variation will increasingly unbalance it, often in ways that are difficult to control. Since the system will eventually unbalance itself through variation, we would never be able to productively use all the capacity in the system anyway, so the local efficiency of some parts would suffer.

If we were to try to load the system to match the capacity of the most capable resource, all we would do is create queues at some of the less capable ones, and we'd still have unused capacity at others — as long as these partially idle resources didn't find something else to do to look busy.*

---

* People are very good at inventing things to do — things that no one really needs — just to show their supervisors that they're busy all the time!

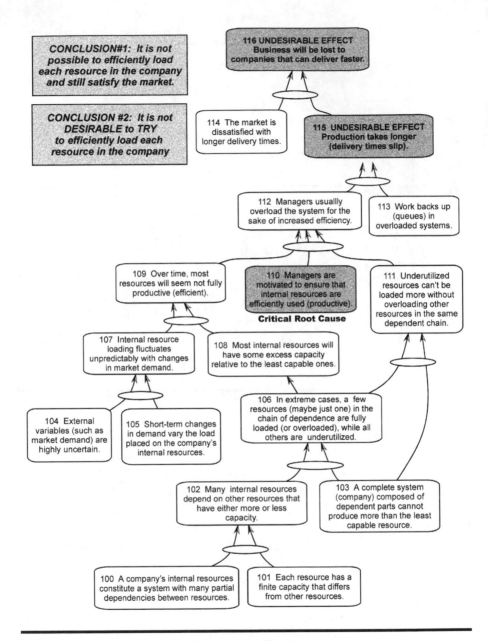

**CONCLUSION#1:** *It is not possible to efficiently load each resource in the company and still satisfy the market.*

**CONCLUSION #2:** *It is not DESIRABLE to TRY to efficiently load each resource in the company*

**116 UNDESIRABLE EFFECT**
Business will be lost to companies that can deliver faster.

114 The market is dissatisfied with longer delivery times.

**115 UNDESIRABLE EFFECT**
Production takes longer (delivery times slip).

112 Managers usuallly overload the system for the sake of increased efficiency.

113 Work backs up (queues) in overloaded systems.

109 Over time, most resources will seem not fully productive (efficient).

110 Managers are motivated to ensure that internal resources are efficiently used (productive).
**Critical Root Cause**

111 Underutilized resources can't be loaded more without overloading other resources in the same dependent chain.

107 Internal resource loading fluctuates unpredictably with changes in market demand.

108 Most internal resources will have some excess capacity relative to the least capable ones.

104 External variables (such as market demand) are highly uncertain.

105 Short-term changes in demand vary the load placed on the company's internal resources.

106 In extreme cases, a few resources (maybe just one) in the chain of dependence are fully loaded (or overloaded), while all others are underutilized.

102 Many internal resources depend on other resources that have either more or less capacity.

103 A complete system (company) composed of dependent parts cannot produce more than the least capable resource.

100 A company's internal resources constitute a system with many partial dependencies between resources.

101 Each resource has a finite capacity that differs from other resources.

**Figure 2.2    Assumption #3: Current Reality Tree**

Here's a different way of looking at assumption #3 (see Figure 2.2). This is a current reality tree (a cause-and-effect tree from the Thinking Process). As with Figure I.1, we read the tree from bottom to top. Precede the cause (the tail of each arrow) with the word "If..." and the effect (the head of each arrow) with the word "...then...". Multiple causality arrows enclosed with an ellipse are read with AND between them. For example: "IF (100) a company's internal resources constitute a system with many partial dependencies between resources, AND (101) each resource has a finite capacity that differs from the other resources, THEN (102) many internal resources depend on other resources that have either more or less capacity." Continue reading this way until you reach to the top of the tree.

There are two key lessons from this tree. First, striving for high local efficiencies everywhere actually bogs down the whole system, and second, it's not possible to achieve full efficiency at each resource in the system and still meet our customers' expectations for timely delivery. Clearly, if we con-sistently fail to satisfy our customers' expectations, they'll eventually go to our competitors. If they do that, we end up losing money, which is not conducive to achieving our goal!

So, if we want to keep (or improve) our market share — a necessary condition to achieving our goal — we'd better not chase local efficiencies everywhere in the system.

We've spent a lot of time talking about assumption #3. There's a good reason for this — it's the most critical assumption underlying constraint theory. Not only is chasing local efficiencies a confusing waste of time, energy, and effort, but it's actually detrimental to the system to do so!

## The Theory of Constraints Approach to System Management

So, if striving for local efficiencies is not the right thing to do, what is? The theory of constraints suggests a rational, effective approach to managing complex systems, which manufacturing companies are.

The first step is to determine the limits, or boundaries, of the system in question. The system boundary is conceptual, not physical — where is the imaginary line that separates outside from inside? Usually, this is an organi-zational boundary — a plant, a division, or the whole company.

Once the system has been defined, the next question to answer is, "What is the goal of the system?" In the case of most commercial companies, it's probably safe to say that making money now and in the future is the common goal of almost every part of the company.

The next step — a little more difficult — is to determine what the critical success factors are. What are those necessary conditions that must be satisfied in order to achieve the goal? Three of these might be competitive advantage, satisfied customers, and employee satisfaction. There might be others as well, but remember that there should only be a few.

Once the necessary conditions are established, constraint theory prescribes applying five focusing steps in order to continuously proceed inexorably toward satisfying those necessary conditions.

## The Five Focusing Steps

Goldratt created the five focusing steps as a way of making sure management "keeps its eye on the ball" — what's really important to success: the system constraint. In one respect, these steps are similar to the Shewhart Cycle (plan-do-check/study-act).[1] They constitute a continuous cycle. You don't stop after just one rotation.

### Identify

The first step is to *identify the system's constraint.* What limits system performance now? Is it inside the system (a resource or policy) or is it outside (the market, material supply, a vendor ... or another policy)? Once the system constraint is identified, if it can be broken without much investment do so immediately, and revert to the first step again. If it can't be easily broken, proceed to the second step.

### Exploit

*Decide how to exploit the system's constraint.* "Exploit" means to "get the most" out of the constraining element without additional investment. In other words, change the way you operate so that maximum financial benefit is achieved from the constraining element. For example, if the system constraint is market demand (not enough sales), it means catering to the market so as to win more sales. On the other hand, if the constraint is an internal resource, it means using that resource in the best way to maximize its marginal contribution to profit. Exploitation of the constraint should be the kernel of tactical planning — ensuring the best performance the system can draw *now.* For this reason, responsibility for exploitation lies with the line managers who must provide that plan and communicate it, so that everyone else understands the exploitation scheme for the immediate future.

## Subordinate

Once the decision on how to exploit the constraint has been made, *subordinate everything else to that decision.* This is, at the same time, the most important and the most difficult of the five focusing steps to accomplish. Why is it so difficult? It requires everyone and every part of the system not directly involved with the constraint to subordinate, or put in second place, their own cherished success measures, efficiencies, and egos. It requires everyone, from top management on down, to accept the idea that excess capacity in the system at most locations is not just acceptable — it's actually a good and necessary thing!

Subordination formally relegates all parts of the system that are not constraints (referred to as "non-constraints") to the role of supporters of the constraint. This can create behavioral problems at almost all levels of the company. It's very difficult for most people to accept that they and/or their parts of the organization aren't just as critical to the success of the system as any other. Consequently, most people in non-constraints will resist doing the things necessary to subordinate the rest of the system to the constraint. This is what makes the third step so difficult to accomplish.

What makes the constraint more critical to the organization is its *relative weakness.* What distinguishes a non-constraint is its *relative strength,* which enables it to be more flexible. So the current performance of the organization really depends on the weak point. While the other parts of the system could do more, because of that weak point there is no point in doing so. Instead, the key to better performance is wisely subordinating the stronger points so that the weak point can be exploited in full.

Subordination actually redefines the objectives of every process in the system. Each process is supposed to accomplish a mission that's necessary for the ultimate achievement of the goal. But among processes there may be conflicting priorities, such as competition for the same resources. Subordinating non-constraints actually focuses the efforts of every process on truly supporting the organization's goal. It allows the constraint to be exploited in the best way possible.

Consider a raw material warehouse. What is its objective? The storing and releasing of material is needed as a "bridge" between the time materials arrive from vendors and the time the same materials are needed on the production floor. When a specific work center is the constraint, any materials needed by that particular work center should be released precisely at the required time. But if market demand is the only constraint, any order coming in should trigger material release.

However, even if no new orders enter the system, shop foremen often like to continue working, to keep their efficiency high. But if the non-constraints in a production system are properly subordinated, material should *not* be released. The material release process must be subordinated to the needs of the constraint, not to arbitrary efficiency measurements. Leaving materials in the warehouse when there is no firm order for them is part of the subordination process. Work for which there isn't any immediate requirement should be treated as a lower priority than the quick release of materials the constraint will soon need.

Subordination serves to focus the efforts of the system on the things that help it to maximize its current performance. Actions that contradict the subordination rationale should be suppressed.

## *Elevate*

It's possible that, after completing the third step, the system constraint might be broken. If so, it should be fairly obvious. Output at the system level will usually take a positive jump, and some other part of the system will start to look like a bottleneck. If this is the case, go back to the first step and begin the Five Focusing Steps again. Identify which new factor has become the system constraint, determine how best to exploit *that* component and subordinate everything else.

If the original constraint is still the constraint, at this point the best you can be assured of is that you're wringing as much productivity out of it as possible — it's not possible for the system to perform any better than it is without additional management action.

If this case, it's necessary to proceed to the fourth step to obtain better performance from the system: *Evaluate alternative ways to elevate the constraint* (or constraints, if there are more than one). "Elevate" means to increase capacity. If the constraint is an internal resource, this means obtaining *more time* for that resource to do productive work. Some typical alternatives for doing this might be to acquire more machines or people, or to add overtime or shifts until all 24 hours of the day are used.

If the constraint is market demand (lack of sales), elevation might mean investing in an advertising campaign, or a new product introduction to boost sales. In any case, elevating invariably means "spend more money to make more money."

Notice that we use the word evaluate in this step. We emphasize this action for a good reason. From the preceding examples — buying more equipment or adding shifts, or overtime — it should be clear that there's more than one way to skin a cat. Some alternatives are less expensive than others. Some alternatives are more attractive for reasons that can't be measured directly in financial terms (easier to manage, for example). In any case, a choice of the means to elevate will usually be required, so jumping on the first option you think of may not necessarily be a good idea.

One of the reasons to favor one elevation alternative over another is the identity of the next potential constraint. As we've seen, constraints don't go away per se. When a constraint is broken, some other factor, either internal or external to the system, becomes the new system constraint. It's possible that the next potential constraint might be more difficult to manage than the one we currently have — it might reduce the margin of control we have over our system.

It's also possible that two different choices of alternatives might drive the system constraint to different locations — one of which might be preferable to the other. Or, it could be that dealing with the potential new constraint may require a much longer lead time than breaking the current constraint. In this case, if we decide to break the current constraint, we would want to get a head start on the tasks needed to exercise some control over the new constraint.

## Ineffective Elevation: An Example

For example, one company involved in the manufacture of solid-state circuit boards found its constraint to be the first step in its process: a surface-mount (gaseous diffusion) machine. Without considering which other resource might become the constraint, they opted to purchase another surface-mount machine. This certainly relieved the original constraint. But the automated test equipment (ATE) — about eight steps down the production line — became the new constraint, and managing the constraint at this location was no easy task. It was more complex to schedule at that point, and it suffered more problems. Moreover, moving the constraint out of the ATE section was even more challenging. Buying more ATE was more expensive than buying additional surface-mount equipment. Finding qualified ATE operators was also more difficult.

In short, it took more time, effort, and money to break the ATE constraint than it did to break the surface-mount constraint. Had the company been able to anticipate that ATE would become the system constraint, they could have chosen to either (a) leave the constraint where it was — at the surface-mount machine, or (b) begin long lead-time acquisition of ATE and hiring of ATE operators to boost the ATE section's capacity *before* increasing the surface-mount capacity. Doing so would have increased system performance, yet preserved the system constraint at a location that was far easier to manage.

Another important factor to consider is return on investment. Once the company broke the surface-mount constraint, there was potential to generate more throughput, but how much? If the ATE's capacity was only slightly more than that of the original surface-mount machine, the company might have gained only a small increase in throughput relative to the cost of the new surface-mount unit. This would be a definite disappointment.

As long as the next constraint poses a substantially higher limit than the existing one, it's probably safe to say that the company did the right thing. Even if exploiting the ATE is more difficult, the increase in throughput may be worth the aggravation. The ATE can always be loaded a little less, and the company will still realize more money. What's the lesson here? Assessing the real return on investment from an *elevation* action requires an understanding of constraint theory, where the next constraint will be, and how much throughput will increase before hitting the new constraint. So, as you can see, the "evaluate" part of the elevation step can be extremely important. We need to know where the new constraint will occur, because it can affect our decision on how to elevate.

## How to Determine Where the Next Constraint Will Be

The easiest way to do this is to apply the first three of the five focusing steps in our heads, before we actually elevate for the first time. In other words, identify the next most-limiting factor, inside or outside the system, that will keep the whole system from achieving better performance after the current constraint is broken. Then determine what actions will be necessary to exploit that new constraint in the future, and how the rest of the system will have to act to subordinate itself to the exploitation of the new constraint.

When we've done this, we'll have a pretty good understanding of the ramifications of each alternative to elevate, and we can make a better-informed decision about which alternative to choose — and it might not be the obvious choice, or the cheapest one!

## Go Back to Step 1, But Beware of Inertia

Even if the *subordinate* step does not break the system constraint, the *elevate* step very likely will, unless a conscious decision is made to curtail elevation actions short of breaking the constraint. In either case, after the *subordinate* or *elevate* steps, we must go back to the first step (identify) to be sure we know where the new system constraint is, or to verify that it has not migrated away from the original location.

Sometimes a constraint moves not as a result of our intentional actions, but as a result of a change in the environment. For instance, a change in preferences of the market might drive us to change our product mix to such an extent that the constraint moves elsewhere. While such external changes don't happen very frequently, it is important to go back to the first step from time to time, just to verify that what we believe to be the constraint still is, in fact, the system's limiting factor.

The warning about inertia means that we should not become complacent. There are two reasons for this. First, when the constraint moves, the actions or policies we put into place to *exploit* and *subordinate* to the old constraint may no longer be the best things to do for the benefit of the whole system. If we don't re-evaluate where the new system constraint is, we would never notice this deficiency. Second, there is often a tendency to say, "Well, we've solved that problem. There's no need to revisit it." But today's solution eventually becomes tomorrow's historical curiosity. If we're too lazy (or dis-tracted by other demands for our attention) to revisit old solutions, we can be sure that eventually — probably sooner, rather than later — we will not be getting the best possible performance from our system.

## The TOC Perspective: A Summary

In summary, organizations live or die as complete systems, not as a collection of individual, isolated processes. Effective exploitation requires that we con-sider a whole system perspective — in other words, what is the *system's* constraint? If we expect to improve the output of our whole system, we must be prepared to optimize the system, not just maximize the performance of its individual parts.

This means that only the system constraint(s) can be exploited to full capacity, and all non-constraints (most of the system) must be subordinated to support exploitation decisions. By virtue of the fact that they are not system constraints, the non-constraints will always — and should always — have substantial excess capacity. Decisions to fill up that excess capacity should be made only with the utmost care to ensure that doing so does not inadvertently force the system constraint to a different place.

## Ramifications of the Five Focusing Steps

If these five focusing steps constitute a valid approach to effectively managing our manufacturing systems, there are several conclusions we can draw about our management environment.

First, only a very few key nodes of our system need continual close attention. Second, most of the data we collect and have access to isn't significant to the performance of the organization. Many times it's "noise," rather than "signal." In other words, it's more likely to confuse than clarify our situation. Third, we should expect nearly all internal components of our system to have significant excess capacity — and this is not a bad thing! In fact, it's required if we are to be flexible and competitive. Finally, measuring and striving for local efficiencies anywhere in the system except for the constraint run the risk of suboptimizing the whole system.

But if we shouldn't emphasize local efficiencies everywhere, how should we assess the performance of our system and the decisions we make to improve it? This is our next topic.

## References

1. Deming, W. Edwards, *Out of the Crisis*, Cambridge, MA, MIT Center for Advanced Engineering Study, 1986.

# 3 | Assessing System Success

With the underlying principles and the prescriptions of the five focusing steps in hand, the next stone in the foundation of constraint theory is assessing the success of decisions. As we will see shortly, one of the biggest obstacles to successful management of complex systems is the inability to determine whether (and how) day-to-day local decisions support the system goal and progress toward its achievement. The theory of constraints provides a means to do so.

## Evaluating Operating Decisions: The Traditional Approach

If the world around us were static, if nothing changed very much, the task of managing would be relatively easy. But that's not the way the world is. Things don't stand still. The competitive environment around us is always evolving. Internal improvements are required to remain competitive. The ancient Greek, Heraclitus, once observed that the only constant in the world is change. Constant change drives a need for continual decisions about what to change, what to change it to, and how to make the change happen.

In for-profit companies, the quality of a decision is usually measured financially, and financial measures are usually the yardstick for differentiating the favorability of competing options. In the corporate environment, the financial standard for most decisions is profit. A good decision results in higher profit; a bad decision hurts profit, or causes a financial loss.

In evaluating management decisions, the two key measurements are Net Profit (NP) and Return on Investment (ROI). The first gauges to what degree the decision makes money. The second compares the investment required with the profit generated.

Net profit and return on investment are not easy to apply to the daily operating decisions required of most managers. It's not easy to quantify the effects of many decisions in financial terms. Neither is it easy to know how a decision made at a departmental level will affect the financial situation of the company as a whole. The theory of constraints provides a bridge between local operating decisions and the company's financial well-being.

## Evaluating Operating Decisions: The TOC Approach

The financial yardsticks provided by constraint theory are throughput (T), inventory or investment (I), and operating expense (OE). These yardsticks are predicated on the assumption that the organization's goal is to make money, now and in the future. If that is *not* the company's goal, operating expense and inventory may still be used, and expressed in financial terms, but throughput will require some modification. It must be defined in some other non-financial term pertinent to the situation. Since the focus of this book is manufacturing, and since most manufacturing organizations are for-profit businesses, we'll confine our discussion of throughput to financial terms. The following definitions come from *The Haystack Syndrome.*[1]

### *Throughput (T)*

Throughput is defined as the *rate* at which an organization generates money (usually through sales of product or service). It represents new money coming into (and retained by) the system — the added financial value the system generates by its activity.* It might be easier to visualize throughput as the *added value* the system infuses into the product. That added value is generated by turning the raw materials, purchased from other organizations, into something that has more value to the customer than the original raw materials.

Mathematically, throughput is the difference between sales revenues and truly variable costs. It's typically measured at the whole-company level, but it's also measured by units of product, by whole product lines, or by a specific sale transaction. For example, the throughput of an individual unit would normally be the selling price of that unit minus the cost of materials that

---

* Transfer pricing between plants or divisions of the same company should not be considered throughput. It's the equivalent of moving money from one internal account to another.

went into it. The throughput of a product line would be the total revenue from the sales of all such products over some period of time, minus the total cost of consumable raw materials and any other costs (such as sales commissions and warranty returns) that are incurred only as a result of selling the product. At the company level, throughput might be total sales revenue for all products over some period of time, minus the cost of raw materials that went into them and all the other truly variable costs (costs that would not have been incurred if the product had not been sold).

Throughput is central to the TOC philosophy because it links local activity to the goal of the organization. It's similar in concept to the term "contribution," which is used mainly in economics. However, the traditional definition of contribution considers direct labor as a variable cost, while TOC rejects this notion. In summary, TOC attaches great importance to throughput. It's tied to many daily decisions in all functions, as we'll see later.

## Investment, or Inventory (I)

Investment, or inventory, is defined as the money an organization spends on things it intends to sell at some point. It's money tied up within the system — financial value that is not easily liquidated, and is used to produce throughput. Investment/inventory would include capital assets, facilities, equipment, and raw materials intended to be converted to finished products for subsequent sale. The test to determine whether a financial factor would be considered inventory or investment: If you'd use it for collateral, it's probably "I".

## Operating Expense (OE)

Operating expense is at the opposite pole from throughput, which makes both terms controversial. Every expense that is not included in the throughput definition (meaning it's not truly variable with units of sale) is included with OE. It's often characterized as the money flowing out of the system. Operating expense includes most categories of overhead (fixed expenses) — in other words, the cost of opening the doors for business each day. What makes OE controversial is that it also includes labor, both direct and indirect. Traditional cost accounting allocates direct labor to units of product sold (or projected for sale). In TOC, labor, both direct and indirect, is considered a fixed cost and is segregated from OE. Why?

The TOC rationale is that direct labor is not a direct expense. Labor is normally purchased in units of *time* — by compensating people for hours per week or month, or, in the case of salaried employees, for a year. Because of the interdependencies inherent in systems, not all the direct labor hours are actually used, and certainly not all of them are used for generating true added value. Consequently, a decision to produce, or not to produce, something — thus committing direct labor to it — does not incur any additional cost. Any direct labor time incurred is taken from the pool of hours for which fixed costs have already been incurred. Therefore, this really makes them an operating expense.

Any expenses paid or incurred on the basis of units of product sold are considered variable expenses, and therefore grouped in the throughput calculation. Traditional full-absorption accounting methods allocate a piece of these fixed costs (which also include other elements of overhead besides labor) to every unit of product made and sold. TOC suggests that this is a conceptually flawed approach. This is where the controversy usually arises. In Chapter 13, we'll discuss this controversy in a little more detail, as we talk about throughput-based decision support.

## Relation of T, I, and OE to Traditional Business Measures of Merit

We've referred to the TOC benchmarks as a bridge between local operating decisions and the corporate level financial measure of success. Now it's time to see how that bridge works. Net profit (NP) is equivalent to throughput minus operating expense. Throughput is the difference between total sales revenue and total truly variable costs (see Figure 3.1). Notice that the TOC calculation of profit does not ignore the expenses that traditional accounting normally allocates to units of product — it merely subtracts them after all the sales have been accounted for. The net profit answer should be the same.

Return on investment (ROI) is equivalent to net profit divided by the inventory or investment required to generate it (see Figure 3.1). The level of throughput that can be achieved is limited by the system constraint. Operating expense is generated primarily by non-constraints.

By now it should be clear where we're going with the bridge concept. We're not going to ask managers to try to measure their decisions against net profit and return on investment directly. Instead, were going to ask them to use T, I, and OE as assessment tools and translate them into effects on NP and ROI. We can improve NP and ROI by making T go up, and by making

$$\text{Net Profit} = \text{T} - \text{OE}$$

$$\text{Return on Investment} = \frac{\text{T} - \text{OE}}{\text{I}}$$

**Figure 3.1   Net Profit and Return on Investment**
(From Goldratt, Eliyahu, The Haystack Syndrome, Croton-on-Hudson, NY, The North River Press, 1990, 53. With permission.)

OE and I go down. As we'll see later, it's much easier for managers, supervisors, and operating level people to visualize the effects their efforts have on T, I, and OE than on NP and ROI, because many daily decisions impact only one of the three measurements.

## What Should Our Priorities Be?

The key question is, "Where should we place our management emphasis?" On reducing operating expense? On reducing investment? Or on increasing throughput? Traditionally, management has put the highest priority on reducing costs, which in most cases means reducing operating expense (see Figure 3.2). There are two compelling reasons for this. First, costs are easy to measure and relatively easy to control. Second, every dollar of cost saved goes directly to the bottom line (net profit).

| TRADITIONAL MANAGEMENT | JAPANESE MANAGEMENT ("JIT") | CONSTRAINT MANAGEMENT |
|---|---|---|
| 1. OE ↓ | 1. I ↓ | 1. T ↑ |
| 2. I ↓ | 2. T ↑ | 2. I ↓ |
| 3. T ↑ | 3. OE ↓ | 3. OE ↓ |

**Figure 3.2   Management Priorities**

The second priority for managers is usually inventory reduction. This is important because managers are painfully aware of the costs associated with maintaining high levels of inventory. But there is somewhat less pressure to eliminate excess inventory than to reduce operating expense because it appears as an asset on the financial balance sheet. The real importance of trying to eliminate excess inventory is that it can hurt throughput. Too much inventory inhibits response to market requirements and can slow introduction of new products even more. This reduces the amount of throughput that can be generated.

Increasing throughput usually seems to be last in priority, probably because managers think they have so little control over it — "T" comes from sales, which, of course, depend on external customers. And customers are often mercurial, capricious, and always highly uncertain. Better to concentrate on what we can directly control.

The Japanese saw the value to be achieved in reducing inventory, which was a key motivator in the development of Just-in-Time. To do that, they had to keep the pipeline flowing — a *pull* phenomenon — which meant that increasing throughput assumed a greater (though secondary) importance as well (see Figure 3.2).

Constraint theory suggests that increasing throughput ought to be the first priority. Reducing inventory, or investment, should be second. And reducing operating expense should be the last priority.

Why does constraint management emphasize increasing throughput? What's the rationale for putting throughput first, inventory second, and operating expense third? In its simplest form, the answer lies in another question: "Are we in business to save money or to make money?"

Take a look at the bar graph in Figure 3.3. The three bars represent operating expense, inventory, and throughput, in that order. The theoretical upper limit of the graph is infinity. The theoretical lower limit is zero. Operating expense and inventory can't be reduced below zero, and throughput can't be increased to infinity. But the practical limits for reducing OE and I are actually much higher than zero, because we have to spend some money to make money. The practical limit for increasing T is also much less than infinity, but its potential for adding to the bottom line is still significantly more than the potential for doing so by cost-cutting (OE and I reductions).

Moreover, there's a risk associated with cost-cutting. Because there's a fine line between spending enough and spending too little, if we cut OE and I too much, we hurt our ability to generate T. And in our efforts to slash these costs, who can say for sure exactly where that line is, and when we've crossed it? Remember the airplane analogy in Chapter 2? Just as a control change in

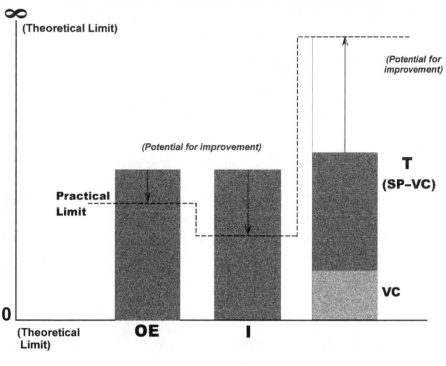

**Figure 3.3   Limits to T, I, and OE**

one axis can affect performance in one or more of the other two, so can a change in I or OE affect T. They're not entirely independent of each other.

Any organization that has been involved in some kind of TQM-based continuous improvement effort has probably made a significant dent in reducing OE and I already. There may not be much more water in that well. Increasing throughput offers the best real opportunity for most companies to improve profitability, now and in the future.

So the overarching strategy of constraint management is to focus primarily on increasing throughput. In doing the right things to make this happen (exploiting the constraint, subordinating non-constraints), inventory/investment is allowed to seek its own natural level. Usually this is a lower level than before constraint management was applied. Finally, constraint theory suggests capitalizing on opportunities to reduce operating expense.

However, in doing so we must ensure that whatever decisions we make don't compromise our capacity to generate T. We should also not waste time or endanger future T by actively searching for ways to reduce operating expense today. For these reasons, constraint management makes reducing OE a definite third priority.

## T, I, and OE: An Example

Let's see how the concepts of throughput, investment, and operating expense we've just discussed apply in the real world. Take a moment to read the article in Figure 3.4.

You can see where the emphasis is at Boeing. And you can see what the short-term effects are. But where in this article is increasing throughput (i.e., generating more sales) mentioned? Take a look at Figure 3.5.

Here's the mention of throughput! (Figure 3.5) Draw your own conclusions: Is Boeing doing the right thing by focusing exclusively on cutting costs and inventory/investment? They're using heavy cost-cutting to improve short-term profits, without any improvement (actually a decline) in sales. Between now and 2001 they will slash $2.7 billion in costs, trim their workforce (OE) by 20%, and facilities (I) by 23%. Yet only 2 years ago, they couldn't find enough skilled workers or floor space to fulfill orders for their 737 aircraft on time! And now they've lost significant sales to Airbus — their only competitor in the world! Will their reductions in OE and I offset their losses in T? Stay tuned . . . only time will tell. Could they have done things differently, with better results?

## Throughput (Constraint) Accounting

Managing by financial measures, usually cost, is what traditional management accounting is all about. Practitioners of constraint management refer to the use of T, I, and OE as *throughput accounting,* or sometimes *constraint accounting.* In actuality, T, I, and OE are decision support aids. They don't really qualify as an accounting method — at least, not yet — because the detailed quantitative rigor needed to satisfy the other requirements (external reporting to investors and tax agencies) has not yet been developed.

Moreover, we don't suggest that traditional accounting practices should be discarded in any event, as they effectively support the external reporting requirements previously mentioned. We do, however, suggest that managing by traditional cost-accounting principles delivers suboptimal results for whole business systems. Consequently, we recommend confining the use of generally accepted accounting procedures to external reporting only. But

---

Boeing sees earnings soar up, up, away    *USA Today*, Friday, July 16, 1999, p. 1B

Cost cutting cited in 172% increase in second quarter

by David Field, USA TODAY

NEW YORK — Boeing's earnings leaped 172% in the second quarter as cost-cutting steps began to work, Chief Financial Officer Debby Hopkins said here Thursday. In one of her first appearances since joining Boeing in December, Hopkins unveiled a quarterly report card to gauge its progress in turning around the commercial aircraft business.

The turnaround is under way, she said, second-quarter net income rose to $701 million, or 75 cents a share, compared with $258 million, or 26 cents a share, a year ago. Its operating income was $793 million, up from $416 million in the 1998 period. Across all of its operations — airliners to space to defense — revenue rose 13% to $15.13 billion from $13.39 billion a year ago. Its profit margin rose to 4.6% from 1.9% in 1998 second quarter.

Hopkins' efforts are winning favor on Wall Street. Boeing shares sagged by one-third in 1998, but by Wednesday had set an 11-month high of $47. Shares dipped 7/8 Thursday on profit-taking to $46 3/4. One way to boost share price is cutting jobs, she said. Boeing will lop about 48,000 jobs by the end of next year from a 1998 peak of 238,600 workers.

Its key tools for tracking Boeing's improvement are four bench-marks that will be reported quarterly in a "value scorecard." The measures:

- **Factory space.** "When you look at the facilities we now have, it's just staggering." Hopkins said of Boeing's 124 million square feet of factory space across the country. Her goal is to get that to 122 million square feet by Dec. 31, to 109 million by the end of 2000 and eventually to 95 million square feet.
- **The number of suppliers.** Boeing wants to cut that from 31,500 now to 31,000 by Dec. 31 to 25,000 next year and eventually to 18,000.
- **Inventory turnover.** Boeing will raise the number of times a year that it replaces supplies by trimming the manufacturing process. The higher the turnover, the faster it uses parts, saving storage. It wants to raise turnover from 2.5 a year now to 2.9 by year's end, 3 in 2000 and eventually 4 a year. "The more they do, the more cash they'll have," says JSA Research analyst Paul Nisbet.
- **Overhead.** Boeing will cut $600 million from costs this year. $1.6 billion more in 2000 and, eventually, $2.1 billion more.

---

**Figure 3.4    Boeing Article #1 (*USA Today*)**

---

**Airbus shoots ahead of Boeing on new jet orders in first half**
> —Printed in the *Seattle Times*, Business News, July 20, 1999

by Andrea Rothman and Peter Robinson, Bloomberg News

TOULOUSE, France — Airbus Industrie shot ahead of rival Boeing in winning airplane orders in the first half of 1999, racking up sales of 234 planes against 120 for Boeing, the two companies said.

The strong showing for the European aircraft maker, the world's second-largest after Boeing, comes as both manufacturers are bracing for a steep decline in orders over the next few years, partly the result of airlines ordering greater-than-expected numbers of planes in the last three years amid fierce price-cutting in the race for market share.

In the past 18 months, Airbus has snatched some of Boeing's most reliable customers, which analysts attribute partly to their frustration over late deliveries as Boeing struggled with production bottlenecks. Orders for big jetliners, a Boeing mainstay, are also down because of the slump in Asia's economy.

"The six-month numbers are confirmation that Airbus is on a high just now, and that Boeing still hasn't shaken off its production hangover," said Doug McVitie, managing director of Arran Aerospace, an aviation-forecasting and consulting company based in Scotland.

The figures don't include a 50-plane order from International Lease Finance for Boeing that was announced in June but won't be signed until this month.

Even as Boeing beat forecasts when it reported a 55 percent jump in second-quarter profit last week, McVitie said the earnings report gave no indication that Boeing was doing a better job of winning orders.

---

**Figure 3.5 Boeing Article #2 (*Seattle Times*)**

there is still a pressing need for a rational, effective way to help managers make the right tactical and operational decisions. The purpose of measures like T, I, and OE is to help managers make decisions that will advance the organization toward its goal. To that end, T, I, and OE are better characterized as *Throughput-Based Decision Support,* and that's the way we'll refer to them hereafter.

# References

1. Goldratt, Eliyahu M., *The Haystack Syndrome,* Croton-on-Hudson, NY, The North River Press, 1990, 53.

# 4 Constraint Management Tools

uccess or failure in any endeavor often relies on the selection and proper use of the right tools. Constraint management is no different. While the Five Focusing Steps are effective guidelines for the tactical and strategic management of any kind of system, in specific situations the nature of the constraints and the problems associated with them call for different tools and procedures. Exploiting a constraint would be done differently in a service environment than in a production process. Subordination would be different in a heavy manufacturing company that produces standardized products than it would in a small job shop. Knowing which of the tools of constraint management to apply requires a prior understanding of the different types of constraints and their characteristics.

## Types of Constraints

In their initial exposure to constraint theory, people are often bewildered by the wide variety of factors that could constrain an organization. On closer examination, however, almost anything that might be identified as a constraint falls into one of seven categories.

1. The *market* is always a prime candidate to be a constraint. Anytime sales demand is less than the system's capacity to handle that demand, we consider a market constraint to be active.

2. *Resources* are another obvious type of constraint. We're referring here to the people, equipment, or machines that do the work of producing a product or service. When an internal resource isn't able to respond to all the requirements the market demand imposes on it, that resource is considered an active constraint. Support (indirect) functions fall into this category of constraint, too.

3. A *material* constraint exists when a system can't obtain enough raw material or supplies to do its manufacturing or service job. We're talking about external material shortages, or the inability to obtain sufficient quality material, not unreliable suppliers.

4. *Vendors/suppliers* can also be a constraint. Their delivery reliability is bad, or their quoted lead times are so long that they discourage market demand for finished products. As you can see, this is different from non-availability of material or supplies.

5. Everybody always says they're financially constrained. But in reality, what they mean is they're budget-constrained. A true *financial* constraint occurs only when a company doesn't have the financial resources to meet its obligations — a cash flow problem. For example, some small companies are financially constrained when they need to sell (and be paid for) products so they can use that money to buy raw materials to fulfill other orders. If there isn't enough cash, any other constraints might not matter.

6. A *knowledge or competence* constraint is similar to a resource constraint. A knowledge constraint occurs when the organization doesn't know how to do what needs to be done to succeed. For example, not knowing how to produce high-quality, precision parts may limit a company's future success. It may also be that the company doesn't have enough competence in tasks that need to be performed, such as engineering, marketing, or information management. We consider competence to be a constraint only when an existing competence is used to its limit, and any improvement in that particular competence will result in more profit.

7. The last, and most pervasive, type of constraint is *policy*. A policy might be a written document, although it doesn't have to be. Policies may be no more than ways of thinking, or cultural mores. "That's not the way we do things around here!" is essentially a policy constraint, even if it's not written down anywhere. "We've always done it this way," is the other side of the same coin. "Not invented here" is another example of a tacit policy constraint. We consider cultural constraints

— the norms and values that limit improvements to organizational performance — as policy constraints, too.

Policy constraints are the most insidious of all, because in the final analysis almost every other type of constraint is driven by some kind of policy. Consequently, the changes needed to properly identify, exploit, or elevate constraints, and to subordinate non-constraints, will inevitably require changing policies somewhere within the organization. To the extent that this is difficult to do, the policy, rather than the physical resource, is likely to be the real system constraint.

We've said that very few factors constitute true system constraints. In fact, at any given time, there might be no more than one active constraint. How can we know when one of these constraint types is currently the active one? Here's a simple rule of thumb: If any change in the activity of a system element will directly (and quickly) impact the bottom line, that factor can be considered an active constraint. For example, an unreliable vendor is probably not an active constraint, even though its inferior performance may cause us a lot of trouble. For a vendor to be a constraint, we need to demonstrate by direct cause-and-effect logic that improvement in that vendor's reliability will have a significant, relatively immediate positive effect on the bottom line. Beware of quickly defining as constraints all kinds of limitations that seem undesirable, but don't directly limit the achievement of the company's over-all goal.

## Constraint Types: Examples

Here are some typical examples of the constraint types mentioned above.

*Market constraint.* The occupancy rate at a vacation resort drops from nearly 100% in August to less than 30% in October and November (not enough sales).

*Resource constraint.* Orders for barbecue grills increase to the point that a sheet-metal fabrication company has to delay promised delivery dates, because the shop floor can't produce the grills fast enough (capacity limitation). The delay causes some potential customers to look somewhere else for their barbecue grills.

*Material constraint.* Timber harvesting (and lumber production) is slowed or stopped because the Bureau of Land Management ran out of

*Peninsula Daily News* (Associated Press), Port Angeles, WA,

**Monday, Aug. 2, 1999, p. A5**

**Delays in spray paint delivery curtail Forest Service harvests**

Associated Press

Logging in federal forests is down by as much as 25 percent this year in regions outside the Northwest because the U.S. Forest Service can't find enough of the paint it needs to mark trees for cutting. The agency says that it will try to make up the logging deficit by next year at the latest.

The paint shortage so far has not had an impact on timber sales in Washington and Oregon. "We still have paint, but we're running low — and we have an emergency order in," spokesman Rex Holloway said.

Timber sales in the five-state Rocky Mountain region are down between 15 and 25 percent because of the paint shortage, forest officials said. Many of the other nine regions are in "roughly the same ballpark," although they could catch up before the end of the year, said Ann Bartuska, director of forest management for the Forest Service in Washington, D.C. "People are coping perfectly well," she added.

Some foresters are marking trees the old fashioned way while they wait for the paint — using a hatchet to notch the trees, Bartuska said.

The agency on May 15 stopped using, oil-based paint to mark the trees it plans to cut down, after workers blamed the paint on an increase in miscarriages and other ailments. But Bartuska said the transition to water-based paint was more difficult than expected. There was an explosion at a paint factory, procurement delays by the General Services Administration and delays in getting the forest workers' union to approve the new paint.

"Everything that could go wrong has gone wrong," she said, adding that the Forest Service is rushing as much paint out to forests as it can.

Timber sales in the Rocky Mountain region — South Dakota, Nebraska, Kansas, Wyoming and Colorado — will be down between 30 million and 51 million board feet this year, regional forester Lyle Laverty said, in a letter earlier this month. That disclosure prompted a letter last week from six senators to Forest Service Chief Make Dombeck.

"These downfalls are not acceptable," the senators from Wyoming, South Dakota and Colorado wrote.

**Figure 4.1    BLM Paint Article**

environmentally friendly paint with which to mark trees that may be cut. (See accompanying article, Figure 4.1.)

*Vendor/supplier constraint.* A supplier of rubber seals routinely ships 2000 seals to satisfy a customer order for 1000 because 50% of the seals in any one order are bad, and the supplier can't figure out how to separate the good ones from the bad ones (quality/reliability). These quality problems directly cause loss of substantial market share the company could have served with their existing capacity.

*Financial constraint.* A small vendor of precision machined parts quotes a 3-week delivery time for an order, not because it actually takes that long to build the order, but because the vendor must wait for payment from a previously delivered order to have enough cash to buy the stock for the current order (cash flow) These quotes cause the loss of potential business.

*Knowledge/competence constraint.* A small manufacturer loses sales because customers require some special heat treatment, and the company is not very good at doing it (competence). Another manufacturer fails to export to other countries because no one in the company knows how to open a subsidiary in a foreign country (knowledge).

*Policy constraint.* A company's board of directors rejects a product development proposal because it does not deliver an internal rate of return exceeding 22% within 2 years (historically established standard).

## The Logical Thinking Process

With so many different kinds of constraints, and with policy constraints underlying most of them, how can we identify the specific changes we should be working on? Many of these constraints aren't easy to identify. Often, they're not physical, or they're not easy to measure. They sometimes extend beyond the boundaries of production processes alone, although they still affect manufacturing, and sometimes — especially if they're policies — they pervade the whole organization.

To facilitate the analysis of complex systems, Goldratt created a logical thinking process. The thinking process is composed of six logic diagrams, or "trees." The Current Reality Tree (CRT) is designed to help identify the system constraint, especially when that constraint is a policy of some kind. The Evaporating Cloud (EC) — a kind of conflict resolution diagram — helps resolve hidden, underlying conflicts that tend to perpetuate the constraint. The Future Reality Tree (FRT) tests and validates potential solutions. The Negative Branch, which is properly a subset of the FRT, helps identify and avoid any new, devastating effects that might result from the solution. The Prerequisite Tree (PRT) helps to bring to the surface and eliminate obstacles to implementation of a chosen solution. It also time-sequences the actions required to achieve the objective. The Transition Tree (TT) can facilitate the development of step-by-step implementation plans.

These tools are specifically designed to help answer the three major questions inherent in the first three of the five focusing steps: *What* to change, what to change *to*, and how to *cause* the change? It is not the objective of this book to address the construction and application of the logical thinking process. There are other books better suited to that task.* However, you'll notice that several of the thinking process logic trees are used in this book to communicate various conclusions about manufacturing and business issues.

Though we won't be getting into how to build these logic trees, it is necessary to understand how to read them. The Current Reality Tree, Future Reality Tree, Negative Branch, and Transition Tree are cause-and-effect trees. They're read using "If... then...", as you did with Figures I.1 and 2.2 (Generic Manufacturing Current Reality Tree and Assumption #3, Current Reality Tree). The Evaporating Cloud and Prerequisite Tree are read a little differently. They're what we call "necessary condition" trees and are read using "In order to have... we must...". For example, "*In order to* make more money, now and in the future, *we must* increase Throughput." Figure 4.2 shows how this statement is graphically represented in a necessary condition relationship.

## Critical Chain

Another valuable asset in the constraint management toolbox is called "critical chain." Also the title of a book by Goldratt,** the critical chain concept provides an effective way to schedule project activities by accommodating uncertainty and resolving simultaneous needs (contentions) for the same resource. The result of applying critical-chain scheduling and resource allocation is a higher probability of completing projects on time, and, in some cases, actually shortening total project duration.***

---

* Refer to:
1. Dettmer, H. William, *Goldratt's Theory of Constraints: A Systems Approach to Continuous Improvement,* Milwaukee, WI, ASQ Quality Press, 1997.
2. Dettmer, H. William, *Breaking the Constraints to World-Class Performance,* Milwaukee, WI, ASQ Quality Press, 1998.
3. Scheinkopf, Lisa J., *Thinking for a Change: Putting the TOC Thinking Processes to Use,* Boca Raton, FL, St. Lucie Press, 1999.
** Goldratt, Eliyahu M., *Critical Chain,* Great Barrington, MA, The North River Press, 1997.
***For more details on how the critical chain concept works in actual application, refer to:
Leach, Lawrence P., *Critical Chain Project Management,* NY, Artech House, 2000.
Newbold, Robert C., *Project Management in the Fast Lane: Applying the Theory of Constraints,* Boca Raton, FL, St. Lucie Press, 1998.

**Evaporating Cloud**                    **Prerequisite Tree**

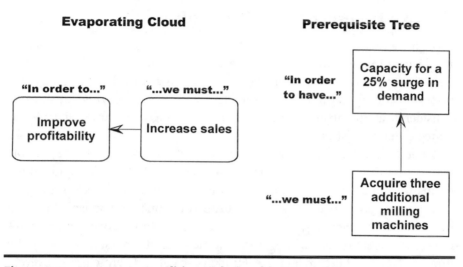

**Figure 4.2    Necessary Condition Relationship (Example)**

## Drum-Buffer-Rope Production Scheduling

Probably the best known of the constraint management tools developed by Goldratt is "Drum-Buffer-Rope." The origin of this name dates back to the analogy Goldratt and Cox used in *The Goal*[1] to describe a system with dependencies and statistical fluctuations. The analogy was a description of a boy scout hike. The drum was the pace of the slowest boy scout, which dictated the pace for the others. The buffer and rope were additional means to ensure all the boy scouts walked at approximately the pace of the slowest boy.

Goldratt and Fox, in *The Race*,* describe in detail the manufacturing procedure that stems from the concepts of a drum, a buffer, and a rope originally introduced through the boy scout hike. The Drum-Buffer-Rope (DBR) method sets the means for synchronizing an entire manufacturing process with the pace of the least capable resource. This book introduces a simplified version of the original Drum-Buffer-Rope developed by Goldratt and compares the two versions.

---

* Goldratt, Eliyahu M. and Robert E. Fox, *The Race*, Croton-on-Hudson, NY, The North River Press, 1986.

## The Five Focusing Steps Revisited

Though we've already discussed the five focusing steps as basic principles of the theory of constraints, they can be considered tools as well. The use of the word "steps" connotes a kind of cookbook procedure, but these steps are more of a conceptual framework for identifying and managing constraints. Considered at the abstract level, the five focusing steps have tactical and strategic characteristics.

Exploitation and subordination improve *today's* throughput. They enable us to realize more from our existing resources. When we exploit and subordinate, we should expect throughput to increase, but we should not expect operating expense to decrease — it probably won't. But it isn't likely to increase, either. Inventory, or investment, is likely to go down naturally — or we may safely reduce it. But under some circumstances, it may stay the same, too. It is not likely to increase. Hidden capacity is likely to be uncovered, which permits throughput to increase without incurring additional cost. Exploitation and subordination may be said to "squeeze blood from a stone."

Identification and elevation are concerned with improving *future* throughput. Besides telling us where the system constraint lies today, the identification step can also predict where the constraint will go in the future. After exploiting and subordinating, there is no more "blood" to be extracted from the stone. Our only option is to find more stones! That's what elevation does for us. But when we elevate, we should *expect* operating expense, inventory/investment, or both, to increase — after all, we're acquiring more new capacity, and that does not come for free. But we should also expect a significant increase in throughput, enough to more than offset the increase in OE and I.

To briefly summarize (Figure 4.3), the *exploit* and *subordinate* steps can be considered tactical activities. They are designed to maximize today's throughput. In other words, they tell us where the constraint is *today* and what we should do about it. The *identify* and *elevate* steps can be considered strategic activities. Determining where the constraint is today and taking steps that can move it somewhere else tomorrow definitely affects system-level strategy. Elevation is intended to maximize future throughput. In other words, these steps tell us where the constraint will be tomorrow, and what should we do about it.

Appendix A describes a tabletop exercise called "The Dice Game" that demonstrates the importance of optimizing the whole manufacturing system and shows the impact of variability (statistical fluctuation) on dependent events.

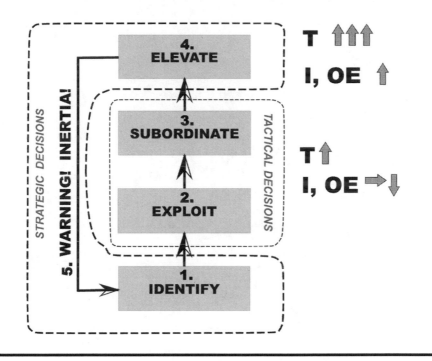

**Figure 4.3    Five Focusing Steps: Strategic as Well as Tactical**

# Reference

1.  Goldratt, Eliyah M. and Jeff Cox, *The Goal*, 2nd ed., Croton-on-Hudson, NY, The North River Press, 1992, 103–119.

# 5   How Work Flows through a Manufacturing Process

N ow that we've completed our first look at constraint theory and had the opportunity to see a relatively simple application in the dice game (Appendix A), we're ready to find out how it applies in a more realistic manufacturing environment.

The flow of work through a manufacturing process has a direct bearing on how we exploit an internal constraint and subordinate non-constraints. Manufacturing processes differ by their structure and the nature of the flow of work-in-process through that structure. While constraint theory applies to all types of work flow, it is applied a little differently in each type.

Nearly all manufacturing processes fit into at least one type, and sometimes a combination of them. The four basic types of work flow are referred to as "A," "V," "T," and "I." This taxonomy is based on the graphical representation of their respective flows.

## The "A" Flow

The "A" flow is so named because it resembles the letter "A." In Figure 5.1, the "A" is turned on its side. "A" flows typically begin with a larger number of raw materials that are combined in some way as they proceed through production, ending in a fewer number of finished products. Most "A" flows

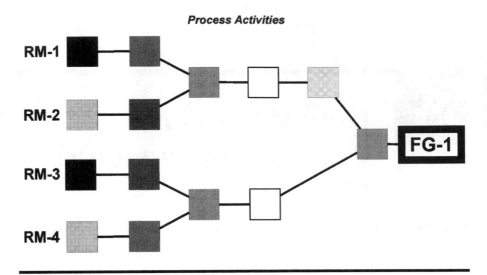

**Figure 5.1    "A" Flow**

are typical assembly operations, such as job shops, aircraft construction, and consumer electronics.

## The "V" Flow

The second type of flow is the "V," so named because it resembles a letter "V." In Figure 5.2, the "V" is laid on its side. A typical "V" flow begins with very few raw materials — maybe only one. The flow of materials through a "V"-shaped process diverges as it proceeds through production, resulting in many more different kinds of finished goods. A capacity-constrained resource (CCR), if there is one, is usually located near the beginning of the process. "V" plants are characterized by expensive equipment and long setups.

Some examples of "V"-type industries include steel-making, plastics, wood products and paper, and oil refining. Some kinds of food processing fit the "V" characterization as well. Potatoes can become packaged hash browns, french fries, or home fries, as well as a wide variety of potato chips.

## The "I" Flow

"I"-type flows are so named because they resemble a straight line from a few raw materials to a few finished products (see Figure 5.3). These are often dedicated assembly lines. In typical "I" flows, the line produces only a limited

**Process Activities**

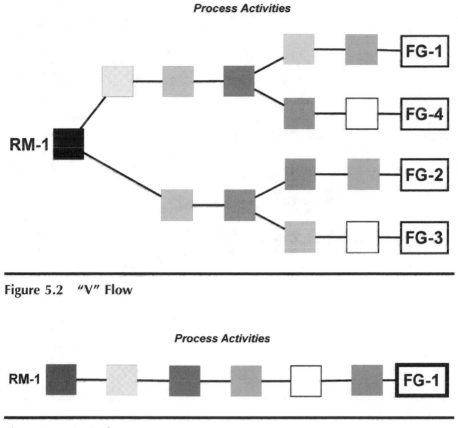

**Figure 5.2** "V" Flow

**Process Activities**

**Figure 5.3** "I" Flow

number of products, and it works on only one product at a time. Examples of "I" flows include food and chemical industries, sheet-metal fabrication, and some kinds of consumer goods.

## The "T" Flow

"T"-shaped flows are so named because they resemble the letter "T" (see Figure 5.4). A "T" flow reflects a limited number of components that can be assembled in a wide variety of ways to create a very large number of finished products — far more than the number of original components. This latter part of the process, starting with the components, is similar to the "V" flow. However, the front end of the process — the making of the components — is usually composed of somewhat independent flows which may resemble either an "A" or an "I." Consequently, "T" flows are essentially combinations

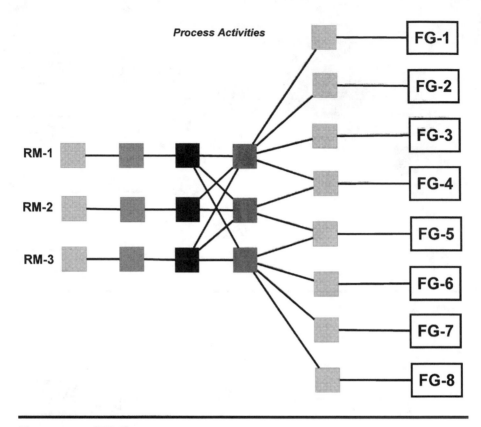

**Figure 5.4    "T" Flow**

of "V" and "A" or "I" flows. In Figure 5.4, you can see that the process starts out looking like an "I." It transitions to an "A" at the assembly points (in the middle), and it becomes a "V" at the end.

In a "T"-type plant, no real CCR dominates, because this structure is too complex, demand for given end products usually fluctuates, and there is a need for excess capacity everywhere in the system. In "T" plants, final assemblies experience the most problems, even though they have excess capacity, because of starvation due primarily to stealing,* and ineffective or improper subordination. Examples of "T"-type flows include automobile manufacture and circuit card assembly.

---

* Stealing in this case is not actually a crime. It refers to the deliberate or inadvertent misdirection of common parts at a divergence point. For example, if a manufacturing process step produces a motor-driven compressor for each of two different end products, and a batch of compressors scheduled to go to the first product is taken by a machine operator at the succeeding step to build the second product, we say that stealing has occurred.

Each of these types of flow presents its own unique challenges to management, but constraint theory can be effectively applied to any of them.

## Various Manufacturing Environments and Their Specific Problems

Besides the differences presented by "A," "V," "T," and "I" work flows, another kind manufacturing environment exists in every production organization. This environment results from the customer fulfillment strategy the company chooses. Any production organization can be characterized as *make-to-order, make-to-stock or to forecast,* or *assemble-to-order.* Some authors on production management suggest that "A" plants tend to be make-to-stock while "V" plants are make-to-order. Their rationale is usually based on the relatively fewer products resulting from an "A" than from a "V." However, these days most "A" plants produce a greater number of different kinds of products than ever before. Some of them are job-shops with full customization, meaning there is no way to effectively make-to-stock. On the other hand, many "V" plants employ make-to-stock, often assisted by forecasting, because their customers demand very fast response.

It seems there's little correlation between the type of flow and whether the manufacturing strategy is make-to-stock, make-to-order/make-to-forecast, or assemble-to-order. The nature of the problems associated with any of the "make-to…" environments is different from the problems resulting from the type of flow.

What category your organization falls into is, to a certain extent, a voluntary choice. In some cases, however, the market situation may push a company toward one fulfillment strategy rather than another. For example, some types of businesses voluntarily choose to be make-to-order. They don't build products until (and unless) they have a firm order for them. On the other hand, many organizations have customers who demand exceptionally fast response to their requests — faster than the company can build and deliver an order. These companies are usually forced to manufacture some stock ahead of time to be able to ship immediately upon request. Those same organizations usually use forecasts to decide how much to build ahead of time.

Some companies avoid making to stock by building partial assemblies — usually common ones — that are stored for use when a firm order comes in. This is a way of getting a head start on a long manufacturing process. By building these partial assemblies ahead of time (before there is an actual demand for them), companies often can significantly cut manufacturing lead time.

## Make-to-Order: The Preferred Way, Whenever Possible

The theory of constraints encourages a *make-to-order* philosophy to the maximum extent possible. There are several good reasons for this.

1. Subordinating to a market constraint is easier and more efficient in make-to-order than it is in make-to-stock or make-to-forecast, because the relationship with the customer is direct. There's no need to guess what is needed now and what's not.
2. Exploitation of an internal constraint — also known as a capacity-constrained resource (CCR) — is also better. The system produces only what the market really requires and does so according to real priorities.
3. True levels of capacity and load are more visible in make-to-order, because no one is confusing the issue by producing something that isn't absolutely needed right now.
4. Finally, the risk of obsolete inventory is dramatically reduced.

One of the most devastating mistakes a manufacturing organization can make is to turn a make-to-order operation into a make-to-stock in a misguided attempt to smooth the load on the system (that is, to make non-constraints more efficient). A second serious mistake an organization can make is to fail to move toward a make-to-order operation when it has the capability to do so, even if only partially, because its managers don't think it can be done.

## Make-to-Stock

If make-to-order is such a good way to operate, why do companies voluntarily choose to make-to-stock? One reason is that it is a relatively convenient, stable business operation. We always know how much we're going to produce next week, next month, and next quarter. This makes production scheduling much easier to do.

Another reason is that confirmations to customers can be made on the basis of what is in stock, — i.e., ready to deliver now — not on promises from production. Also, off-the-shelf delivery to customers is a faster response.

The real motivation for making to stock, however, is that usually our actual production lead time is longer than the customers can or will wait for delivery. The objective of constraint management in manufacturing is to enable lead times short enough that the company can make-to-order as much as possible and still deliver in time to meet the customer's needs. For example, if a customer requires delivery in 2 days, and you have the capability to make-to-order in that time, why would you ever maintain more than a minimal "insurance" amount of finished goods inventory? The theory of constraints aims to bring the production operation as close as possible to make-to-order by enabling the reduction of actual manufacturing lead time.

The reason TOC favors a make-to-order approach is that there are several sticky problems associated with making to stock. First, finished-goods stock costs money — real money, not pure paper figures — that isn't required in a make-to-order mode. In make-to-stock, funds must be expended for the raw materials to manufacture the finished stock. These fixed costs tie up money so that it can't otherwise be spent on activities that directly generate throughput, because the company is committed to holding inventory. Moreover, a certain percentage of inventory often "dies" — it becomes obsolete before it can be sold. It must then be scrapped or sold below the variable cost of manufacture just to clear it out of the warehouse.

Second, introducing new products becomes much more complicated because of the need to get rid of old product inventory first. The switch between the old and the new must be effectively planned, so no unsold old finished goods will remain.

Third, trying to identify changing market trends from stock consumption data is not easy. In a make-to-order environment, the backlog directly reflects the exact current demand. But in make-to-stock, the volume of sales per product in different time windows must be observed to detect a change in the market's taste.

Finally, it's not easy to exploit an internal constraint in a make-to-stock environment. Exploitation means maximizing the throughput generation of a constrained resource, but when that resource's time is divided between manufacturing what is needed now and what isn't, the management of priorities becomes more complicated.

It should also be noted that once you're in a make-to-stock mode, it's very difficult to get out of it. The warm, fuzzy feeling of convenience it provides motivates people to stay in that comfort zone.

Though make-to-order offers definite advantages over make-to-stock, in some situations make-to-stock can't be avoided. This is usually the case when a company's market demands delivery faster than the company can produce. Failing to meet the customer's expectation for fast delivery has both short- and long-term impact. In the short term it's loss of an order (today's "T"). In the long term, it could be loss of a customer (future "T"). However, while we may be forced into some degree of make-to-stock by the behavior of our market, we should not accept make-to-stock as an exclusive way of life. If we can produce faster (shorten manufacturing lead time), we can produce to order more often and eliminate, or vastly reduce, the need to build finished stock. Make-to-stock should be reserved for only those circumstances in which there is no alternative. However, when manufacturing lead time is shortened as much as feasible, rather than accepting make-to-stock as a way of life, we should look for market segments that are prepared to wait a little longer in exchange for more value (e.g., discounts). Waiting longer in this case means not weeks or months, but perhaps days.

## Make-to-Forecast: A Variation of Make-to-Stock

A significant number of companies base their production planning on a forecast of future sales. On the surface, this looks like a superior way — better than traditional make-to-stock — for solving the problem of having to deliver faster than the production lead time. Forecasting is also used heavily for purchasing material. Let's first address the role of forecasting in production planning, then we'll talk about it's role in purchasing.

The rationale for forecasting is simple and straightforward. We wish we could produce just to order. But sometimes this isn't possible, because the customer's patience is shorter than our manufacturing lead time. If we can't persuade our customers to relax their requirement for immediate delivery and we can't shorten the manufacturing lead time to match our customers' requirements, we're forced to produce finished products before we have a firm order in hand. There seem to be two ways to do this. One is to make-to-stock. As we have seen, this way involves determining a fixed re-order point, which should be based on a gross estimate of future demand. The other, much more sophisticated way, is to make-to-forecast. This requires predicting future sales and producing according to that prediction.

The advantage of make-to-forecast over make-to-stock is that it affords us much further visibility into the future, providing the opportunity to better smooth the load throughout the year. It also allows us to hold many fewer finished goods in inventory. It is a clear winner. Or is it really?

Make-to-forecast can be a clear winner only if the forecast is *very* reliable. Unfortunately, in the real world, forecasts seldom are. Moreover, decision making based on a forecast isn't simple at all. Let's consider a simple example. Suppose the sales forecast for product P109 for February is 100 units. This is the best forecast we can get anywhere. The production lead time of P109 is about 1 month, and it's now January 1. Let's ignore the fact that sales predictions cover a whole month. How much should we produce? Do we really want to have 100 units of P109 on February 1? Not necessarily. In most cases we should have more on hand.

In order to make a sound decision, we need an additional piece of information that we usually miss, and it is quite crucial: *forecasting error*. Any forecast aims at the expected value. In other words, the average sales expected. But even when the forecast exactly hits the expected value, actual sales may deviate from it. The forecasting error is a measure of the possible deviation from the expected value. The probability that February sales of P109 will be exactly 100 is quite small. Actually, it's likely to be more or less than 100. So what do we do?

The most common solution is to determine a level of safety stock. How much should this be: 10, 20, or 100% of the expected value? The rationale usually is that safety stock should cover one or two standard deviations of forecasting error, depending on the level of service required by management. In reality, the forecasting error is included only very rarely, and a managerial quantitative definition of a service level isn't too common, either.

There are two reasons why we don't see the forecasting error very often. First, when forecasts are based on the intuition of the marketing people, the concept of error simply doesn't exist. An alternative might be to use a reasonable range of sales, specifying the February sales as a range, for instance, between 70 and 130. However, even this simpler, more intuitive concept isn't used frequently.

Second, even when the forecasting error is available, and computerized algorithms are able to assess it, the error may be so large that the whole notion of forecasting seems dubious. Suppose the forecasting error for February is 200, or twice the expected value. It's not uncommon for forecasting errors to be larger than the average. What this means is that the "noise" in the system is such that there is no real value in the forecast itself. Suppose that in reality there is an upward trend of 5% every month. This is a very nice trend, but when the noise of the system is much larger, it may take a very long time before the trend is identified. Moreover, any forecast algorithm is bound to be erratic.

The desire for better forecasts has led companies to base them on aggregated demand. While an aggregate forecast may be much more reliable, the way it is actually used for decision making is really no better at all. Suppose we have a family of products called P100, that contains products P101 to P109. While the forecast for the total sales of P100 may be good (a relatively small forecasting error), most of the detailed production-planning decisions have to consider individual products. Deciding that P109, for instance, is 12% of the total P100 family sales is a very crude forecasting decision, which compromises the reliability of the aggregated forecast. The result is a very unreliable forecast for P109, and a very poor basis for planning.

It's interesting to note, too, that most companies using forecasting as the basis of their production schedule suffer from excessively high inventories and too many shortages at the same time. Most markets experience significant sales fluctuations. In such an environment, make-to-stock is substantially superior, because it allows fast reaction to changes in market demand. As we'll see later, make-to-stock lends itself as a very good control mechanism that can signal when a problem is emerging. One such problem may be that the demand increases sharply, and the current replenishment level may be insufficient.

An active control is not very simple and straightforward in make-to-forecast. In fact, the only real control method in make-to-forecast is constant re-forecasting, which eventually leads to constant reshuffling of planning. It's ironic that the desire for long-term visibility prompted a move toward make-to-forecast, causing more confusion between planning and execution with make-to-forecast than without it, eventually leading to less reliable long-term visibility!

Still, forecasting does have a role in production planning. There is one clear case where a forecast is the only effective tool we have: when huge peaks of sales exist for a very short period of time. In this case, we can't rely on the rules of continuous replenishment to a fixed level. We have a pressing need to decide how much to produce before the peak occurs, and this number can't be derived from current sales. If you absolutely have to depend on a forecast, keep in mind that you need *both* the forecast *and* the forecasting error to make effective decisions. It's certainly nice to know the average sales at peak demand, but knowing how reasonable that average is and how low the actual figure may go can be even more beneficial.

In a make-to-stock environment, the forecast should be considered a control aid. The forecast can give a sense of whether current replenishment levels are adequate. A decision to change the replenishment level should be made only when the forecast is significantly different from the stock level routinely used.

In make-to-stock, the replenishment level serves to buffer or protect us from two independent sources of uncertainty: market demand and actual production lead time variability. A forecast of market demand (including the forecasting error) should be only a partial input to the decision. When a clear seasonal demand pattern exists, we should expect to change replenishment levels accordingly.

Other aspects of production planning have a more pressing need for forecasting. Capacity planning usually considers longer periods. Aggregate forecasting is much more useful in this situation, because we don't need details about the exact products to be manufactured at any given time. The purpose of capacity planning is to estimate approximate magnitude. Forecasts can be effective at this.

## Forecasts and Raw Material Inventories

The challenge of managing raw materials stems from the fact that the time horizon is much longer. Because forecast accuracy drops farther out into the future, the reliability of raw material plans based on a forecast deteriorates, sometimes precipitously. For raw materials that have long, stable shelf lives (usually meaning that they are going to be used for quite a while), managing raw material stocks the same way as in make-to-stock is usually sufficient. This is especially true when a forecast is used to maintain good control by verifying the validity of inventory levels.

Raw materials with restricted shelf-lives need to be based on forecast, tempered with some other inputs before translating the forecast into actions. Don't simply take the result of the forecast in deciding when and how much to buy. Other factors to consider include the forecasting error (or a reasonable range), the price of the item, the anticipated damage resulting from a stock-out, and the response time and reliability of the supplier. Raw material buying decisions are somewhat sophisticated. They shouldn't be just a straightforward result of forecasting input.

There can be a major difference in the relative noise of consumption between different raw materials. Items that go into some end-products are much more stable than others. In any case, bear in mind that material stock is impacted by two nearly independent variables: market demand, which generates demand for materials, and the actual delivery time of raw material suppliers. The "red-line" control mechanism, explained later in this book, when applied to replenishment stock levels, can be very effective in tracking both variables and signaling when a threat to material availability emerges.

In summary, the way forecasting is used today is ultimately to the disadvantage of manufacturing systems. In most cases, a much simpler make-to-stock approach can be more effective than make-to-forecast. In those cases where a forecast is absolutely required, its use should include the forecasting error, or the equivalent notion of the reasonable range. When discrete forecast values are incorporated directly into any production or inventory planning, you can conclude that somebody didn't do their homework.

Goldratt contends that any system can be optimized only to the level of the natural noise within the system, and trying to optimize beyond that level actually damages the system. Deming has made the same point.[1] Relying too heavily on a forecast to represent our reality is the same as trying to optimize the system beyond its natural noise level.

## *Assemble-to-Order*

One alternative to making to stock (or to forecast) is assemble-to-order. This is really a combination of elements of make-to-order and make-to-stock. In assemble-to-order, manufacturing lead time is conserved by pre-assembling intermediate portions of the finished product. This assembly is usually confined to the longest lead-time operations. Assemble-to-order can be useful when intermediate assemblies are common to more than one product. The intermediate assemblies are managed as if they were made-to-stock finished products, but the real finished product is still managed as make-to-order. The principles of TOC apply to both aspects of the assemble-to-order environment.

In summary, make-to-order is the best approach. This philosophy demands shorter production lead times, which TOC is designed to provide. To the extent that make-to-order is not feasible, the first fallback to consider should be assemble-to-order. If assemble-to-order isn't sufficient, make-to-stock is next in priority, and make-to-forecast is a last resort — and only in cases where it is known to be fairly accurate. The use of make-to-stock and make-to-forecast should be minimized as much as possible. Finished stock targets should be designed to cover only the difference between the delivery response time demanded by the market and the shortest possible manufacturing lead time.

## Reference

1. Deming, W. Edwards, *Out of the Crisis,* Cambridge, MA, MIT Center for Advanced Engineering Study, 1986.

# TRADITIONAL DRUM-BUFFER-ROPE

# 6 Applying Constraints Theory to Manufacturing Operations

You'll recall that one of the most important principles we talked about in Part I was the idea that the best efficiency of a whole system is not the sum of the local efficiencies. Improving each part of the process to the $n^{th}$ degree doesn't benefit — and might actual hurt — the system as a whole because of suboptimization.

The "dice game" (Appendix A) shows that variation and dependency affect all systems. It also demonstrates that even if we balance capacity throughout the system, it won't stay balanced for very long because of the combined effects of variation and dependent events. Trying to balance a manufacturing system will create interactive bottlenecks that seem to move from one location to another, maybe even daily. Balanced manufacturing lines eventually put you in a continual reactive mode, chasing problems from one part of the process to another.

We also discussed the Five Focusing Steps, particularly the importance of identifying the constraint, exploiting it, and subordinating everything else to the exploitation of the constraint. And anytime demand or capacity changes significantly, the identity of the system constraint is likely to change.

Now it's time to see how the principles of constraint theory apply to a notional manufacturing organization.

# The Simple Production Organization

Let's look at a simple production organization. We suggest that you now take a break from reading and move to something a little more hands-on. In Appendix C, you'll find a description of Plant 120. On the compact disk that accompanies this book, you have the MICSS program that allows you to manage Plant 120 for half a year.*

Investing the time to go through the Plant 120 simulation will enable you to experience firsthand the dilemmas we're about to discuss. It would be best if you first read Appendix C, then run the computer-based tutorial and read Appendix B (a guided tour). At this point you'll understand Plant 120 well enough to run the simulation according to the First Run Instructions in Appendix C. In this first run, we ask you *not* to change the production policies. As you manage Plant 120 for 6 months (simulation time, of course), jot down the difficulties you have in maintaining excellent due-date performance. Consider, too, whether this company might be able to serve more clients.

Even if you prefer to continue reading now and not spend the time at the computer running the simulation, take a few minutes now to read the description of Plant 120 in Appendix C. Most of you will find this operation to be considerably less complex than the organizations you work for — so simple that you might consider it unrealistic. For learning experiences, it's usually a good idea to keep things simple. Too many complexities and variables can distract from the basic lessons. Even so, you'll find that running even this simple a manufacturing company won't be easy. Concerning realism, keep one thing in mind: A methodology that works well in a simple environment might not translate easily to a more complex situation. But, for sure, if it doesn't work in a simple setting, it won't work in a more complicated one.

Let's begin with a general situation and work down to specifics. Figures 6.1a and b show the same current reality tree we saw in the introduction. It doesn't describe any particular situation. Rather, it characterizes the generic causality common to many different manufacturing organizations. Take a moment to read through it. Do you see any similarities here with your own situation? Especially the "drowning in information" part?

---

* You must follow the registration instructions in order to use the program, but it will be well worth your time and effort to do so. After registering your copy of the MICSS, we recommend that you go through the tutorial included in the software.

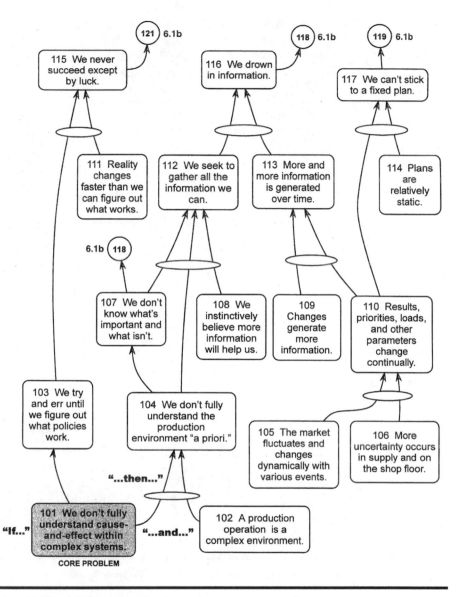

**Figure 6.1a    Generic Manufacturing Current Reality Tree**

Figures 6.2 a and b show a different current reality tree. This one addresses the specific experience of running Plant 120. When we've conducted workshops and allowed the participants to run the Plant 120 simulation, we've consistently observed the undesirable effects (UDE) noted in entities 112, 203, 206, and 207. Those of you who ran the Plant 120 simulation in the

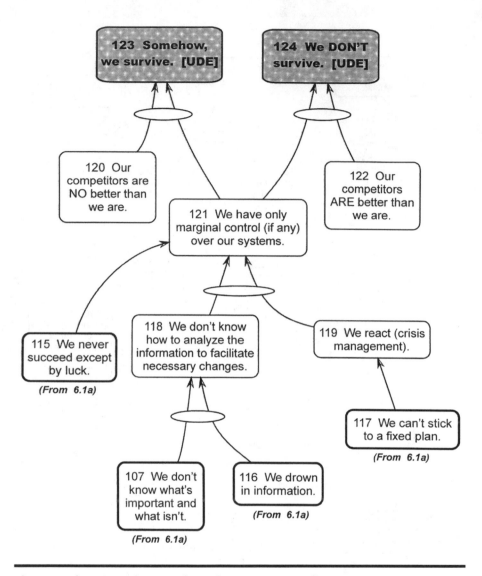

**Figure 6.1b   Generic Manufacturing Current Reality Tree**

MICSS program probably noticed those effects. While some of you may not have seen all of these effects in your own environment, between this current reality tree (Figure 6.2) and the generic manufacturing tree, you have probably experienced most of them at one time or another.

There are three root causes inherent in Plant 120 problems:

1.  Information overload (we don't know where to look for the important things).

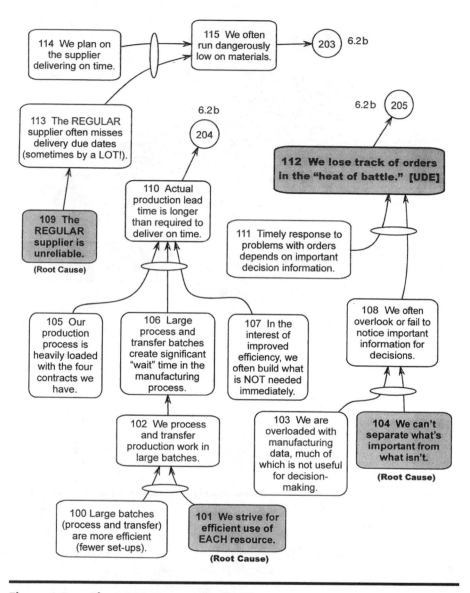

**Figure 6.2a   Plant 120 Current Reality Tree**

2. An unreliable supplier.
3. An emphasis on efficiency at each step of the production process. This preoccupation with local efficiency manifests itself in the use of large process batches, minimum set-up changes, and large transfer batches (transferring complete work orders).

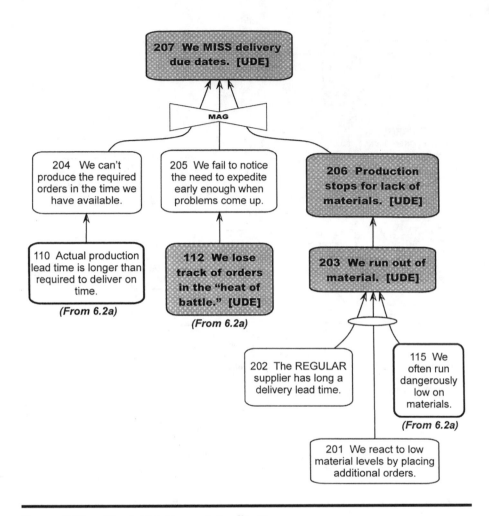

**Figure 6.2b    Plant 120 Current Reality Tree**

One thing we can be relatively sure of is that if these *are* the policies that are causing our problems, changing them won't be easy. Typically, there will be persuasive arguments not to change them. Would you willingly stick your neck out to change such policies and be held accountable if the change fails? In the constraint management paradigm, we typically reflect such differences of opinion through one of the logic trees of the Thinking Process, a diagram for resolving conflicts that Eli Goldratt named the evaporating cloud. Let's look at three such conflict resolution diagrams that explain the nature of the resistance to changing these production policies.

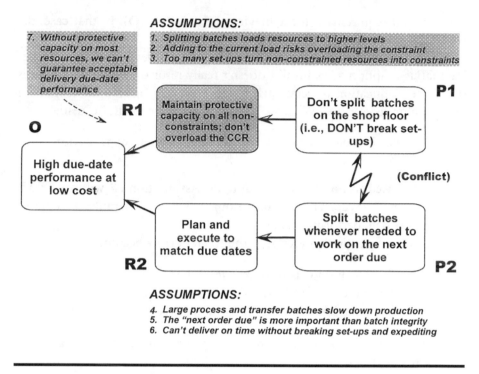

**Figure 6.3    Conflict #1: Local Efficiency**

## *Conflict #1: Local Efficiency*

This might be termed the efficiency conflict (Figure 6.3). There will be strong arguments not to split batches. Most of these arguments are inherent in the assumptions shown in this diagram. But these arguments are invalid — they, in turn, are based on the erroneous assumption that high local efficiencies are good. If you recall, we addressed that fallacy when we talked about the implications of TOC basic assumption #3. Remember our conclusions?

1. You can't fully load all parts of the system and still satisfy your customer (the market).
2. It's dangerous to even try to do so, because of the damage it can do
   to your flexibility, response time, and on-time delivery performance.

What does that mean with respect to this conflict? It means that the most critical invalid assumption in this diagram is #7 — the one that tries to justify high efficiency at all resources. If assumption #7 is invalid, then R1 is not really a valid requirement for achieving the objective (O). In that case, the whole top side of this conflict collapses.

The local efficiency conflict is a common one. However, merely recognizing that assumption #7 is invalid doesn't really resolve the conflict; there is still some justification to retain P1, because we can't ignore the impact of nearly unlimited set-ups. What we need to do is to revise R1 to read:

> R1: Maintain protective capacity on all non-constraints; don't overload the CCR.

We also need to revise the assumptions. Assumption #7 will now read: Without protective capacity on most resources, we can't guarantee acceptable delivery due-date performance.

And the assumptions underlying the P1–R1 arrow become:

1. Splitting batches loads resources to higher levels.
2. Adding to the current load risks overloading the constraint.
3. Too many set-ups turn non-constrained resources into constraints.

Even with these revisions, the more common conflict is still intact here (Figure 6.3, revised).

## Conflict #2: Unreliable Supplier

Here's the second conflict (see Figure 6.4). This could be considered the unreliable supplier conflict. Like the efficiency conflict, this one, too, centers on the obsession with cutting costs in every possible area. The arguments (assumptions) for not using the faster supplier are all based on (a) incremental cost savings on the purchase price of raw materials, and (b) what seems to be a significant difference in shipping cost (though it's only a difference of $500 per order).

If these cost savings drive us to behaviors that result in late deliveries (due to stock-outs), which, in turn, may result in losing our contracts to more reliable competitors, how significant are those costs, really? Can we incur those costs and still make money? Or perhaps make even more money than we do already?

## Conflict #3: Information Overload

Here's the third conflict (Figure 6.5). We might call this the information overload conflict. This conflict plays to our instinctive reaction to look for

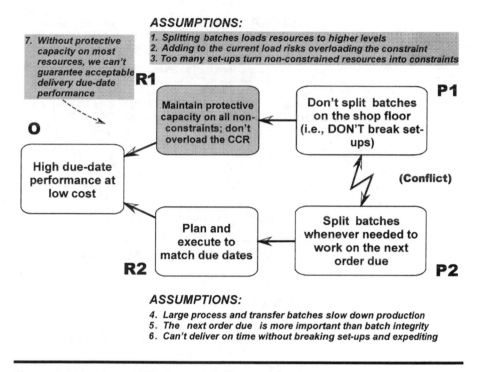

**ASSUMPTIONS:**

7. **Without protective capacity on most resources, we can't guarantee acceptable delivery due-date performance**

1. *Splitting batches loads resources to higher levels*
2. *Adding to the current load risks overloading the constraint*
3. *Too many set-ups turn non-constrained resources into constraints*

**R1**

**O**

Maintain protective capacity on all non-constraints; don't overload the CCR

Don't split batches on the shop floor (i.e., DON'T break set-ups)

**P1**

High due-date performance at low cost

**(Conflict)**

**R2**

Plan and execute to match due dates

Split batches whenever needed to work on the next order due

**P2**

**ASSUMPTIONS:**

4. *Large process and transfer batches slow down production*
5. *The "next order due" is more important than batch integrity*
6. *Can't deliver on time without breaking set-ups and expediting*

**Figure 6.3(r)    Local Efficiency Conflict (Revised)**

more information when we're confused, rather than trying to separate out the important information from all that we already have. (Which would you rather have: *more* information, or the *right* information?)

In *The Haystack Syndrome*, Goldratt defines information as "...the answer to the question asked."[1] Everything else is merely data. Before we can get the answers to our questions, we must know what questions we should be asking. So, what are the questions we should be asking about Plant 120? What should we be watching to detect problems in time to prevent bad outcomes? What can we do to keep these problems from happening? Data alone don't tell us the answers to these questions. At best, they give us a big pile to sort through, from which we can synthesize information.

# Injections: Breaking Conflict #1

What should we do about the efficiency conflict? Goldratt coined the word "injections" to describe the actions that should be taken to break a conflict. His analogy was a doctor injecting a drug of some kind to cure a disease. In

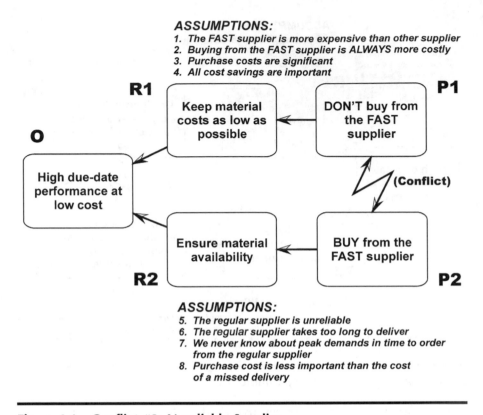

**Figure 6.4    Conflict #2: Unreliable Supplier**

the case of conflicts, an injection is something that is not currently present in the situation — something we have to introduce.

Normally, our injections would replace one or both of the conflicting prerequisites (P1 or P2). We can do this with the revised conflict statement (Figure 6.3 revised). In this case (the commonly encountered first conflict), the injections are intended to replace the top-side prerequisite (P1): "DON'T split batches on the shop floor." The injections are relevant for the two ways to verbalize the conflict between P1 and P2.

So, in addition to preserving P2, we also want to plan smaller batches into the master production schedule in the beginning. In the specific case of Plant 120, the obvious size for a batch is the one that is the exact size of the order to be delivered, not a fixed batch — a batch size that would be smaller than the current fixed process batch used in Plant 120. Smaller process batches in the master production schedule will, in fact, generate the need for additional machine set-ups at most resources. So when we know where the system constraint (CCR) lies, we'll be careful how many additional set-ups

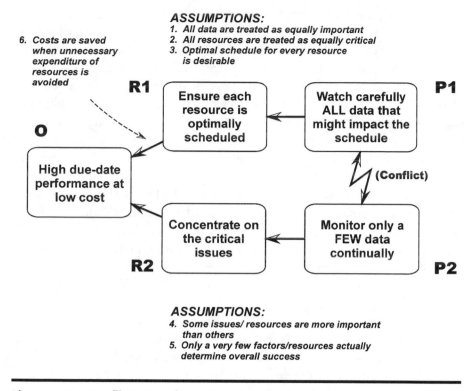

**ASSUMPTIONS:**
1. All data are treated as equally important
2. All resources are treated as equally critical
3. Optimal schedule for every resource is desirable

6. Costs are saved when unnecessary expenditure of resources is avoided

**R1**

**O**

**P1**

Ensure each resource is optimally scheduled

Watch carefully ALL data that might impact the schedule

High due-date performance at low cost

(Conflict)

Concentrate on the critical issues

Monitor only a FEW data continually

**R2**

**P2**

**ASSUMPTIONS:**
4. Some issues/ resources are more important than others
5. Only a very few factors/resources actually determine overall success

**Figure 6.5    Conflict #3: Information Overload**

we allow at that resource. But we won't worry too much about time lost in additional set-ups at other locations except when such additional set-ups come close to fully loading our resources — in other words, when a non-constraint actually starts to *become* a constraint. As long as we have some excess capacity nearly everywhere in the manufacturing process (as indicated in machine utilization rates and rough-cut capacity), we won't concern ourselves too much about additional set-ups. In order for us to do this, however, we need to have a way of identifying the emergence of a new constraint before it becomes a serious problem.

# Transfer Batches

There is yet another policy that should be changed. Plant 120's management has been allowing resources to begin work on an order only when all the parts are available for the whole order. This has the same effect as transferring in batches that are the size of complete work orders. This is a very common policy. Work-in-process is routinely moved between work centers in complete batches. MRP basic logic assumes that batches are moved as whole units, as well.

Dedicated assembly lines behave differently. While the line works on a specific product, between the work stations the material moves by a quantity of one. The classic example of this is Henry Ford's moving assembly line, where one car at a time moved from work station to work station. But can we apply that policy in a job shop? Certainly! In TOC, the term for the smallest number of parts that are allowed to move between work centers is "transfer batch."

One of the most important characteristics of TOC, and other methods such as lean manufacturing, is that the size of the transfer batch need not equal the "process batch." As a matter of fact, the size of the transfer batch should be, in most cases, one unit, or as close to one as possible. This doesn't mean that every little part must move immediately to the next work center. But shipping just one part to the next work center should be possible (and authorized) whenever needed.

The usual explanation for why production managers transfer work-in-process only as whole batches is that otherwise it would be difficult to handle the paperwork and control the location of particular work orders. But ask yourself these questions: Do we *really* want to make simplified paperwork the constraint of the whole organization? Do we *really* lose control when we let work orders bridge several work centers? Running Plant 120 (and later ADV200) can give you an idea of the high price, in lead-time and due-date performance, we pay for the policy of moving work-in-process in batches equal to the amount processed.

So we want to transfer work-in-process between work centers in smaller batches (overlapping batches). In the MICSS software, every part processed by a work center is automatically transferred to the next work center. However, unless the next work center is authorized to begin processing partial work orders, this transfer of just one unit at a time has no consequence. By changing the *WO Acceptance* policy to a *Partial Work Order* transfer policy (refer to the "Machine Policy" under "Policies" in the "Production View" of the MICSS program), we're allowing resources to start work on an order without having all the parts present. This has the same effect as transferring in smaller batches, even though we're not establishing a particular transfer batch size. Try this yourself to see the huge impact changing this policy has.

The transfer-batch-equals-process-batch policy, which we challenge here, is indirectly related to the efficiency conflict. Using small transfer batches

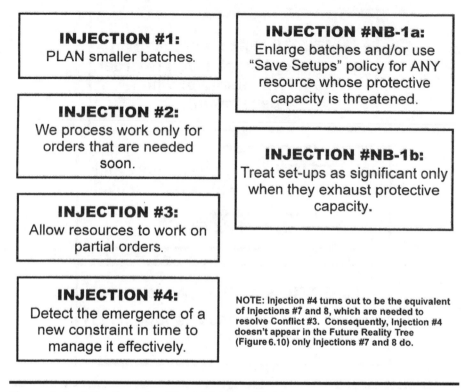

**INJECTION #1:**
PLAN smaller batches.

**INJECTION #2:**
We process work only for orders that are needed soon.

**INJECTION #3:**
Allow resources to work on partial orders.

**INJECTION #4:**
Detect the emergence of a new constraint in time to manage it effectively.

**INJECTION #NB-1a:**
Enlarge batches and/or use "Save Setups" policy for ANY resource whose protective capacity is threatened.

**INJECTION #NB-1b:**
Treat set-ups as significant only when they exhaust protective capacity.

NOTE: Injection #4 turns out to be the equivalent of Injections #7 and 8, which are needed to resolve Conflict #3. Consequently, Injection #4 doesn't appear in the Future Reality Tree (Figure 6.10) only Injections #7 and 8 do.

**Figure 6.6   Injections for Plant 120 Conflict #1**

may cause a work center to set up another process batch before it finishes the current process batch, because the additional parts are stuck in upstream operation. Consequently, the desire to save set-ups may be relevant here as well. But the more common reason for this erroneous assumption is the desire for efficiency, of both the paperwork and the resources we use to do the transferring. So the root cause of this policy is the drive for efficiency everywhere, which is the essence of the first conflict.

The four injections needed to resolve the first conflict are summarized in Figure 6.6. Two additional injections, NB-1a and NB-1b, are required to preclude potential negative outcomes from Injection #1 (Figure 6.11, later in this chapter).

## Injections: Breaking Conflict #2

This type of conflict (Conflict #2) is very real in many organizations, whether we're talking about suppliers or other outside subcontractors. The least-cost suppliers are preferred because of low prices, but their reliability may leave

INJECTION #5: Establish an "emergency" stock level; re-order from FAST supplier when penetrated.

INJECTION #6: Emergency stock is set to a level at which it's not likely to be exhausted within the FAST supplier's QLT.

INJECTION #NB-2: Accept raw material cost increases as long as $\Delta T$ remains positive.

**Figure 6.7    Injections for Plant 120 Conflict #2**

much to be desired, and their lead times may be long. It's a case of getting what you pay for.

As with any conflict resolution, we're looking for a way to satisfy the low cost requirement yet still be assured that we have the material available when it's needed. This means that we'll probably have to accept some increase in raw material costs as insurance for availability. The challenge will be to keep material costs under control while we do that. In this case, we will need three injections (see Figure 6.7):

1. Establish an emergency stock level and order as required from the fast supplier to ensure that we don't run out of materials, which would stop production.
2. Set the emergency stock to a level at which it's not likely to be exhausted within the fast supplier's quoted lead time.
3. Accept some incremental increase in the cost of raw materials as long as the added sales revenue minus the change in raw material cost remains positive. This additional injection, NB-2, is needed to pre-

clude the negative consequence of paying a premium for faster delivery (Figure 6.12, later in this chapter).

We must distinguish here between emergency stock and traditional safety stock. For most inventory managers, safety stock is considered any amount above the average use rate. For instance, if the average weekly consumption rate is 50 units and we hold 80 units in stock, we have 30 units as safety stock. An emergency level is the amount necessary to sustain production of firm orders against stock-out stoppage. This means that when the stock drops below the emergency level, we have to issue an emergency order. We then depend on the emergency order to arrive before the current stock is exhausted.

Let's consider an example. Assume that our average weekly production for the past year is 50 units of products A1 and A2, and that our fastest supplier can usually deliver within 2 days. How much raw material should we hold as an emergency, or "red-line" level for raw materials Y1, Z1, and Z2. Let's not forget that Y1 is used for both products. Two days of production at 50 units per week would require 20 units each of Z1 and Z2, and 40 units of Y1.

But what about "Murphy" and an unpredictable market demand? Even faster suppliers experience unexpected production delays, and a rapid spike in market demand may exceed our planned production level while we're waiting for a fast delivery. How can we mitigate the risk of running out of raw materials? We would probably be safe in holding an emergency level equivalent to twice the average demand during the expected 2-day period required for resupply. So our emergency levels for Y1, Z1, and Z2 might be 80, 40, and 40, respectively.

One might argue that we don't need that much protection for Y1, because seldom will both products experience such high demand. Generally speaking, that's probably true. But in this particular example Y1 is somewhat cheaper, and the damage to our throughput resulting from not having material when required is significantly higher (starvation of the whole shop floor), so the decision seems sound enough.

## Safety Stock vs. Emergency Stock

We must distinguish here again between emergency stock and traditional safety stock. For most inventory managers, safety stock is considered any amount above the average use rate. For instance, let's assume that the average monthly consumption rate is 220 units, the regular replenishment frequency is once a month, and our stock target for the start of each month is 300 units. Under these conditions, our plan provides for 80 units as safety stock.

An emergency level is something quite different. It's defined as the amount necessary to sustain production of firm orders against stock-out stoppage. This means that when the stock drops below the emergency level, we have to either put pressure on the supplier to ship the order already in the pipeline as fast as possible, or issue an emergency order to the fastest supplier we have. We then depend on the emergency order to arrive before the current stock is exhausted.

So, dropping below the emergency level clearly initiates emergency actions to bring in material as quickly as possible. The emergency level should be significantly lower than the safety stock. Safety stock is intended to protect against deviations from average consumption. Emergency stock is specifically intended for situations in which most of the safety is gone, and there's a real danger of exhausting all raw material unless emergency measures are taken. The emergency level depends mostly on what remedial measures we have at hand to fill the shortfall.

Let's consider another example (Figure 6.8). Assume that the average consumption of material Z1, which is needed for product A1, is 250 units per month. Suppose the normal inventory levels are 750 for replenishment and 500 for re-order. This means every time the inventory drops below 500, an automatic purchase order is issued for the regular (cheapest) supplier to replenish the inventory to 750.

Now suppose that the supplier's average lead time for delivery is 6.5 weeks. This means that every time an order is issued we'll need, on average, about 375 units to cover the average demand The safety stock is about 125 units, bringing the reorder level to 500. Once the stock drops below 500, a purchase order is issued, but the actual inventory continues to go down until the shipment from the supplier arrives. As the market demand may be considerably higher than the average and/or the supplier may be late with the shipment, there's a good probability that we may exhaust all our remaining stock before we receive a delivery from our supplier. We'd certainly prefer to do something before that happens. But what can we do?

Suppose we have a supplier that's able to respond, on average, in 2 days. In an emergency, we can issue an order to that supplier. But this supplier is also more expensive than our regular one, so we'd like to avoid having to do that, if possible. Instead, we'd prefer to establish inventory management policies that allow us to keep stocks as low as we can, while still safeguarding us from having to use the expensive (but fast) supplier.

How much raw material should we hold as an emergency, or red-line level for Z1? If the average monthly consumption is 250, then the average for 2 days is 24. But what about "Murphy" and an unpredictable market

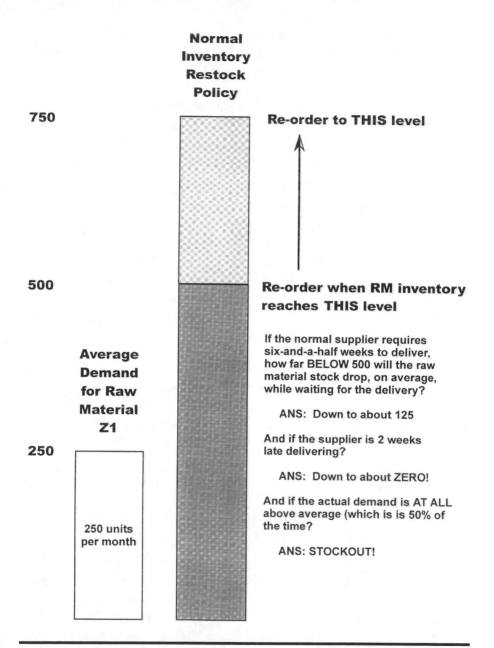

**Figure 6.8    Safety Stock vs. Emergency Stock: An Example**

demand? Even faster suppliers experience unexpected production delays, and a rapid spike in market demand may exceed our planned production level while we're waiting for a fast delivery. How can we mitigate the risk of running out of raw materials? We'd probably be safe in holding an emergency level equivalent to *twice the average demand* during the expected 2-day period required for re-supply by the fast supplier. So with an expected 2-day demand of 24, our emergency level for Z1 might be 50. That means that if the actual inventory of Z1 drops below 50, we would issue an emergency order to the fast supplier to protect against the possibility of stock-out.

## Injections: Breaking Conflict #3

This conflict is related to the generic manufacturing current reality tree — the one that centers on information overload. Obviously, we'd like a solution that allows us to pay most of our attention to the factors that are really important to a system's success. But we can't ignore the fact that even minor parts of the system can occasionally degrade system performance.

Our injections (see Figure 6.9) for this conflict are unique to constraint theory. First, we're going to *identify* the system constraint. Then we're going to watch it closely to be sure that it doesn't become either overloaded or starved for work. This is another way of saying, "*Exploit* the constraint." Second, we're going to pay only limited attention to the non-constraints in the system — the parts that have significant excess capacity to respond to variation and uncertainty. We'll watch them closely only when they show signs of stress associated with impending overload, but we won't worry about them at all if they are underutilized (as long as the CCR is well utilized). This is another way of saying, "*Subordinate* the non-constraints to the exploitation of the constraint."

## Future Reality Tree: Plant 120

These injections might seem adequate, but obviously we haven't tested them yet. We can apply them in Plant 120, but in the real world we may feel a little more confident about them if we test them logically first. If our assessment has been correct, we should be able to demonstrate that the injections logically produce the outcome we want. At the very least, we might find that they won't be effective *before* we expend time and energy trying to change the policies. And we might even identify some new problems that these injections create — ones that don't exist now.

So if we were to apply these injections properly, Figures 6.10a and 6.10b show how we can expect the future to unfold. It would appear from this Future Reality Tree that our proposed injections will, in fact, deliver the

```
┌─────────────────────────────────┐
│  INJECTION #7:  Identify the    │
│  constraint and watch it closely.│
└─────────────────────────────────┘
```

```
┌─────────────────────────────────┐
│  INJECTION #8:  Monitor non-    │
│  constraints only when they are │
│  in danger of losing their      │
│  protective capacity.           │
└─────────────────────────────────┘
```

**Figure 6.9     Injections for Plant 120 Conflict #3**

results we desire. But they also deliver something else: two possible new problems.

Our first injection (plan smaller process batches) also produces a new undesirable effect when we apply it. This new chain of cause-and-effect is shown in Figure 6.11. In order to keep this new undesirable effect from happening, we need to take some preventive action ahead of time. That preventive action is embodied in two injections. One of these, injection #NB-1b, has already been identified: Treat set-ups as significant only when they consume protective capacity. The second injection is an additional one (NB#1a): Enlarge batches and/or conserve set-ups for any resource whose protective capacity is threatened. If we do these things in addition to the original injection (#1), we should still be able to realize the desired effect and avoid this new undesirable effect.

Our second injection (establish an emergency stock level; re-order from fast supplier when penetrated) also produces a new undesirable effect (see Figure 6.12). In this case, another cause besides injections #5 and 6 — "Murphy" — may produce this undesirable effect, too. So, in identifying and trimming this negative branch, we actually do ourselves the additional favor of preventing the same effect from a completely different cause that we hadn't anticipated. The injection we'll use to do this is #NB-2 (accept some raw material cost increases as long as $\Delta T$ remains positive).

Are you ready to try out the injections in the Plant 120 MICSS simulation? Go ahead. Change the production policies in accordance with the injections from the Plant 120 Future Reality Tree, and run the simulation again, using the "Second Run Instructions" in Appendix C. Notice any differences?

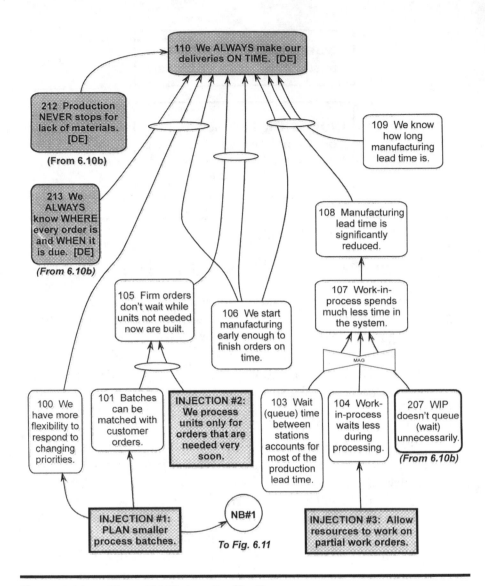

**Figure 6.10a    Plant 120 Future Reality Tree**

# Generic Manufacturing Conflict

Sometimes, even in diverse situations, different conflicts have common elements. Though the words describing one particular conflict may differ from another, the meaning of those words is generally the same. Moreover, the root cause of diverse problems within a single organization may be the

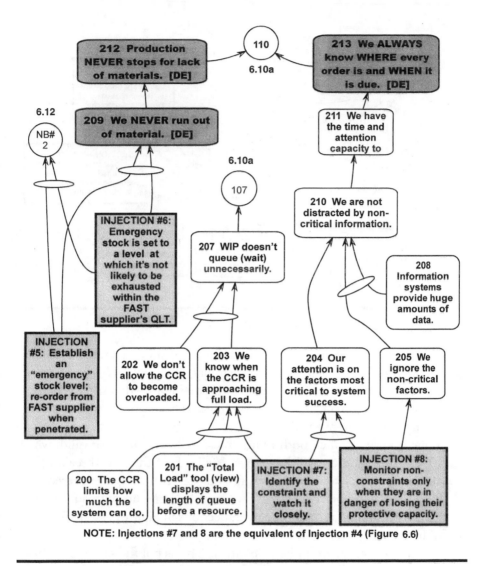

**Figure 6.10b    Plant 120 Future Reality Tree**

same, yet can cause seemingly different conflicts. When we find such situations, we try to generalize a conflict statement that characterizes the core conflict behind all the other conflicts. We refer to this as a *generic conflict.*

The conflict in Figure 6.13 summarizes the other three, and it's fairly common to all manufacturing systems. Have you seen it in yours? Even if you haven't, keep it in mind. You might be able to identify it more quickly in future situations.

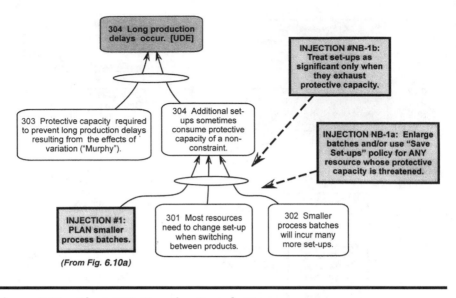

**Figure 6.11    Plant 120 Negative Branch #1**

How do we resolve this generic conflict? The short answer is, "With a generic solution that will work in most similar situations." This can be powerful information to know. It means that if you identify this situation in the future, you can go directly to a solution that has been proven to work in the past — no need to reinvent the wheel.

In the generic conflict, both requirements (R1 and R2) are valid, which means that our solution will have to satisfy both of them. In breaking this conflict, we'd really like to preserve prerequisite #2 and replace prerequisite #1. But in replacing prerequisite #1, we have to come up with solutions to ensure that R1 is still satisfied. The two injections in Figure 6.14 are intended to do that.

Note that the key word in R1 is "control." This is not the same as "reduce" or "allow no increase." The first injection suggests that we ignore the cost of capacity when making our operating decisions, because those costs don't change with most operating decisions. Moreover, there is a pre-existing need for some minimal capacity level to provide a specific product mix and to maintain a minimum service level. Beyond that minimal level, non-constraints need some excess capacity to ensure effective subordination to the constraint. And we inevitably end up with even more capacity, because capacity can be purchased only in chunks. For example, you can't acquire 38% of an operator or machine. All of these factors create a certain level of expense

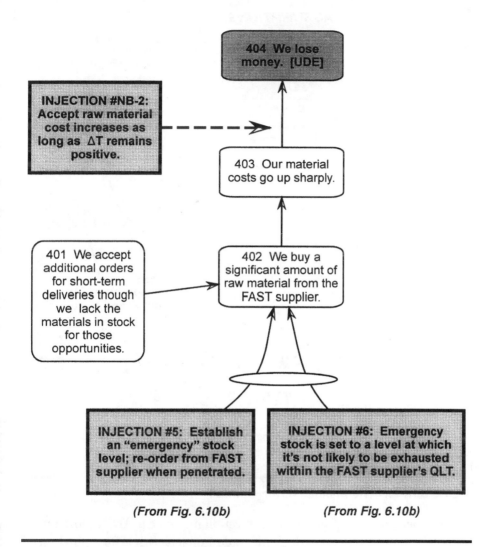

**Figure 6.12    Plant 120 Negative Branch #2**

that is *not* impacted by daily decisions, such as giving priority to one particular work order or doing more set-ups.

Of course, there are two presumptions here. One is that such daily decisions won't require us to *add* capacity — we'll simply use the excess capacity we already have. The second is that the decision should not turn a particular resource into an internal constraint. So since we've already paid for our existing capacity, no additional out-of-pocket costs are incurred if we choose to not use it fully — only opportunity costs.

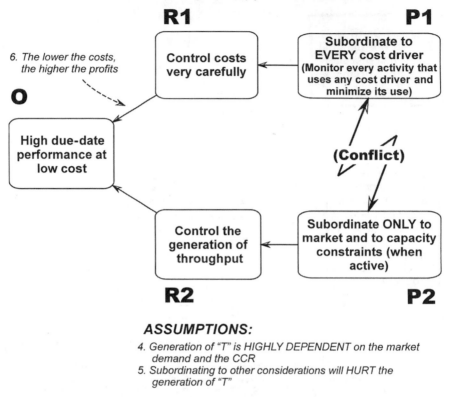

**ASSUMPTIONS:**

1. *Every cost driver offers the potential to save money*
2. *Every opportunity to save money is important*
3. *Costs will go up sharply if we don't subordinate to cost drivers*

**ASSUMPTIONS:**

4. *Generation of "T" is HIGHLY DEPENDENT on the market demand and the CCR*
5. *Subordinating to other considerations will HURT the generation of "T"*

**Figure 6.13 Generic Manufacturing Conflict**

Another way of interpreting this injection might be to say, "Ignore capacity costs in daily decision making unless additional *real* capacity is purchased."

The second injection suggests that our rule of thumb for decision making at the operating level should be to maintain a positive difference between the change in expected throughput and the change in expected operating expense. As long as that number is positive (and overall "T" does not go down), the decision contributes to the organization's goal. Since the decision not to fully utilize a resource adds no cost, $\Delta T$ minus $\Delta OE$ remains positive.

In summary, the traditional policies that support local efficiencies degrade satisfaction of customers. We risk losing business if this happens. Large batches, either process or transfer, may look good from an efficiency

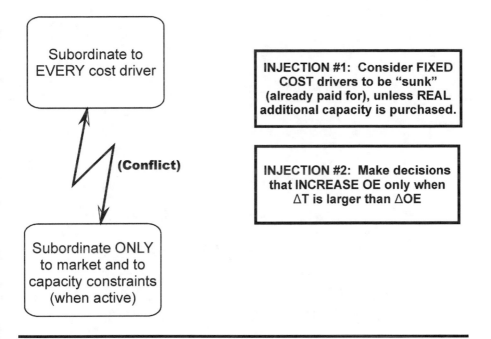

**Figure 6.14    Injections for the Generic Manufacturing Conflict**

standpoint, but they hurt our flexibility to respond to fast-breaking changes. They also clog production capacity with work that does not absolutely have to be done now — capacity that could otherwise be employed to produce more throughput. In many cases, minimizing set-ups isn't nearly as important as most people think it is. Finally, even with a good plan, a means of control — anticipating and preventing problems before they have a chance to develop — is critical to success.

# Reference

1. Goldratt, Eliyahu M., *The Haystack Syndrome: Sifting Information from the Data Ocean*, Croton-on-Hudson, NY, The North River Press, 1990, p 6.

# Traditional Drum-Buffer-Rope

The first questions we should probably dispense with are, what is "drum-buffer-rope," and why are we calling it traditional? Drum-Buffer-Rope, usually referred to by its abbreviation DBR, is a method of manufacturing production scheduling originated by Goldratt in the 1980s. The theory of constraints grew out of manufacturing applications of this method, similar to the situation Goldratt and Cox described in *The Goal*.[1] DBR itself was first described in detail by Goldratt and Fox in *The Race*,[2] and in even more detail in *The Haystack Syndrome*.[3]

The "drum" in DBR was first considered to be the internal capacity-constrained resource (CCR) that limited the overall production of a company. Later, it came to represent the production schedule for the CCR. The constraint is likened to a drum because it establishes a pace, or frequency, to which the whole organization synchronizes itself. By using the capacity of the most limited (constrained) resource in a dependent chain as the drum, the whole process is safeguarded against overloading, which slows down the flow of work. When no CCR is active, the drum is merely the list of shipments due to customers.

The "buffer" in DBR is a protective mechanism. Goldratt recognized that if a system's CCR determines the best performance the system can hope to achieve, none of the CCR's capacity to perform should be wasted. This means that it should be protected from having too much idle time (nothing to do). Goldratt conceived of the idea of a buffer of work waiting in front of the CCR, so that it would never be starved for work. However, in DBR, the buffer is a little different than most people might conceive it. The buffer is *time*, rather than *things*. Instead of planning to keep a stack of work-in-process (WIP) in front of the CCR waiting to be done, units of WIP are planned to arrive for processing some period of time before the CCR is scheduled to begin working on them.

Finally, the "rope" is, in effect, a communication device. Conceptually, it stretches between the CCR and the initial material release point in the production process. The rope is the mechanism that regulates the release of materials. Materials are normally planned for release at the same pace as the CCR operates. They are precluded from faster release to avoid swamping, or overloading the CCR. The tangible form of the rope is usually a material release schedule, which is adjusted or updated as real-world changes to the pace of the CCR (the drum) occur.

The "rope" may seem to be just a technical device, but there's an important concept behind it. The more work-in-process (WIP) there is on the floor, the longer lead time is. Moreover, excessive WIP can confuse production personnel about priorities. Work centers can face huge amounts of work, yet fail to notice that some of it is due much later, if there is a customer requirement for it at all. The impression is "every work center is a bottleneck." Foremen react by trying to be more efficient — they often merge orders to save setups. The result is a slow and unreliable response to market requirements. The "rope" forces the production floor to process only what is due shortly. This streamlines the flow, sets the right priorities, and exposes excess capacity that has been hidden within the system.

The reason we're calling this form of DBR traditional is that it was the original version and has not changed materially since it was conceived. We're distinguishing it from a newer, simplified version you'll read about in Chapter 10, which we'll call simplified DBR. To fully understand and appreciate the advantages the newer version offers, we'll first discuss traditional DBR and its associated concepts.

## What DBR Does

What is traditional DBR intended to achieve? First and foremost, it's designed to satisfy existing market demand — to deliver all orders on time, as promised. Second, it's designed to move work-in-process through production as fast as possible. Third, it is intended to reveal the nature and extent of capacity that might be hidden, capacity we're not currently able to take full advantage of. In other words, it should allow us to do more than we think we're able to do without disrupting current delivery performance.

Finally — and we emphasize finally — it *may* facilitate the saving of some costs. However, consider this a happy coincidence when it happens. It is not the primary objective of DBR — generating more throughput is!

## What DBR Does Not Do

In pursuing its mission, DBR does not concern itself with local efficiencies. The reasons for this should be clear from our earlier discussions. It doesn't reduce so-called non-value-added time, such things as numbers of set-ups. The exception to this rule would apply if the additional set-ups turn a non-constraint into a constraint. It also does not consume time on a capacity-constrained resource (CCR) doing work that is not needed right now.

For example, DBR encourages not building to stock or to future delivery requirements while current orders due sooner wait, or smoothing the load (building stock far in advance of peak period demands). Constraint theory does not preclude this tactic, but it does suggest that it be done as little as possible, and only when no other alternative exists. To the extent possible, DBR enables the compression of manufacturing cycle time toward the objective of building to order, rather than to stock. In this way, TOC facilitates the reduction of inventories and operating expense as a side effect (not a primary objective) of pursuing increased throughput.

## Some Basic DBR Principles

Let's reiterate some basic lessons we've already discussed about constraint theory that apply specifically to DBR. We know that only a very few resources can be loaded to or near full capacity and still permit the flexibility needed to manage a changing shop floor environment effectively. Protective capacity is our safeguard against the unexpected.

Most production resources will naturally have excess capacity — and we should usually not look at this as something wrong. We certainly shouldn't tamper with it unless we're sure it won't change the location of the constraint.

We know that Murphy lies in wait continually. Though we can anticipate that it will happen, specific occurrences of internal variation can't be known in advance, and they can be significant. And in keeping with Murphy's Law, they usually happen at the worst possible time. Compounding internal variation is the uncertainty of the external environment — market requirements and demand level.

As loads on the production process increase in response to changes in market demand, and especially because of changes in product mix, more capacity-constrained resources may emerge. When there is more than one such CCR, we refer to the condition as an interactive constraint situation. It creates a huge burden on production management. Control of the system becomes very difficult because changes to variables often confound one another. Interactive constraints usually cause deterioration of due-date performance, and overtime goes up sharply.

## Guidelines for DBR Shop Floor Planning

In the best of all possible worlds, we'd prefer to be able to produce only to order. Inventory management is simpler and less expensive, and the sales force is usually happier. But as good as DBR is at shortening cycle times, it may not be able to reduce them into a make-to-order range in all cases. Though it's not always achievable, this should always be our objective. In cases where it's not possible to do completely, we should minimize as much as possible the amount of making-to-stock that we actually do.

Sometimes there *is* a need to produce to forecast or to stock. We need to do this when the customer's standard for acceptable delivery time is routinely shorter than the shortest possible actual manufacturing lead time we can achieve. For example, seasonal peak demands (or other spikes with some predictable periodicity) may exceed the CCR's capability to produce to order. In such cases, a better alternative than building to stock (finished goods) is to assemble-to-order longer lead time intermediate components. These can usually be assembled in advance of actual need, and are normally built by non-constrained resources.

## DBR Basic Concepts

In terms of the Five Focusing Steps, establishing the drum really constitutes exploitation planning: How are we going to make the best use of the constrained resource we identified? We do this by deciding what to produce, and how the CCR is going to handle the load. Normally, the "how" is expressed in the form of a Master Production Schedule. Establishing the buffer means protecting the exploitation plan from starvation and ensuring the integrity of the scheduled work sequence.

As mentioned earlier, in TOC in general, and in DBR in particular, the buffer is not things — it's time. Instead of piling a lot of stuff (units of work-in-process) in front of the CCR, under DBR we assure that the next unit needed arrives at the CCR a set period of time before it's actually going to be worked on. Establishing (or tieing) the rope means determining a schedule for material release into the production process that does not exceed the rate at which the CCR is currently processing work. The rope protects the CCR from overload. Consequently, no advance release of material is allowed. Figure 7.1 depicts these principles.

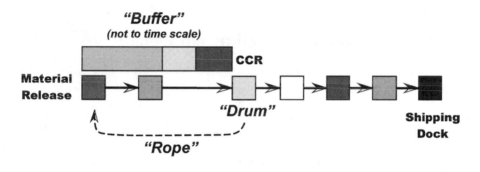

**Figure 7.1    Basic DBR Concept**

The drum — the CCR's capacity to produce, as reflected in the master production schedule (MPS) — establishes the pace of the system. The rope is the signaling device that tells the inventory controller when to release material into the system. Ideally, the material release schedule should be created for the same time period as the master production schedule, and it should be updated or corrected at the same time the MPS is created/updated, or when a reduction in the CCR's capacity occurs (for unscheduled maintenance, or other Murphy factor).

The rope ensures that material enters the system at a rate that is synchronized with the capacity of the CCR. Consequently, the load on non-constraints is regulated so as not to overload the CCR. Additional load is held outside the production floor until the appropriate time for it to be processed.

And the buffer is insurance. It protects the most critical resource — the one upon which the throughput of the whole system depends — from starvation (loss of productive time). It also protects the planned schedule and sequence of events from disruption caused by late-breaking additions to the schedule.

It is important to emphasize that DBR is a *planning* method, not a *control* method. DBR to some degree makes room for internal variation and external uncertainty in the manufacturing environment. But as with any other kind of plan, it can't anticipate and accommodate all possible problems that might interrupt the flow of work through the process.

DBR also provides details for only parts of the system: the master production schedule, the CCR, and material release. It does not detail the rest of the system. The logic of DBR spells out what should be detailed and what should not.

## The Control Conflict: Detail or No Detail?

Almost every organization experiences the control conflict (see Figure 7.2). This conflict essentially says:

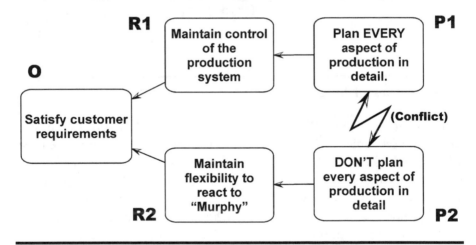

**Figure 7.2   The Control Conflict**

"In order to satisfy customer requirements (O), we must maintain control of the production system (R1). And in order to maintain control of the production system (R1), we must plan every aspect of production in detail (P1)."

"But in order to satisfy customer requirements (O), we must also maintain the flexibility to react to Murphy (R2). And in order to maintain the flexibility to react to Murphy (R2), we must not plan every aspect of production in detail (P2)."

This might be likened to Hamlet's dilemma: To plan in detail, or not to plan in detail ... that is the question. People seem to accept as almost axiomatic that detailed planning and attention to everything contribute to better control. This might be the case where uncertainty doesn't play a significant part. But where uncertainty does enter in, detailed planning can be a waste of time and, in some cases, can do more harm than good. Military strategists and tacticians have learned this lesson. The uncertainties of the battlefield are even more pronounced than those in business, so military plans go into very little detail beyond stating objectives, allocating forces (resources), identifying command relationships, and specifying initiation times. We'll re-visit this conflict in just a moment to come up with a solution, but first we need to discuss some other issues that bear on the conflict.

For the following discussion, we'll consider Figure 7.3 to represent a typical manufacturing process. Some are obviously more complex than this, while others are perhaps less complex.

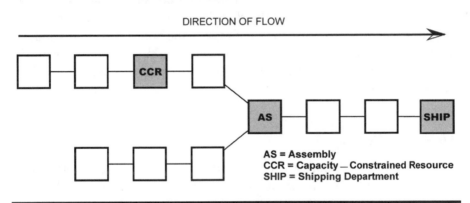

**Figure 7.3    A Typical Manufacturing Process**

## Buffers: Traditional DBR

The buffer part of Drum-Buffer-Rope is the one aspect of the method that makes it unique from other production management approaches, such as Just-in-Time. Buffers protect the system's delivery commitments from the negative effects of internal variation and external uncertainty. In traditional DBR, there are three types of time buffers:

1.  A shipping buffer, which protects the shipping due date;
2.  A CCR buffer, which protects the capacity-constrained resource from starvation; and
3.  An assembly buffer, which protects the flow of parts from a CCR against interruption for lack of a part coming from a non-CCR.

## The Shipping Buffer

The shipping buffer is defined as a *liberal estimation of the manufacturing lead time from the CCR to the completion of an order*. If a CCR is not involved in the chain (i.e., the process is not internally constrained), the shipping buffer is the lead time from the release of raw materials to order completion. Figure 7.4 is a graphic representation of a shipping buffer in several different configurations. Notice the use of the words "liberal estimation." As we'll see shortly, this liberal estimation includes more than just pure processing and transfer time.

Although we'll be using the top configuration as a continuing example, the shipping buffer concept applies as well to production lines where the assembly point is *in front* of the CCR, and to production lines where there is no active CCR at all. In each case, the definition is the same, but the part of the process encompassed by the shipping buffer may be different. Along the side of the process where the CCR resides, the buffer encompasses all the time it takes, after the CCR has finished with it, to arrive at the shipping dock. When there is no CCR, the shipping buffer extends all the way back to the material release point.

## The CCR Buffer

The CCR buffer is *a liberal estimation of the manufacturing lead time from the release of raw materials to the site of the CCR* (see Figure 7.5). The constraint (CCR) buffer includes all the time required to move work-in-process from the raw material release to a point where it stands immediately in front of the CCR, waiting to be processed. As with the shipping buffer, liberal estimation here also includes more than just processing and transfer time, as we'll see in a moment.

## The Assembly Buffer

The assembly buffer is *a liberal estimation of the manufacturing lead time from the release of raw materials to an assembly point where CCR parts and non-CCR parts are combined*. Figure 7.6 shows what the assembly buffer looks like. As you can see, it encompasses all the time required to move work from the release of materials to the point where the partially processed piece is ready to be combined with another part coming from the path in which the CCR lies. In this case, too, more than just processing and transfer time is included.

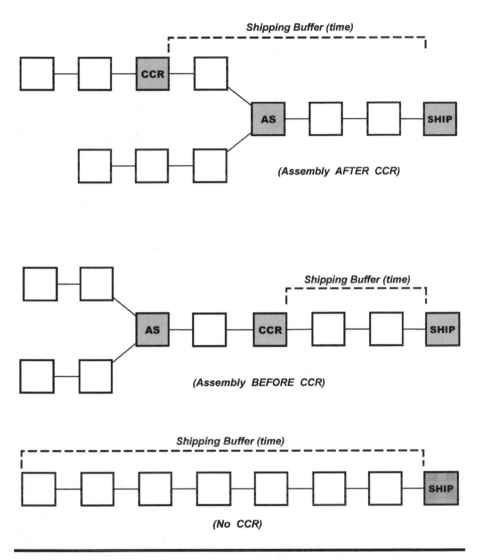

**Figure 7.4   Shipping Buffer**

## Preliminary Actions

Now it's time to see how we go about applying DBR to a manufacturing process. We'll assume that two basic management tasks pertaining to any manufacturing process have already been accomplished:

1.  A map of the flow of material through the manufacturing process for each product has already been developed. This is not a physical layout

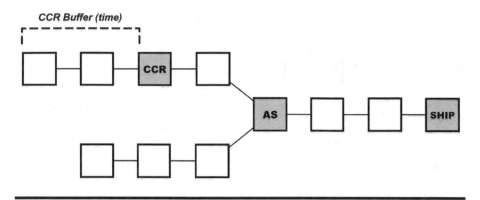

**Figure 7.5    CCR Buffer**

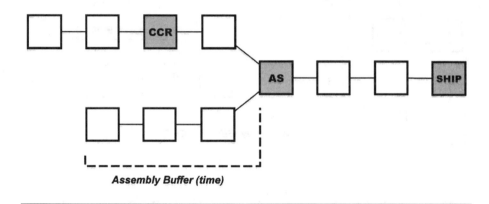

**Figure 7.6    Assembly Buffer**

    of the shop floor — it's an activity flow, similar to the "All Products Routing" information window in Plant 120 (refer to Appendix B, Figure B.12). Figure 7.7 also shows a typical material flow map.

2. Reasonably accurate estimates of task duration (time-per-part) for a single unit of product by each resource (or, when necessary, time-per-batch) have been established. These are pure processing times for each manufacturing step in the material flow map for each product. For the CCR, these estimates should be as accurate as possible. Neither set-up time nor transfer time (from one work center to another) has been included.

3. Estimates of set-up times, especially for the CCR, have been established.

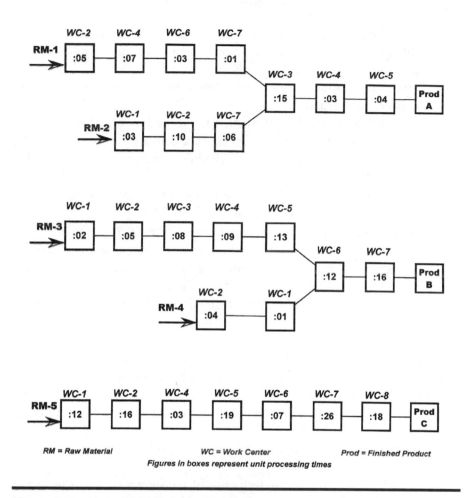

**Figure 7.7   Material Flow Map by Product**

Although these tasks aren't mandatory, you may find them useful in visualizing the "big picture" of the production process. Once these tasks are completed, we're ready to start our traditional DBR plan.

## Traditional DBR Planning Procedure

1.  The first step* in planning a traditional DBR schedule is to start with what we might call an optimistic master production schedule. This

---

* Much has been written about traditional DBR by a number of different authors (refer to the bibliography at the end of this book for a partial list). There is likely to be some variation between the different references in describing the procedures that follow, but the basics will be essentially the same from one source to another.

is a schedule that is unconstrained; it assumes you can build every-thing that goes into it and deliver on time. Our optimistic MPS will be based on firm orders only, required due dates, and only the minimum forecasted orders absolutely required to satisfy on-time delivery requirements.

2. Sort the entries in the optimistic MPS according to their due dates. At the top of the list should be the next delivery.

3. Gather data to construct a CCR schedule. For every entry in the date-sorted MPS:

   ■ Determine whether the CCR is required to process each order, and skip orders that don't pass through the CCR.*

   ■ Write the name(s) of the operation(s) the CCR performs beside each entry in the MPS. Distinguish any work orders that require more than one operation from the CCR. Exclude any work orders that are already downstream from the CCR.

   ■ Also write the number of units the CCR will process for each entry in the MPS.

At this point there are two ways to proceed. We'll refer to one as the simpler CCR scheduling algorithm, and the other as the more sophisticated algorithm. The simple one suffices for most manual implementations. The more sophisticated one is the backbone for any computerized production scheduling system.

If you're using the *simpler* CCR scheduling algorithm:

4. Schedule the CCR in the sequence of the operations for the sorted MPS (in order of due dates). Start with the earliest order that still needs the CCR. Assign the necessary time for set-up and processing time for all units required in the order. Continue forward in time, scheduling all the orders in the MPS.

If you're using the more sophisticated scheduling algorithm:

4a. Start with the last entry of the sorted MPS. Assign the appropriate time on the CCR, including set-up and processing times, so that when the CCR finishes the last part, the shipping buffer time remains until

---

* Some orders may already have passsed through the CCR. Some products may not require any of the CCR's time. They are referred to as "free products."

the due date. If the required CCR start time is already taken by a previous order, move the operation backward in time until you find a free spot. This is essentially backward scheduling.

If an order should have been started before "zero time" (i.e., in the past), that particular order and all subsequent orders must be pushed forward in time. The order with the earliest due date should be started immediately. All subsequent orders that use CCR time should follow this one, maintaining their original sequence.

> NOTE: *When the CCR is fully loaded, the simpler algorithm yields the same results. But when the CCR isn't fully loaded, the more sophisticated algorithm will allow some orders to be worked later, while ensuring enough protection (a full shipping buffer) for due dates.*

The remaining steps are common to the two scheduling algorithms.

5. Validate that the first tasks the CCR must perform already have inventory waiting for processing at the CCR. In the ideal situation, the CCR will have work waiting that is equivalent to half the CCR buffer time. When there is less than this amount of work-in-process queued at the CCR, determine whether there is work for orders later in the schedule that the CCR might do now. If so, rearrange the production sequence to produce these orders earlier.

6. Verify the feasibility of the due dates. Look for orders that will consume more than half of the shipping buffer time. These would be orders that, if started at the CCR in the sequence and at the time previously determined, would leave the CCR having used more than half of the planned shipping buffer. This situation is too close for comfort and threatens on-time delivery.

7. When some orders are found to be in danger of missing their delivery due dates, take action to prevent a missed delivery. One way to do this is to try to save set-up time by merging some orders. Another is to plan overtime or subcontracting as required. The objective is to enable completion of orders that were pushed too late in the CCR schedule. If overtime, extra shifts, subcontracting or saving set-ups are not feasible, return to the MPS and delay the problematic orders.

8. Once the MPS has been scrubbed and is deemed doable, schedule the release of materials that pass through the CCR. Material release time

should be backed up before the planned start time at the CCR by the value of the CCR buffer time.

9. Schedule the release of materials that do not pass through the CCR. First determine the material release time for the assembly buffer. These are the materials that will be assembled with CCR-processed parts but do not, themselves, use the CCR. The safest course of action is to schedule the release for the assembly buffer based on the due date of the order minus the sum of the shipping buffer time and the assembly buffer time.

10. Materials for products that do not use the CCR at all are released at a time equivalent to the shipping due date minus the shipping buffer.

## Traditional DBR: The Big Picture

Figure 7.8 depicts what we've just covered. The shipping schedule is protected by the shipping buffer. That schedule minus the shipping buffer indicates the time that a particular order should come out of the CCR.

The MPS is the drum. It determines what the CCR works on and when it should work on it. The CCR buffer protects the integrity of the MPS.

The material release schedule is the rope. It determines when materials should be released to the production floor. The MPS date/time for each order minus the CCR buffer determines the material release time for each entry on the material release schedule.

## What to Do with Non-Constraints in a DBR Environment

We've already seen that there is a great temptation to try to plan everything everywhere in the system in great detail. This is a difficult temptation to overcome, and TOC/DBR in some ways makes this even more difficult, because it presents us with a situation in which there are a lot of system components that don't need to be (and probably shouldn't be) scheduled. The question always arises, "What do we do about non-constraints in a DBR operation?"

The answer is that in DBR, no schedule is produced for non-constraints. Our basic assumption is that buffers, coupled with excess capacity at non-constraints, provide enough flexibility for non-constraints to react in the best way to provide whatever support is needed. A good example might be a fire department. They perform an indispensable function, but nobody schedules

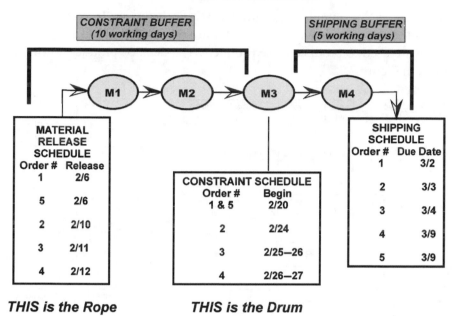

**Figure 7.8   Traditional DBR: The Big Picture**

them to put out fires at specific times — when a fire needs to be put out, they put it out. And they can do this because they usually have a lot of excess capacity (idle time).

Under DBR, in the absence of a schedule for non-constraint resources, these work centers are expected to conform to a standard policy: When work arrives, do it as expeditiously as possible, and move it onto the next step in the process. This is often referred to as the "roadrunner" approach, after the cartoon character who had only two speeds, full speed and full stop.

The important thing to keep in mind is that efficient use of the non-constraints is not what you're in business for. Since the needs of the external customer depend on the efficiency and effectiveness of the constraint (CCR), the objective of the non-constraints must always be fast satisfaction of the needs of the CCR.*

---

\* This is a behavioral issue (rooted in organizational culture) of the highest importance. At some point, measurements and appraisals will have to be aligned with this objective.

## An Example of Traditional DBR Scheduling

Let's consider an example of traditional DBR scheduling. In our example, four different products (A, B, C, and D) are produced and sold. Ten work centers are used to produce these products. The detailed product routing is shown in Figure 7.9.

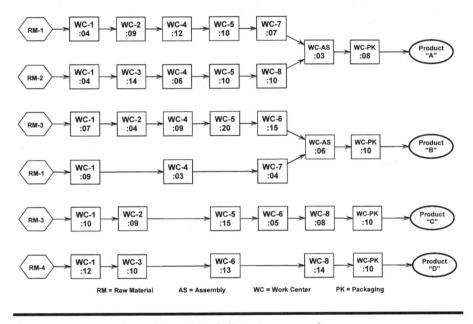

**Figure 7.9   Traditional DBR Scheduling: An Example**

The CCR is work center number 5 (WC-5). Notice, however, that WC-5 is not used in the manufacture of product D. Only four different raw materials are used to manufacture all four products. This is a true make-to-order environment and the lead time promised to the customer is 3 weeks. Consequently, the schedule horizon is 3 weeks.

Let's assume the date is 12/31/99. The last year of the old millennium starts tomorrow. Fortunately, we didn't have to shut down our plant between Christmas and New Year. We have shipments due in the first 3 weeks of January, as shown in Table 7.1. This table represents the Master Production Schedule, unless we find that we're unable to complete it.

The next step is to schedule the CCR by forward loading it according to the due dates (using the simple method, described earlier, in scheduling the CCR). We can skip the first three work-orders as they no longer need WC-5. Work orders 4 and 5 are already at WC-5, so our nominal CCR can start working immediately. The materials for the rest of the orders are yet to be released.

**Table 7.1    Master Production Schedule**

| Work Order | Due Date | Product | Quantity | Status |
|:---:|:---:|:---:|:---:|:---:|
| 1 | 1/03/2000 | A | 90 | Completed |
| 2 | 1/05/2000 | C | 72 | Completed |
| 3 | 1/06/2000 | D | 24 | At WC-8 |
| 4 | 1/07/2000 | C | 96 | At WC-5 |
| 5 | 1/10/2000 | B | 72 | At WC-5 |
| 6 | 1/11/2000 | D | 36 | Not released |
| 7 | 1/13/2000 | A | 24 | Not released |
| 8 | 1/14/2000 | B | 24 | Not released |
| 9 | 1/17/2000 | D | 30 | Not released |
| 10 | 1/17/2000 | C | 64 | Not released |
| 11 | 1/18/2000 | C | 32 | Not released |
| 12 | 1/20/2000 | A | 48 | Not released |
| 13 | 1/20/2000 | D | 30 | Not released |
| 14 | 1/21/2000 | B | 24 | Not released |

The CCR buffer is 5 days. The assembly buffer is assumed to be only 3 days. It exists only for the assembly of Product B, where the lower leg produces a part that does not pass through WC-5. The other leg of Product B is a CCR part, as WC-5 is used in the fourth operation.

Product A uses WC-5 in both its legs, so no assembly buffer is needed. Certainly no assembly buffer is required for Product C, because it has no assembly operation.

The shipping buffer for Products A, B, and C is assumed to be 5 days. This buffer covers the entire product routing from WC-5 through completion. However, the shipping buffer for Product D is 8 days. The reason Product D has a different shipping buffer is that it's a "free" product (in other words, it doesn't pass through a CCR). Notice in Figure 7.9 that in the absence of a CCR buffer, the flow of Product D has more operations to protect from variability (Murphy).

The lead time for Products A, B, and C is equivalent to the sum of the CCR buffer, the processing time on the CCR, and the shipping buffer. So, in our case it should be 10 working days plus the days the CCR needs to work on the order, which may be 1 to 3 days. In determining the quoted lead time for the customers, we also need to take into account the possibility that the CCR may be scheduled to begin work on a particular order later than desired because of the load imposed by other orders due earlier. Let's see how this might happen in this particular example.

## The CCR Schedule

We'll assume no set-up is required for WC-5 in this case. We'll also assume only 1 shift per day of 8 hours. In processing Work Order #4 (96 units of Product A), the total processing time per piece is 20 minutes. Processing for all 96 units takes 24 hours — 3 working days. We translate every work order to hours of work. For the sake of simplicity, in this example we've established quantities that would exactly fill whole shifts. The CCR schedule appears in Table 7.2.

**Table 7.2   CCR Schedule**

| Working Days | 1/3 | 1/4 | 1/5 | 1/6 | 1/7 | 1/10 | 1/11 | 1/12 | 1/13 | 1/14 | 1/17 | 1/18 | 1/19 | 1/20 | 1/21 |
|---|---|---|---|---|---|---|---|---|---|---|---|---|---|---|---|
| WC-5 work order # | 4 | 4 | 4 | 5 | 5 | 5 | 7 | 8 | 10 | 10 | 11 | 12 | 12 | 14 | |

We can see immediately that we have a problem. If the CCR processing time for Work Order #14 is 1 day, and the CCR doesn't begin work on it until 1/20, there's no way it can be ready to ship on 1/21. Even though the MPS horizon covers a window of 3 weeks, we expect the CCR to finish all orders ahead of the shipping date by an amount of time equal to the shipping buffer. Since we allow half of the shipping buffer as a minimum time to protect the original due date, the CCR should complete all of its work orders no less than 2.5 days before the end of the horizon. One option might be to advise the customer of a delivery delay of just 1 day, then take steps to expedite the order.

Table 7.3 shows an original due date for all work orders, the expected date of completion (conclusion of WC-5 processing, plus 5 days shipping buffer), and the earliest possible completion date (conclusion of WC-5 processing plus 2.5 days). Product D can be considered late only if the due date is less than half the buffer and the materials have not been released. But this is not the situation in this case, so all Product D shipments are assumed to be on time.

It seems the situation is even worse than our initial assessment. The worst problem is Work Order #5, which is due to ship on 1/10. The earliest date possible, even with expediting (urgent completion) is 1/13 — 3 days later than promised! In fact, the constraint (WC-5) won't even finish processing this work order until 1/10, the original due date. What can we do?

**Table 7.3   Work Order Status**

| Work Order # | 3 | 4 | 5 | 6 | 7 | 8 | 9 | 10 | 11 | 12 | 13 | 14 |
|---|---|---|---|---|---|---|---|---|---|---|---|---|
| Due Date | 1/6 | 1/7 | 1/10 | 1/11 | 1/13 | 1/14 | 1/17 | 1/17 | 1/18 | 1/20 | 1/20 | |
| Planned Completion | 1/6 | 1/12 | 1/17 | 1/11 | 1/18 | 1/19 | 1/21 | 1/24 | 1/25 | 1/20 | 1/21 | |
| Expedited Completion | 1/6 | 1/10 | 1/13 | /11 | 1/14 | 1/17 | 1/17 | /19 | 1/20 | 1/21 | 1/20 | 1/25 |

One option might be to advise the customer of a one-day delivery delay. Take a look at the work-in-process routing (Figure 7.9). Notice that after the constraint there are two additional operations for Product B. The constraint is scheduled to start processing Work Order #5 on 1/6. If we use a transfer batch of *one* and the parts from the other leg already reside at the assembly point, we may assume that by the end of 1/10 most of the order will be completed, and only the last few units will still need to pass through the last two operations. If this is the case, there's a good chance we can ship the order on 1/11.

We should clarify two things about the option above. We're assuming the non-constraint parts needed for Product B are already at the assembly point, because this is as far as they can go without the constraint's parts. We're also assuming that there's adequate excess capacity on that leg to make it possible for them to be there. If for any reason those parts are still upstream of the assembly point, this option isn't feasible.

Is it realistic to expect that we can rush an order for 72 units of Product B to completion? We can assume so only if we expedite those parts and ensure that the remaining work centers required for Product B, the ones after the CCR, are available. Can we guarantee this?

In general, when multiple products are involved, it's best to be very careful in committing to delivery dates earlier than half the shipping buffer *after* the date the CCR is supposed to finish processing.

We really have only two options: we can either change the original Master Production Schedule (and advise the customer accordingly), or we can add capacity at the constraint. If we add three second shifts at WC-5 before January 10, we significantly improve the chances of finishing Work Order #5 on time, and the subsequent orders as well.

One warning, though: If we add capacity to WC-5 only, can we be certain that a different resource won't become a temporary constraint? By adding second shifts to WC-5 we actually elevate the constraint (increase capacity) for a while. Whenever we elevate a constraint we'd better determine whether a new CCR has emerged. A computer-based scheduling system could easily answer this question by monitoring the total load on the non-constraints for the period of time in question. However, very accurate data on the non-constraint are required for this, and such data aren't always available.

If we want to preclude the emergence of a new constraint, we can add a second shift to the next most heavily loaded work centers, and possibly other resources as well. This can give us confidence that, within the buffer time, all non-constraints are able to do everything required to support the best exploitation of the CCR. In our example, we have a number of orders faced with an almost totally consumed shipping buffer, and we'd like to reduce the pressure on the non-constraints as well. So adding three second shifts to all the resources seems like a good idea.

When the time comes to actually add second shifts on the first 3 working days, another problem occurs. Let's change the schedule first (see Table 7.4). The last working day for the constraint is 1/17, which is expected because every order is supposed to be past the constraint and into the downstream operations in the last 5 days (the shipping buffer). But we'd also like to have 5 days for the released materials to reach the constraint. The parts for Work Orders #7 and #8 haven't been released yet. Even if we release those parts on the morning of 1/3, they'll have only 3 and 4 days, respectively, to reach the constraint.

**Table 7.4    Revised Shift Schedule**

| Working Days | 1/3 | 1/4 | 1/5 | 1/6 | 1/7 | 1/10 | 1/11 | 1/12 | 1/13 | 1/14 | 1/17 | 1/18 | 1/19 | 1/20 | 1/21 |
|---|---|---|---|---|---|---|---|---|---|---|---|---|---|---|---|
| Shifts added | 1 | 1 | 1 | | | | | | | | | | | | |
| WC-5 work order | 4 | 4&5 | 5 | 7 | 8 | 10 | 10 | 11 | 12 | 12 | 14 | | | | |

On one hand, we can hope that half the CCR buffer might be enough. On the other hand, if we assume the second shift will be used for all resources, and if we remember that the original 5-day buffer assumed only 1 shift per day, we'd better measure the buffer in shifts, rather than in days, so that we won't create problems for ourselves with material release.

We can now create a raw-material release schedule (Table 7.5). Note that the non-CCR materials for Product B, specifically Work Orders #8 and #14, are released only 3 days before the CCR start processing time, because the assembly buffer is only 3 days.

**Table 7.5   Material Release Schedule**

| Release Dates | 1/3 | 1/4 | 1/5 | 1/6 | 1/10 | 1/12 |
|---|---|---|---|---|---|---|
| RM-1 | 24 - WO#7 | | 24 - WO#8 | 48 - WO#12 | | 24 - WO#14 |
| RM-2 | 24 - WO#7 | | 32 - WO#11 | 48 - WO#12 | | |
| RM-3 | | 24 - WO#8 | | | 24 - WO#14 | |
| | | 64 - WO #10 | | | | |
| RM-4 | 36 - WO#6 | | 30 - WO#9 | | 30 - WO#13 | |

While the MPS covers a 3-week horizon, the CCR schedule reflects only 2 weeks and 1 day. The material release schedule is even narrower, covering only 1.5 week. These differences reflect the impact of the buffers.

This simple example demonstrates the approach of DBR to scheduling. Notice that the schedules include only the due dates, the CCR operations, and the release of materials. Non-constraint operations aren't scheduled at all.

## The Control Conflict Revisited

Let's return to that conflict we considered earlier — whether to plan everything in detail or not (see Figure 7.10). Based on what we've just seen, there are two injections that can break this conflict. These injections will replace P1 (plan everything in detail).

The first injection is to plan in detail only those activities that have no flexibility or excess capacity, and those from which the system can't tolerate a mistake. These are the master production schedule, the CCR schedule, and the material release schedule.

If the material release is too early, protective capacity is wasted doing things that are not needed now. If it's too late, it will be impossible to recover from the unexpected ("Murphy," demand changes, etc.).

The second injection is to not schedule any resource with significant excess capacity or flexibility. The only guidance for such resources is

1. Work as quickly as practical (and still satisfy quality standards).
2. Work only on what is needed now — don't let them take it upon themselves to keep busy producing what is not needed to fill firm

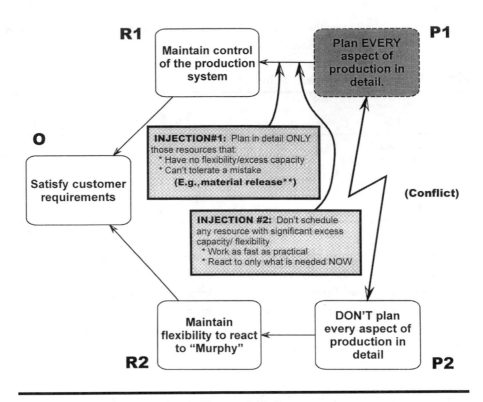

**Figure 7.10   The Control Conflict Revisited**

orders. The only exception to this is a conscious decision to assemble-to-order or make-to-stock in anticipation of a known, short-term future demand that has not yet appeared but will overload the system.

3. If more than one order is present for processing at a non-constraint, the one with the earliest time on the CCR schedule or the earliest due date should be started first.

## Managing Non-Constraints in a DBR Environment

Remember: the second injection says, "Don't schedule any resource with significant flexibility/excess capacity." This begs the question, "How much flexibility is enough?"

Whether a non-constraint should be planned or not is a function of its flexibility, which, in turn, depends on the amount of excess capacity it has. At some point there is not enough excess capacity to respond to changes (break set-ups, change work priorities, and still go back to the original job).

How many such reactions can a non-constraint handle? One? Two? Four? Five or more? Unfortunately, there is no rule of thumb for this. The nature of the specific environment will point to the answer.

When a non-constraint does not have complete flexibility to subordinate, it usually turns into a constraint. In most cases some simple actions — for example, minimal planning to prevent significant waste of capacity, set-up reductions, minimum batch policies or better qualified operators — can prevent this from happening. All of these means are subject to a critical question: *Does this non-constraint really have the capability to subordinate?* Only when the answer is "no" should other measures (including minimal planning of non-constraint activities) be considered.

In a turbulent market environment, or if equipment is frequently unreliable or unavailable, non-constraints need much more flexibility, and the threshold for considering this flexibility loss will be much lower. In such a case, you might consider flexibility to be compromised even when 30% of the non-constraint's time is still available. Whatever minimums you establish for required flexibility (excess capacity), keep in mind that only inflexible resources should be planned. Any resource with enough excess capacity (a judgment call on your part) should be left to react in real time when all pertinent information is available.

# References

1. Goldratt, Eliyahu M., *The Goal*, (2nd revised ed.), Croton-on-Hudson, NY, The North River Press, 1992.
2. Goldratt, Eliyahu M. and Robert E. Fox., *The Race*, Croton-on-Hudson, NY, The North River Press, 1986.
3. Goldratt, Eliyahu M., *The Haystack Syndrome: Sifting Information Out of the Data Ocean*, Croton-on-Hudson, NY, The North River Press, 1990.

# 8 Traditional Buffer Management: The DBR Control Mechanism

I n our discussion of traditional DBR so far, we've glossed over the topic of buffers somewhat in the interest of presenting the whole DBR concept. However, the role of the buffers is critical for ultimate success in an uncertain environment. Consequently, proper understanding of buffers is a must for robust planning. But even more important, understanding buffers and the way they behave in reality is crucial for proper control in executing plans. We refer to the method used to control continuing operations after traditional DBR is established as buffer management (BM). It's the key to the success of DBR, so we need to address some specific questions about it, particularly:

1. How do time buffers work?
2. How do we decide what buffer duration is enough?
3. What do we do with the buffer once we've established it?

We're going to answer all of these questions in this chapter.

## The Buffer Concept

Time buffers are the TOC way of protecting systems and processes against the effects of special cause variation (which is often referred to as "Murphy," after Murphy's Law) and uncertainty. For our purposes, special cause variation is disruption to internal process activities. Examples of such disruption might be unexpected human absences, equipment breakdowns, longer than expected set-ups, unanticipated quality problems, fires, broken water pipes, short duration electrical power losses, etc.

We'll consider uncertainty to be external, rather than internal. The biggest external uncertainty we usually have to accommodate is changing market demand, although there might be other uncertain external variables as well (supplier reliability, material availability, etc.).

In TOC, and under DBR in particular, buffers are not composed of things (items to be worked on) — they constitute a period of time. A buffer is only a planning factor. We incorporate time buffers in our plans based on our best guess of the flexibility we'll need to respond to variation or uncertainty.

The use of the term buffer in constraint management is unique in two respects. First, the buffer is expressed as time, rather than units of work-in-process. Second, we refer to the buffer as a liberal estimation of the whole production lead time (usually from the raw materials to the CCR), rather than distinguishing between an average lead time and then adding extra safety time to it (which might normally be considered a buffer).

The reason buffers (in the DBR vocabulary) are defined as the whole lead time and not just the safety portion is that in most manufacturing environments there is a huge difference between the sum of the net processing times and the total lead time. When we review the net processing time of most products, we find it takes between several minutes and an hour per unit. But the lead time may be several weeks, and even in the best environments several days. Consequently, each unit of product waits for attention somewhere on the shop floor for a much longer time than it actually takes to work on it. The magnitude of that waiting time depends on the overall load on resources and planning policies. So it makes sense not to isolate the net processing time, but to treat the whole lead time as a buffer — the time the shop floor needs to handle all the orders it must process.

But buffers alone are not enough. It's not unusual for a situation to exceed the buffer's capability to absorb variation/uncertainty. So even with a buffer in place, we must be ready to identify situations when the buffer will be unequal to the task and respond with effective corrective action before the situation gets out of hand. An effective buffer can significantly reduce the number of such exceptional responses we need to make, giving us a more stable system in the long run. But all the fire prevention in the world doesn't obviate the need for firemen once in a while.

## Buffer Management

The immediate purpose of the buffer is to absorb minor deviations to our plan. The ultimate objective of buffer management is to reveal and warn us of major threats to our plan — deviations so large that even the buffer can't handle them — in time for us to act to avoid disaster.

The state or condition of the buffer at any given time indicates the degree of threat to successful on-time delivery. In a DBR-based system, a late delivery implies that somehow all the protection that we built into the system has been exhausted. In other words, the buffer has been overrun. So in order to understand the true nature of the uncertainty we face and the degree of threat to on-time delivery, we should analyze the state of the buffers.

## DBR Buffers: Three Zones

We've defined a DBR buffer as a fairly long (liberal) estimation of the actual lead time between two points in the internal supply chain. We're going to divide that time into three approximately equal parts. The buffer is analogous to a shock absorber, and the three zones to different degrees of compression (Figure 8.1).

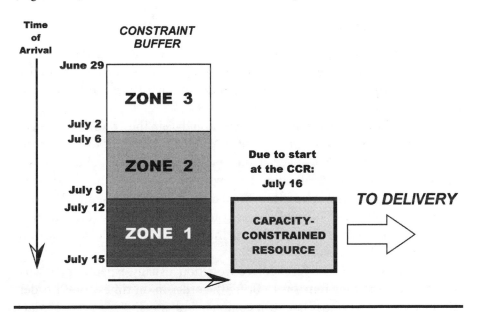

**Figure 8.1    DBR Buffers: Three Zones**

Normal road vibration consumes a relatively small part of the shock absorber's compression capability. This is equivalent to Zone 3.

Moderately sized bumps or potholes — which don't occur as frequently as normal road vibration — compress the shock absorber somewhat more, but not completely. This would be comparable to Zone 2.

Occasionally we hit bumps or potholes that are so big, they bottom out the shock absorber. They might even bend the rim of the wheel. Such bumps in a manufacturing environment would consume all of Zone 1's compression capability.

In a manufacturing situation, Zone 3 is the top end of the buffer. It's much longer than the net processing time of one unit but it is short enough that many orders consume most of it. Quite often it takes even longer than that, penetrating Zone 2. Zone 3 might be considered equivalent to normal road vibration. Zone 2 is the middle of the buffer. Variability or uncertainty occasionally consumes part or all of this segment — this might be equated to a moderately sized pothole. Zone 1 is the bottom of the buffer. This is the "tooth-jarring" bump that fully compresses the shock absorber. We don't ever want to see this part fully consumed. Any penetration of this zone constitutes a danger flag.

## Holes in a Buffer

When an order is not present at the protected site (CCR, assembly point, or shipping point) at the time it's required to be there, we refer to this condition as a "hole" in the buffer. There can be holes in any of the three zones (see Figure 8.2).

A hole in Zone 3 means that the order should be in the production process somewhere, but we don't worry about it. We don't even look for it. Material release should have taken place at the beginning of Zone 3, and we might check to be sure that it really did. It always requires some time for an order to move from material release to a protected area (CCR, assembly). A hole in Zone 2 results from normal process variation and is cause for attention, but not action. A hole in Zone 1, on the other hand, indicates a serious problem with the order.

Only holes in Zone 1 trigger corrective action, usually expediting, because only a very short time remains to bring the order in on time. Zone 1 orders can be considered almost late. If a complete buffer (all 3 zones) is 15 days, we are fairly certain that this is enough for normal delivery, and most orders

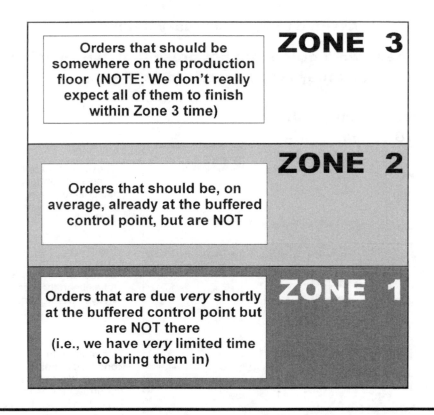

**Figure 8.2    Holes in a Buffer**

are ready in less than 10 of those days. Any orders that exceed those 10 days should be expedited.

## Holes in a Buffer: An Example

Here's a simple example. Let's assume we've established three buffer zones, as depicted in Figure 8.3. Each zone is 5 days long. Let's assume today is January 3. The time is 8:00 a.m. We have four jobs pending on the production floor:

- Work Order 47 is scheduled to be shipped on the morning of January 4.
- Work Order 48 is scheduled to be shipped on the morning of January 11.
- Work Orders 49 and 50 are scheduled to be shipped on the morning of January 18.

**Assume today is January 3 (8:00 a.m.)**

**These work orders are not present on the shipping dock, and they are expected to SHIP on...**

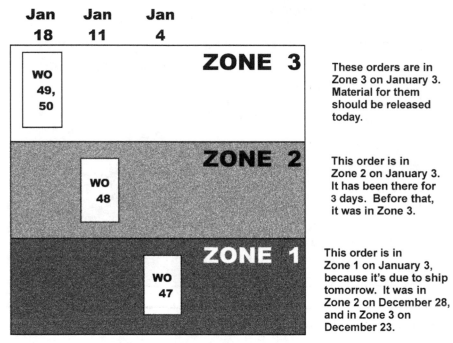

| Jan 18 | Jan 11 | Jan 4 |
|--------|--------|-------|

ZONE 3 — WO 49, 50 — These orders are in Zone 3 on January 3. Material for them should be released today.

ZONE 2 — WO 48 — This order is in Zone 2 on January 3. It has been there for 3 days. Before that, it was in Zone 3.

ZONE 1 — WO 47 — This order is in Zone 1 on January 3, because it's due to ship tomorrow. It was in Zone 2 on December 28, and in Zone 3 on December 23.

**SHIPPING BUFFER**

*NOTE: For simplicity, we're assuming a 7-day work week, 5 days in each zone of the buffer, and shipping on the morning of the day indicated.*

**Figure 8.3    Holes in the Shipping Buffer**

The first thing we do is to take attendance at the shipping dock — we physically check to see what work orders have been completed and are waiting for shipment. We do this daily. Since today is January 3, if we don't find Work Order 47 there, we have a hole in Zone 1, because it's due to be shipped tomorrow! This is a serious problem, because this order is now almost late. We have to locate that work-in-process (if we don't already know where it is) and we have to expedite it, or it will very likely be delivered late. In reality, we shouldn't be surprised by this situation, because Work Order 47 has been in Zone 1 for the past 4 days, and we would have taken action to expedite it earlier — probably on December 29.

We should also expect to find Work Order 48 there as well, even though it's not due to be shipped until January 11. If it's not there, we have a hole in Zone 2. This is not a serious problem — yet — but it bears watching. We might try to locate the work on the production floor (i.e., Where is it now?) and determine how close it is to arriving at the shipping dock. Is it likely to be there before January 7, at which time it enters Zone 1? If so, we need not take any action. It will arrive at the shipping dock in time for its scheduled shipping date. All we need do is monitor it, to make certain it doesn't suffer any further delays. If it won't arrive on the shipping dock before January 7, we have to take some action to speed up work on it.

We should not expect to find Work Orders 49 and 50 there. They are still likely to be in the production process — probably between the shipping dock and the preceding buffer-protected point (CCR, assembly, or even the material release point). However, if they don't appear at the shipping dock on January 8 (the Zone 2 date for those work orders), we'll start looking for them, too, just as we did for Work Order 48.

Here's another way to look at it (see Figure 8.4). Let's consider Work Order 49 alone. If it's not present at the shipping dock by January 7, don't worry about it! We don't expect it to be there. It's still somewhere in the manufacturing process. However, if it's not on the shipping dock by January 8, we've got a hole in Zone 2, and we should start looking for it, but take no action, unless we can see that it will surely become a hole in Zone 1. And if for any reason it does not show up at the shipping dock by January 13, we'd better do something fast! This order is now a hole in Zone 3 and in imminent danger of being delivered late.

## How a Hole in the Buffer Appears in the Master Production Schedule

Abstract pictures are nice to look at, but let's translate what we've just seen to the real world. Figure 8.5 shows an example of a simple master production schedule. As before, we'll assume that today is January 3, and that each zone of our shipping buffer is 5 days. To identify the holes in a buffer, we would go out onto the shipping dock and look at the finished goods sitting in front of it.

If we don't find Work Order 47, in its entirety, sitting at the shipping dock, it's possible that it has already been shipped. This is usually easy to find out. However, if Order 47 was neither shipped nor waiting to be shipped, we must waste no more time! It should be shipped tomorrow – this is a hole

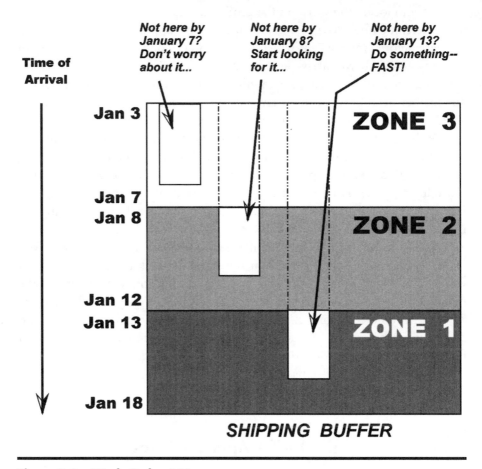

**Figure 8.4    Work Order #49**

in Zone 1. We need to locate and expedite it right now. In fact, we should already have noticed its absence on December 24, as a hole in Zone 2, and on December 29, as a hole in Zone 1. We would also have had to mentally prepare ourselves for the possibility that it might not be on the shipping dock in time to ship on time tomorrow.

We would also expect to see Work Order 48, either partially or in its entirety. If we did not find it there, we would backtrack through the manufacturing floor to find out where it is. This is a hole in Zone 2. As long as it is reasonably close (within one or two process steps) of the shipping dock,

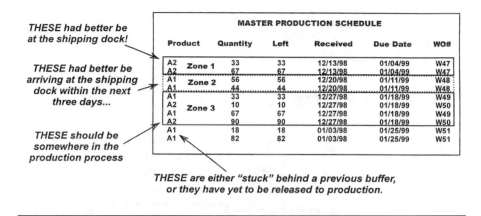

THESE had better be
at the shipping dock!

THESE had better be
arriving at the shipping
dock within the next
three days...

THESE should be
somewhere in the
production process

THESE are either "stuck" behind a previous buffer,
or they have yet to be released to production.

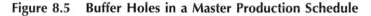

**Figure 8.5    Buffer Holes in a Master Production Schedule**

we would not take any action. We'd just wait for it to arrive at the shipping dock sometime within the Zone 2 window.

We would not expect to see Work Orders 49 and 50. The materials for these should be on the manufacturing floor. But we should not expect to see them on the shipping dock very shortly. If we're especially paranoid, we might check with the inventory manager to confirm that the materials were, in fact, released to the production floor at the scheduled time. But we'd take no other action at this point. Order 51 is either on its way to the CCR or assembly point, or, if no CCR is active, materials will not be released for another week. Notice that the due date for Order 51 is January 25, and the shipping buffer is only 15 days long.

# DBR Buffer Zones: A CCR Example

Let's consider an another example (Figure 8.6). We'll use a constraint buffer for this. Suppose our master production schedule calls for the CCR to start on Work Order 95 in the early morning on July 16. We'll assume our CCR buffer is 12 working days (there are 2 intervening weekends and a national holiday to consider).

If release of material is scheduled for June 29, the three zones would break down this way:*

---

\* There is a 3-day weekend between Zones 3 and 2, and a 2-day weekend between Zones 2 and 1.

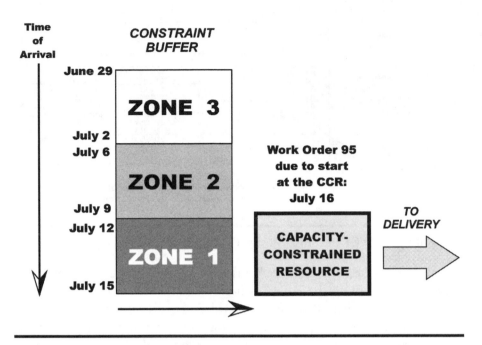

**Figure 8.6    Hole in a CCR Buffer**

Zone 3: June 29 to July 2.
Zone 2: July 6 to 9.
Zone 1: July 12 to 15.

Here's a visual picture of what the three zones in this example might look like. (Figure 8.7) Zone 3 is the top part of the CCR buffer. Any order that appears in this zone should have been released to the manufacturing floor for processing. We expect this zone to be fully consumed by actual production lead time. In our example, the boundaries of this zone are June 29 and July 2. If everything goes normally, we would expect the order to arrive at the CCR for processing by the end of the day on July 2.

Zone 2 is the middle of the CCR buffer. An order released on June 29 for production might use some of this buffer zone if any variability was experienced during actual production activities between material release and the CCR. If an order due to start processing by the CCR on July 16 is not in place there by July 6, we would start looking for it. We'd find out where in the preceding part of the process it currently resides, and do nothing but monitor it, unless we can immediately see that it won't arrive at the CCR by the beginning of its Zone 1 time.

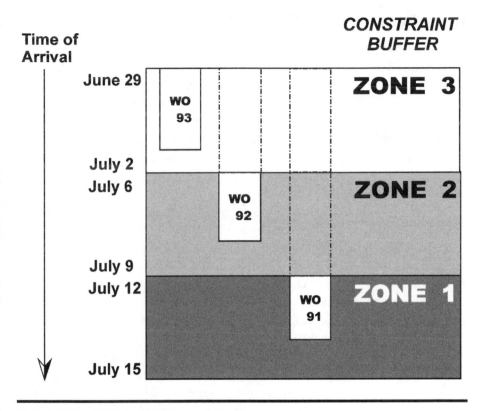

**Figure 8.7   DBR Buffer (Example)**

Zone 1 is the bottom part of the CCR buffer. An order that was released on June 29 but has not arrived at the CCR by July 12 is in danger of being delivered late — but there may still be time to save it. An order in this zone requires immediate action to begin expediting it.

To summarize, as long as orders have been released as scheduled, *ignore* orders in Zone 3 — we don't expect orders in this zone to be waiting at the shipping dock, the CCR, or the assembly point. *Monitor* orders that haven't arrived at the CCR by Zone 2 time. Determine the location of the errant order, but don't take action if it is expected to arrive at the CCR before Zone 1 time begins. *Expedite* any orders that don't arrive at the CCR by their Zone 1 time — and don't expedite any orders that are not in Zone 1, unless you are absolutely certain that there is no way they will arrive at the CCR before Zone 1 expires.

## Three Benefits of Buffer Management

There are three benefits to buffer management that make it worth doing. First, it signals management that an order is almost late, usually in time to do something about it, but it allows us to limit expediting to only those situations when it is truly necessary. An ancillary benefit is a significant reduction in the stress level of production managers!

Second, it alerts management when the whole production system is starting to lose stability. More than one work order in Zone 1 at a time is an indication that the system is destabilizing. Even if only one work order at a time enters Zone 1, if this happens many times during a short period, the system is still likely to be destabilizing. Here's an analogy. If school starts at 8:00 a.m., and the teacher has instructed the students to be in their seats at 7:55 a.m. (the beginning of Zone 1), the teacher won't be too concerned if one student (work order) comes in at 7:57. But if two more come in at 7:58 and another at 7:59, the teacher will start to become concerned about class discipline (system stability), even if none of the students actually arrives after 8:00 (a late shipment). So multiple Zone-1 penetrations in a short period of time can prompt managers to examine the load on the whole system and decide what actions to take to restabilize the production system.

Finally, buffer management can help managers identify an emerging constraint — one that is different from the known CCR. If DBR is applied effectively, the known CCR should never be overloaded. If we observe many work orders penetrating Zone 1, it might indicate that some other resource — a non-constraint — may be losing its protective capacity.

## How to Realize the Benefits of Buffer Management

Here's how to realize the benefits buffer management can provide.

1. Look for Zone 1 holes in buffers. Monitoring deliveries due for that period quickly points out incomplete orders that are in danger of being late. Expedite to preclude such orders from becoming late.

2. Analyze the data on any order that enters any Zone 1 (CCR, assembly, or shipping buffers). Increased pressure on the system is indicated by a large, or increasing, number of holes in Zone 1. Besides the action needed to deliver the specific order on time, take action to relieve the stress on the overall system. In most cases, this means adjusting either capacity or demand as required.

3. Whenever a Zone-1 order is expedited, identify and note for the record the resource that holds the last of the order's units. After several Zone-1 penetrations, a Pareto chart can indicate the most likely resource to become the next system constraint. For example, a low yield from a resource with relatively large excess capacity might point to a target for continuous improvement efforts. Keep in mind that buffer management operates in the *real world,* not in a database. Consequently, it can help identify real time constraints and non-constraints that would not show in the database because of data inaccuracy (or a long data update cycle).

Remember, one hole per month in Zone 1 is not serious, unless that hole represents an exceptionally large order or constitutes a large percentage of the output in a month. But several holes may indicate that the system is losing stability. Flexibility (protective capacity) has been lost, or a new constraint may be emerging — or both.

## Identifying an Emerging Constraint: An Example

Let's say a change in product mix has caused the CCR to shift from machine 10 to machine 23. The load on machine 23 is still growing, but the company's information system does not indicate this change, because either the data in the system are erroneous or the next periodic data system update isn't due for another week or so. How can we tell that the constraint is shifting?

Before the constraint began to shift, the production manager noticed that no more than three orders per week ever entered Zone 1. Now the number is approaching 15 per week, and still growing. In expediting these orders, the production manager notices that three quarters of the Zone-1 penetrations result from orders that seem to be stuck at machine 23.

Based on that information, a production manager knowledgeable in constraint theory would conclude that a new constraint is emerging at machine 23. This means that new *exploitation* and *subordination* procedures must be devised and implemented to ensure that the production system continues to realize maximum throughput.

# 9 Drum-Buffer-Rope (DBR) and Manufacturing Resource Planning (MRP)

I t should be pretty obvious by now that we've been talking about policies and procedures rather than automated tools. DBR can be applied manually in the real world, and it often is in fairly small, uncomplicated operations, like Plant 120. But once the size and level of complexity increases, manual DBR becomes almost impossible — there aren't enough hands to juggle all the balls.

Most companies with manufacturing processes of any size or complexity use some form of computerized Material Requirement Planning (MRP) package. Most current MRP systems are more accurately classified as "MRP-II," the acronym standing for Manufacturing Resource Planning. MRP/MRP-II systems help schedule both material requirements and production operations. One of the big problems with MRP applications is that they're what's referred to as "infinite capacity" systems — the schedules they produce don't consider any capacity constraints. This "infinite capacity" limitation is probably the best-known and most widely discussed disadvantage of the MRP algorithm. However, we'll see later that it's not the only one. Consequently, MRP creates some problems that we'll discuss in more detail below — problems that DBR repairs.

We now know that DBR amounts to finite capacity planning, but we also know that there is probably a considerable investment in MRP software in most companies. Moreover, the development of MRP from an algorithm to calculate net material requirements into a comprehensive manufacturing database makes it difficult to replace. Most Enterprise Resource Planning (ERP) systems are developed around the old MRP concepts. The few DBR computerized systems available work within larger MRP systems, while providing all the necessary DBR scheduling and control.

But if an organization complex enough to require computer scheduling support wants to move to DBR planning and scheduling, does that mean that it would have to scrap its MRP system and install DBR software? The short answer is "no." The investment in MRP software is not lost. Moreover, not having dedicated DBR software shouldn't preclude any shop floor from implementing DBR. There are ways to "force" the standard MRP system to cooperate with the major Drum-Buffer-Rope requirements, but this does require some manipulation to make the MRP software function as a DBR scheduling package.

As it stands today, MRP is really the only standard method for managing material requirements information. And despite its shortcomings, MRP is also the standard for manufacturing information in general. Because most companies recognize that it's risky to use information systems that are not fairly standardized and well documented, MRP is the information system of choice among manufacturing organizations.

## MRP Advantages

Though it does have shortcomings, MRP also has some definite advantages. For most manufacturing environments, MRP's material requirements support is adequate. MRP also integrates information from sales, production, and purchasing, and it accommodates the need to time-phase activities.

Moreover, MRP does not create a false impression of precision. Work is scheduled in time buckets. But MRP provides no detailed sequencing information. It may overload specific time buckets, and only a subsequent check of capacity resource planning will reveal this overload.

Production gains more than it loses from this characteristic of MRP. While the software refrains from overly sophisticated planning, it is also obvious (by exception) which elements are missing. This alerts knowledgeable schedulers to check the omitted factors and exercise human judgment to make realistic choices.

But perhaps the most important advantage MRP offers is that it is flexible enough to provide the kind of information required to support DBR — needs that were not envisioned at the time MRP was conceived.

# MRP Disadvantages

However, if a company's manufacturing objective is to minimize actual production lead times while maintaining a high degree of delivery reliability, MRP has some major drawbacks, too.

First, MRP software is normally batch processed. It doesn't run in real time. MRP runs are not updated with each new order. Rather, they may incorporate many new orders that accumulate over some period of time (days, a week, etc.). Second, MRP does not deal with uncertainty very well. It protects delivery dates by adding more time everywhere in the process. This stretches production lead times out considerably longer than they need to be, and it clogs the system with work that is not immediately needed.

Another problem MRP poses is what might be called "sensory overload." It creates work orders for every level in the bill of materials. This proliferation of work orders results in less visibility for the process as a whole. This tendency to create separate work orders for each level in the bill of materials (BOM) stems from the desire to merge work orders for common parts. Merging the requirements for the same parts that go to different orders and products seems to save a lot of set-ups. But it also reduces the ability to control priorities by reducing the visibility on what parts are needed for specific customer orders. It also results in larger process batches, making it difficult to split batches when necessary. And some of the concepts behind MRP create devastating production management policies.

# MRP Policies That Can Create Problems

One unfavorable policy is the requirement for intermediate due dates at each step in the process. While this may seem to be a common-sense policy — dictating unequivocal activity-ending times that can be closely controlled — it has some definite negative ramifications. One such ramification is that when operators see that it's possible to finish a particular batch much earlier than the scheduled completion time, they may look for other options to be more efficient. After all, they're rated on efficiency, aren't they?

Suppose you're the operator of NC15, a non-constraint resource. Today is Monday morning, and you look ahead at all the work orders that MRP predicts will eventually pass through your work center. You notice Work Order 102, for 100 units. You already have all these pieces at your site, but you need 1.5 hours to set-up your machine. After that, the whole batch requires only 30 minutes to process.

Luckily you notice that Work Order 111, for 230 units of something else, is also on the same list. But being the smart, experienced operator that you are, you know that setting up your machine between those particular work orders will require only 2 minutes because the two operations are similar and use the same tools. So if you combine the work for those two work orders you can be much more efficient.

However, the parts for Work Order 111 aren't yet at your work center. They're due to arrive on Wednesday. Since Work Order 102 isn't really due until Thursday, we can safely delay its processing until Work Order 111 arrives at your site on Wednesday, right?

Wrong! DBR suggests that maximum efficiency is not important for non-constraints. Instead, DBR demands subordination of all non-constraints to the constraint. In other words, when you have Work Order 102 ready for processing at your site, process it immediately.

Intermediate due dates give a false impression that there's no need to hurry. Remember: The whole idea behind buffers is to accumulate them at the right places, so that the extra time can be effectively used when variability hits us hard. At all unbuffered locations, it's important to push the parts through as quickly as possible if we're to realize the advantage the buffer is designed to provide. If every operator waited (i.e., used up slack time) to deliver just at the required time, some work is bound to be late.

Consider what could happen if we decided to delay processing Work Order 102 from Monday until Wednesday, expecting subsequently to pass it on the next day. Now, because of "Murphy," our work center goes down at noon on Tuesday for 1.5 days. By the time we're back in operation (Thursday), many other orders will be competing for its time. If Work Order 102 is done on Monday, it can go safely to the protected area (shipping, CCR, or assembly) without having to be expedited and without creating the artificial impression that the buffer time is too short. This is the essence of the road-runner approach mentioned in Chapter 7. By minimizing the amount of time any given order spends at any one work center, we minimize its exposure to the effects of "Murphy" at that site as well. So the road-runner principle can be considered a risk mitigation practice as well as a contributor to reduced manufacturing cycle times. Intermediate dates, a part of the MRP output and philosophy, are at odds with the road-runner approach.

Another unfavorable consequence of MRP is that it doesn't preclude the early release of materials when the first few work centers have nothing else to do. Such early release is really at odds with the rationale of DBR. It creates huge amounts of work-in-process, disrupts priorities, and increases lead time. While the early release of materials isn't a formal MRP policy, it isn't discouraged by MRP professionals.

Another unfavorable policy is that MRP assumes transfer batches are equal to process batches, an assumption built into the MRP time-phasing algorithm. This means that work-in-process is held (delayed) between process steps until the preceding step has completed processing the whole order. Queues can build up dramatically, slowing the flow of entire orders through the manufacturing line.

## Overcoming MRP's Disadvantages

As indicated earlier, it's not necessary to "throw the baby out with the bath water." MRP can be used to support a DBR operation. To do this, a production manager must first acknowledge the disadvantages of MRP. Obviously, this requires that the production manager know what those disadvantages are and why they are harmful to the production system. Then the inherent flexibility in MRP must be used to manipulate the software to support effective constraint management.

How should MRP software be manipulated? First, we need to force the drum into the MRP. There are several steps in doing this.

1. Initially, we identify the capacity-constrained resource (CCR) and verify processing and set-up times to the best accuracy possible. It's likely that we've already done this.
2. Then we start with an optimistic Master Production Schedule (MPS) — what we'd like to be able to do, if we weren't internally constrained. Unless we already know which work orders require time at the CCR for every entry in the MPS, we need an MRP run to obtain a list of all the operations the CCR needs to do.
3. With this list in hand, we manually schedule the CCR operations in the same way as described in Chapter 7.
4. Determine any required changes in the MPS. For every operation scheduled on the CCR we must verify that the finish time at the CCR allows enough time to complete the rest of the manufacturing process prior to the due date that currently appears in the MPS. Slip the shipping dates when necessary.
5. Force the CCR schedule into the MRP program, and use the updated MPS. *NOTE: If a particular MRP package doesn't allow a schedule to be forced on one resource (the CCR), then the simplified form of DBR*

*(S-DBR), explained in Chapter 10, is the only effective option for man-aging DBR with an MRP system.*

6. Next, insert the appropriate buffers and let MRP generate the material release. To understand how to do this, we need to examine some internal characteristics of MRP.

## MRP Lead Times and Queues

The original MRP algorithm, Material Requirements Planning, was based on exploding the Bill-of-Material (BOM) for every entry in the MPS. Timing for the material requirements was based on fixed lead times between any given part of the BOM and the next level. The lead time expressed an esti-mation of the actual time needed to move the part and process it. The notion of lead time is similar to the concept of a time buffer. It expresses a gross estimate of the time required to move an order through a sequence of oper-ations. The significant difference is that lead time is inserted between every entry in the BOM and the next level, while DBR prescribes time buffers only for the critical areas (CCR and assembly). Consequently, DBR buffers usually cover many parts (and several levels) of the BOM.

### *When Fixed Lead Times Can Be Used*

MRP packages that allow execution according to fix lead times are more easily transformed for DBR. The first thing to do is zero out most of the MRP lead times. The only remaining lead times should be at the origin of the buffers. Parts arriving at the CCR should carry a lead time equal to the CCR buffer. Usually this means that we must ensure that the CCR operation is a separate entry in the BOM. All the BOM entries prior to the CCR operation should have lead times of zero. The same should be done with the shipping and assembly buffers.

The result should be that MRP-directed material release for production aligns exactly with the buffer sizes (time durations). This procedure will also cause upstream operators to think that they are always past due, because the zero lead time makes it appear that the intermediate due date has already passed. Such an impression is not necessarily a bad thing for non-constraint operators to have. It can reinforce the idea that any work reaching a non-constraint should be processed as soon as possible: "When you see that your start–finish has already gone by, get in gear as quickly as possible."

## When Only Dynamic Lead Times Are Used

The more advanced MRP systems use dynamic lead times. This means that the actual time allowed for an order to pass through the sequence of operations defined as an entry in the BOM is calculated, and the size of the order has an impact.

The routing file specifying the sequence of operations and resources needed contains four factors used to calculate the lead time. These are set-up time, run time, move time, and queue time. Again, the notion of queue time is similar to the time buffer, but it has a much narrower interpretation. Queue time is usually much larger than the sum of the other numbers. The only number that considers the size of the order is the run time.

The way to force MRP to implement time buffers only at certain locations is to zero all queue times and move times for all non-constraint operations leading to a protected area (CCR, assembly, shipping point). The CCR operation itself rates a very high queue time, representing the vast majority of the buffer. The only difference in dynamic lead times is that because of the run time we may get somewhat different buffers for different sizes of orders.

Set-up and run times cannot be zeroed because they are a basic part of the capacity requirements planning (CRP) capability of MRP, and we definitely need that feature to provide an additional control on our use of capacity.

## Establishing the Rope

When the CCR schedule, the buffers, and the MPS are all ready, we can run the MRP to create the material release schedule. When the buffers are all in place, the MRP release schedule is close enough to satisfy any DBR implementation. What we need to do now is ensure that no material release is permitted prior to the MRP schedule.

## Problems in DBR Implementation within MRP Systems

The preceding procedure for using an MRP system to implement DBR is doable, but it's not very easy or straightforward. We haven't mentioned buffer management in a DBR/MRP system. It's more difficult than with a dedicated DBR scheduling system. In many cases the MRP software helps very little, and most of the work of buffer management must be done manually.

The basic problem in using MRP to implement DBR is that the MRP is forced to work under a different kind of logic than it was designed to do. Because of this dichotomy, a complete understanding of DBR thinking is crucial. It's very common in production operations to find that new people, well-schooled in MRP logic, replace DBR-trained people because of attrition or transfer. These new people are now faced with what seems like a "crooked MRP" implementation. They tend to do it the way they learned, which means changing MRP back to the way it was designed to operate. When this happens, DBR is essentially erased, and yesterday's norms are back in place again.

In order to maintain effective DBR in an MRP environment, the logic behind DBR and the derived changes to the regular MRP must be clearly documented, and people — both those already on board and those who later join the organization — must be thoroughly trained in DBR.

## DBR-Specific Software and Dynamic Buffers

MRP software can be adequately programmed to handle the tasks DBR requires. But there are definite advantages to computer application packages specifically designed to support DBR operations (i.e., not MRP software). Most of these software applications are compatible with existing MRP/ERP packages. They replace the primary MRP data run (sometimes referred to as "mrp"), but the MRP system is still used to maintain the database, data entry, and some of the tools such as rough-cut capacity planning and capacity requirement planning.

The first advantage of DBR-specific software applications is that most of them can support finite-loading constraint schedules. Second, they can provide a feasibility check by showing (in simulated runs) whether all the non-constraints can really do what they must to support the constraint in the required time.

Third, they can provide the capability to selectively shorten buffer times for better lead times. By using DBR-specific software to analyze actual results, buffer management can be improved. The software can show, for instance, that Zone 2 or Zone 1 were never penetrated. In such a case, the buffer is probably too large and might be safely shortened. Alternatively, this same kind of analysis might show Zone-1 penetrations occurring too frequently, revealing a need to enlarge the buffer.

More buffer time might be advisable when a non-constraint can't cope with constraint support demands, such as periodic seasonal peaks or unexpected demand spikes. Larger buffers may also be required when the variability in quality is high, or if there are many process steps.

The term "dynamic buffering" is used to describe the capability of DBR software to identify temporary load changes on non-constraints. In effect, this segregates internal resource variability from external demand uncertainty, so that the buffers for each can be managed separately. This feature can be extremely useful when internal variation is small enough not to require a very large buffer, but changes in customer demand (external uncertainty) fluctuate much more widely.

In software packages that have a dynamic buffering capability, the user can usually reduce the normal buffer and still protect against "true Murphy," or internal variability. Load fluctuations due to changes in customer demand are noted by the software. When the DBR automated scheduling system identifies a peak demand building on a certain non-constraint, it automatically enlarges the appropriate buffer. In other words, it releases material earlier than usual to allow non-constraints enough time to do their jobs and still allow the work-in-process to reach the protected resource on time. This capability can take such arbitrary peak loads out of the realm of uncertainty and make them predictable at the planning stage, so that appropriate management action can be taken earlier. In other words, the normal buffer can be relatively short, yet be quickly expanded — automatically, by the DBR software — when the need arises.

After a transitory load on a non-CCR is gone, the software will adjust the buffer back to the original level. Other factors (variability in quality, number of process steps) require human intervention to reduce their impacts and further shrink the buffer.


## Summary

Let's review what we've covered in the last four chapters (Part II). Most production managers would agree that a robust plan beats expediting any day. The closer to full load the manufacturing process gets, the more it destabilizes in the face of variation and uncertainty. TOC production policies can liberate hidden capacity in the process. We obtain this extra capacity by:

- Focusing on the capacity constraint (CCR).
    - —Exploiting it and subordinating non-constraints so the CCR won't be starved for work, and
    - —Doing only orders that are needed now.

- Making-to-order whenever possible.
- Completing work-in-process in smaller batches.
- Transferring work between stations in smaller batches.
- Preventing early release of materials for orders due much later.

Additional manufacturing cycle time reduction can be realized by scheduling daily instead of weekly. A daily schedule should add new firm orders to the MPS, while preserving the plan for existing firm orders. And it's better to defer work that isn't immediately needed. In other words, complete firm orders before making-to-stock, even if it means breaking set-ups.

Drum-Buffer-Rope is a way to obtain the best overall system efficiency, safeguard against variation and uncertainty, deliver on time (in the shortest possible time), speed the flow of work-in-process, and attain greater control over the whole manufacturing system.

The "drum" is the schedule for the Capacity-Constrained Resource (CCR). The "rope" is the material release schedule, preventing premature introduction of work-in-process. "Buffers" are the time allowed for work orders to arrive on time at the shipping dock, the CCR, and assembly points, despite "Murphy." Time buffers protect the delivery schedule so that less expediting is needed, and managing the buffers can help in identifying an emerging constraint. But even the best buffers can't provide complete protection against the unexpected. Consequently, we need some kind of control method to warn us of an impending problem before it's too late to do anything about it.

Knowing what's important and what isn't helps control information overload. Constraint theory helps distinguish what's important from what isn't. Due-date reliability depends on control of the system. And finally, buffer management is the key to the success of DBR.

# SIMPLIFIED DRUM-BUFFER-ROPE

# 10 Simplified Drum-Buffer-Rope (S-DBR)

In the preceding part of this book, we examined a basic manufacturing system, Plant 120, and we saw that even with only a few products, work centers, and raw materials, shortening production lead times while maintaining a high on-time delivery record was not easy to do. We also saw the favorable effects on our sensory load when we applied the production principles of the theory of constraints: smaller process and transfer batches, and working on the earliest firm orders first.

We also explored the concept of traditional drum-buffer-rope (DBR) and the critical role that buffer management plays in its success, observing that with or without DBR, perhaps the most critical need in any production management environment is a means of control — a way to anticipate and head off deviations before they seriously destabilize the system.

When you learned basic math, the teacher made you do it the hard way, with a pencil and paper and your own brain. It was an effective way of ensuring that you understood the concepts. However, most of us now use electronic calculators to do math. When was the last time you (without benefit of a calculator)…

- Did a square root on paper?
- Figured a total payout for a 30-year mortgage based on the future value formula?
- Worked out a length you couldn't physically measure using a trigonometric function?
- Or just multiplied two four-digit numbers on paper?

In a similar way, in Part II we devoted a good bit of effort in going over traditional DBR, to ensure your understanding of the the basic principles and concepts. But although traditional DBR *does* work, like manual mathematics, it can be somewhat cumbersome. Now it's time to learn how to use the calculator to come up with the same answers. Simplified Drum-Buffer-Rope (S-DBR) doesn't quite reduce the problem to a few keystrokes, but it is easier to install and use, and it achieves the same effects. By the time you fully understand how to apply S-DBR, you may be asking yourself, "Why didn't we set-up our manufacturing to do this so easily in the first place?"

# Difficulties in Applying Traditional DBR

No system is perfect — some are just better than others. While it is decidedly an improvement over MRP, using traditional DBR does present some difficulties.

## Spreading Buffer Time

Implementing three buffers, while protecting the intended specific points, weakens the global protection. Time assigned to one of the three buffers is not usable — if needed — by either of the other two. Each buffer protects its own area, but if the buffer is not needed at an earlier point, that time can't be saved to protect subsequent points. For example, let's assume that all the steps in production between material release and the capacity-constrained resource (CCR) function normally. A work order arrives at the CCR well before that resource is ready to work on it — and waits. After the CCR is finished with it, the work order moves on toward the shipping dock. Now, although the shipping point has its own buffer, this time is, of course, limited. If something goes wrong between the CCR and the shipping point — something that consumes all of the planned shipping buffer, or more — none of the unused CCR buffer time, which was never used, can help us.

## More Buffer Time

In this example, it should also be obvious that while the actual protected manufacturing lead time under DBR may be less than the equivalent MRP-computed time, three buffers can add more lead time than is actually needed to compensate for the reduced overall protection. Moreover, three buffers can also create conflict between different buffer needs, making the buffers, collectively, more difficult to control. An operator may face a choice between two different orders that have penetrated Zone 1 in two different buffers (e.g., shipping buffer for one, CCR buffer for the other). Which has priority? If the same buffer was penetrated, the choice would be clear: Priority goes to the order with the deepest buffer penetration. But with different buffers, the answer is not clear.

## Schedule Stability

Shifting customer priorities makes it difficult to maintain a stable schedule at the CCR. Suppose we have a schedule for the next 3 weeks, based on firm orders only. Now a new customer comes to us, promising significant additional work, but we would have to ship this new order in the next 2 weeks. Obviously, the only way to do this is to insert the new order into the existing master production schedule somewhere. We'd also have to change the CCR schedule.

It may only be necessary to insert the new order into the schedule and slip processing of all the orders that follow by the duration of the inserted order. We'd need to validate that those later orders would still make their promised delivery dates. If not, we might look for a way to conserve time by saving set-ups at the CCR, but then we'd have to shuffle the entire CCR schedule.

Consider another situation: A customer cancels an order, or delays it for a month. Not an uncommon event, but it does present us with a dilemma. Should we leave the CCR schedule alone, even though we lose the opportunity to generate throughput in the short term? Or should we reschedule the CCR, producing some orders earlier (as long as we're confident that the materials can be there in time) to preserve throughput in the near future? In really complex operations, it can be especially difficult to schedule (or reschedule) the CCR and derive a material release schedule without software support.

## Superfluous Buffer

In traditional DBR the rationale for having an assembly buffer is that once a CCR has worked on some parts (time of the most scarce resource invested), we should ensure flow to the market of these precious parts as fast as possible. They should not wait unnecessarily at a subsequent assembly point for parts that did not use the most critical resource. But parts that pass through the CCR have no special value in themselves — their importance derives only from the irreplaceable time the CCR expends on them. Their real value accrues when a customer is ready to accept — and pay for — the finished product. So assembly of parts from the CCR with parts that don't use the CCR should be accomplished in time to ship them to the customer at the required time. This may be much later than the time the parts were scheduled at the CCR. Since the CCR's capacity must be exploited, some work may have been scheduled at the CCR *much* earlier than its due date. Is there really a need to force the assembly work center, which is not a CCR, to work on these parts too early?

If the whole idea of buffers is to accumulate maximum protection at the weakest points, a case can be made for having a shipping buffer and a CCR buffer, but not an assembly buffer. Materials that pass through the CCR are released based on the constraint schedule. Materials that go into free products (i.e., products that don't use the CCR at all) are scheduled for release based on a shipping buffer. All the assembly buffer really does is add time to the release of non-CCR materials. In fact, the assembly buffer is really no more than an extension of the shipping buffer that provides earlier release of non-CCR materials and earlier arrival at the assembly point.

We might really need this extension, as the original length of the shipping buffer is designed to cover the activities only from the CCR to the shipping point. Because a longer buffer may be required to deal with non-constraint parts, traditional DBR adds that buffer at the operation assembling the constraint parts with the non-constraint parts. Viewed this way, the assembly buffer is not really independent — it's only a part of the shipping buffer.

A common misunderstanding in traditional DBR is to assume the existence of an assembly buffer at *any* assembly. But assembly buffers are established only when assembly points fall *after* a CCR and combine CCR parts with non-CCR parts. Work centers that assemble only non-CCR parts or only CCR parts don't need any buffer at all.

## Uniform Buffer Sizes

Production organizations that apply DBR tend to make the buffers for all products the same size. While traditional DBR does not encourage using different buffer lengths, it does not prohibit it. In certain situations — probably in most environments — different products may have very different lead times and be subjected to different levels of uncertainty. Product A may consists of only two operations, while Product Z may need 200 different operations. Does it make sense to give both the same buffer length?

An appropriate buffer length for Product Z may be 2 weeks, but a buffer of 2 days may suffice for Product A. Should we really use a 2-week buffer for both? Does Product A really need that much protection? There's no reason why products having a significant variance in lead time can't have different buffer sizes for each. If the differences in lead times are minor, however (e.g., 9 days for one, 10 days for the other), there is not much point in having buffers of varying sizes, but if one product has a 3-day lead time, while another's is 12 days, a different size buffer for each may make sense.

## Work Orders

Work orders articulate a requirement for specific outputs, which may be finished products or intermediate parts. Under MRP, every part appearing in the bill of materials merits a work order specifying the quantity to be produced and the operations to be performed on them. In traditional DBR the use of work orders is discouraged to some degree. Material is released in accordance with the master production schedule, which is based mainly on customer orders. Material is allowed to flow freely through the process, but specific units of work-in-process are not assigned to specific work orders. As long as materials have one clear sequence of operations, this works well. It has the advantage of flexibility in reassigning work-in-process from one order to another after production has started. However, this creates a problem for common parts (i.e., parts that support more than one assembly or product): Where do they go? In a non-work-order environment, it's necessary to specify where parts with more than one alternative destination go.

In traditional DBR, the material is allowed to flow freely to a common part (divergence) point. Prior to that point, the flow is deterministic, meaning the people on the shop floor know exactly what to do, given the materials. At the common part locations, the operators are given clear instructions what to do, how much to do, and a specific time to do it.

However, the use of time here is different than in CCR schedule instructions. The time in a CCR schedule is the actual time work should be started. The time for common part (divergence) operations is the earliest time work should start on an order ("not earlier than..."). For example, at a CCR, a work order to process 100 units of part X234 on Wednesday, April 5, at 2:00 p.m. means that the CCR is expected to start work on the order at that time. But if the CCR completes the preceding work order at 12:30 p.m., and if X234 parts are available, the CCR may start on that order early. However, if a non-CCR resource is required to work on the X234 order (a common part), that same work order requires the non-CCR resource *not to start* processing X234 parts before Wednesday at 2:00 p.m. Processing should not start earlier, because the output of common part (divergence) operations may be needed for other products at different times. But the changes in procedure among different resources can create confusion.

## Stealing

This is related to the preceding discussion on work orders. When common parts are processed for something other than what is needed now, we call it "stealing." This is quite a common phenomenon in "V" plants. The traditional DBR-I solution is to assign every divergence operation (where an input may be used in more than one subsequent process step) a definite "don't do before" schedule. However, this is only a partial solution. Let's consider a graphic example of this problem that shows when this solution doesn't work (Figure 10.1).

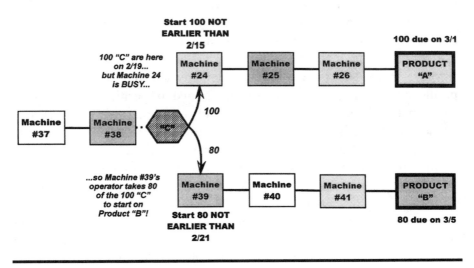

**Figure 10.1     Stealing (An Example)**

Suppose that both Products A and B need common part C. We need 100 of Product A on March 1, and 80 units of Product B on March 5. The "not earlier" time given to Machine 24 for the use of the common part for Product A is February 15. The "not earlier" time given to Machine 39 for the use of the common part for Product B is February 21.

Let's say that the common parts for Product A actually arrive on February 19. But the resource that needs them — Machine 24 (after the divergence point) — is busy, so those parts sit idle (waiting). Without the "not earlier than" requirement, Machine 39 would immediately start processing 80 parts.

However, 2 days later, on February 21, Machine 24 is still busy with the previous job. Machine 39 — the resource assigned to work on Product B — is ready for common part C, but because of some delay, the common parts for Product B will not arrive until February 28. Machine 39's operator isn't aware (or doesn't care) that his parts haven't arrived yet. According to the schedule, Machine 39 is allowed to start working on the C parts. So Machine 39's operator takes 80 of the 100 common C parts intended for product A and processes them for Product B.

When Machine 24 is free to start working on Product A, it finds only 20 units of the common C parts. The rest will arrive later, on February 28. But the shipment of Product A is due the day after the parts originally programmed for Product B are slated to arrive — March 1! So it should be clear that traditional DBR only partially solves stealing problems.

## Operator Confusion

Another problem at divergence points is confusion (see Figure 10.2). Suppose the resource working on Product A is Machine 24, a non-constraint. Let's assume that Machine 24 is needed in 10 different operations, 5 of which work on the common C part. The other five operations don't use common parts at all. Consequently, Machine 24 receives definite "don't-do-before" schedules for *five* of its operations, but *nothing* regarding the other five. Traditional DBR practices direct operations not having a schedule to work when it's available. Operations *with* a schedule should be performed when there is work having a schedule instruction with an earlier or equal date to the current one. But if both kinds of parts arrive at or near the same time, which should Machine 24's operator work on first? This can become quite confusing to the operator.

## Need for Data Automation

Obviously, the more places in the manufacturing process where schedules are needed or used, the greater the dependency on a computerized system. For example, calculating, gathering, and printing common-part schedules need the support of a computerized system. Obtaining these schedules is not easy with a standard MRP system that produces a timetable for every operation.

# S-DBR: Simplified, Effective

What follows is a way to realize all of the benefits of traditional DBR and solve some of its problems at the same time, without creating new ones. We'll refer to this less complicated version as simplified DBR (S-DBR).

S-DBR is suitable for application in most manufacturing environments. It can even apply in situations so simple that traditional DBR would seem to complicate things. There are, however, circumstances in which traditional

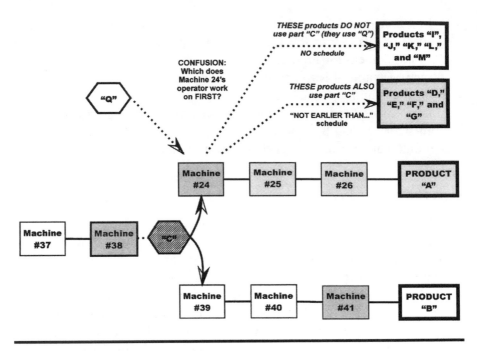

**Figure 10.2    Operator Confusion**

DBR might be preferable to S-DBR, and these cases will be discussed in more detail later. But in general, S-DBR is likely to apply to a wider variety of production configurations more easily than traditional DBR.

S-DBR embodies all of the justification — the logic and basic assumptions — of the original. And perhaps most important of all (to many organizations), S-DBR can be supported by existing MRP software — investment in unique, dedicated software is not required.

S-DBR operates the same way traditional DBR does in the absence of a CCR. There is only one buffer — the shipping buffer — and no detailed schedule for any work center. The chief distinction between traditional DBR and S-DBR is that S-DBR operates the *same way* as when there *is* an active CCR. S-DBR also adds a new control indicator — planned load — to ensure smooth performance during operation.

## S-DBR: Basic Assumptions

As with traditional DBR, there are some basic assumptions upon which S-DBR is founded. The first, and most important, is that market demand is always a system constraint. At times, an internal resource or other part of the system (material availability, etc.) may become interactive with market demand, but the majority of internal constraints are inevitably temporary in nature, and not active constraints all the time. Capacity-constrained resources usually truly limit company performance only at times of peak demand, but not at off-peak times. Fluctuations in market demand make it difficult to fully load any particular resource all the time. The market demand constraint, on the other hand, is always present. The challenge most companies face is to drive (increase) market demand to the capacity limits of one resource.

If internal constraints are usually only temporary, then the second assumption is that sometimes the internal resource that's frequently a constraint often has excess capacity. Likewise, at other times this same internal resource is overloaded. When this happens, delivery due-date performance is degraded, with commensurate risk to customer satisfaction and subsequent loyalty.

Here's an illustration of the preceding two assumptions. Let's say that the graph in Figure 10.3 represents an extended period of time — maybe a whole year. The dotted line represents the capacity of the slowest resource in our operation — the capacity-constrained resource. The solid line represents a fluctuating customer demand for our products. Maybe it's seasonal, or maybe it's tied to some other period (semi-annual, quarterly, etc.).

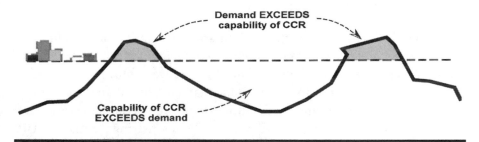

**Figure 10.3   Demand and Capacity**

As you can see, for short periods twice a year, market demand exceeds our capacity to deliver our products in our normal response time. But for much of the year we have more capacity than we're using. Except for true monopolies, this will almost always be the case. In a true monopoly, the market has no other alternative but to wait for the monopoly to provide what the market needs. There is no motivation for the monopoly to obtain excess capacity, because the market can't go to a competitor if the company doesn't deliver a product at the time the customer would prefer to have it.

Naturally, it would be desirable to have a CCR nearly fully loaded throughout the year. Only a sophisticated synchronizing of sales and marketing with operations can achieve such an objective. In other words, we'd like a flexible exploitation of two interactive constraints: the market and a CCR.

# S-DBR: Operating Principles

## *Subordination to the Market*

So if it's accurate to say that organizations actually have excess capacity everywhere in the system most of the time, then market demand is normally the dominant system constraint. And if the five focusing steps prescribe subordinating all non-constraints to the system constraint, then organizations should always subordinate themselves — and their components — to the requirements of the market. It might not be possible to do this completely, but to the extent that it's feasible, subordinating to customer requirements is mandatory if the company is to avoid losing business. Let's test this prescription for validity with a couple of questions:

1. Do we care about customer satisfaction?
2. If so, why?

If you answered "yes" to the first question, you're implicitly admitting that your customer has a choice to go to competitors, to the detriment of your throughput and net profit. If that's the case, your business is probably not a true monopoly, able to dictate to the market, rather than the other way around. Even Microsoft and Intel, with 85% of the operating software and microprocessor markets, respectively, worry about satisfying the market. This implies that their ability to make more money (or retain the profits they make now) is constrained overall by the market, not by any internal resource, in spite of their commanding positions in the marketplace.

However, while market demand may always lurk in the background as an overall system constraint, a company's internal capacity may limit its potential to expand it's current market (i.e., to make more money *now*). If we accept that the market is always a system constraint (an impediment to making more money), we're really saying that the market is part of our system for making money. Recalling the chain analogy we discussed in Chapter 1, it follows that our commitments to the market need to consider the capacity of just one internal resource — or, in some special cases, very few resources.

Sometimes this internal resource is a temporary capacity-constrained resource, meaning that the demand on it temporarily exceeds its ability to produce. At other times, however, it may not be a CCR, though it has less excess capacity than any other resource. In this case, it would be the first CCR to emerge if demand increased. Consider Figure 10.4, for example. Even though the market is currently the system constraint, the load on the internal resources indicates that Resource B would be a prime candidate to become a CCR, if and when demand increases, because its utilization rate is higher than any other resource. In other words, B would reach full loading first.

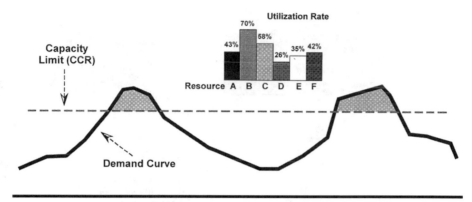

**Figure 10.4　A Potential CCR**

But even if the CCR is fully loaded (the seasonal demand peaks shown in Figure 10.4), this is likely to be a temporary condition that could quickly change (i.e., demand could drop precipitously) if the company fails to subordinate to (satisfy) its market. Are you unable to keep up with demand? Don't worry — just keep disappointing your customers. Pretty soon they'll go to your competitors, and demand will come back down to a point within your capacity, maybe even well below it. Your overload problem will have taken care of itself — but so will your profit!

## Protective Capacity Everywhere

Another crucial principle of S-DBR is that a CCR needs some protective capacity of its own. In other words, even the most heavily loaded resource should not be deliberately loaded up to its full capacity. We'll see why shortly. All the other resources (non-CCR) need considerably more protective/excess capacity. We've seen the reasons for this in our discussions of traditional

DBR. Excess capacity on non-constraints provides the flexibility to respond to changing demands and the protection the CCR needs.

But why do we need to maintain some excess (protective) capacity at the CCR? Let's take a look at a current reality tree (Figure 10.5). Briefly summarized, it's saying that a company needs protective capacity to respond to changing market requirements, but in the interest of internal efficiency and reluctance to cede *any* business to someone else, most companies load all their resources — especially the CCR — as heavily as they can. The net result of this is that neither the market nor the CCR is effectively exploited.

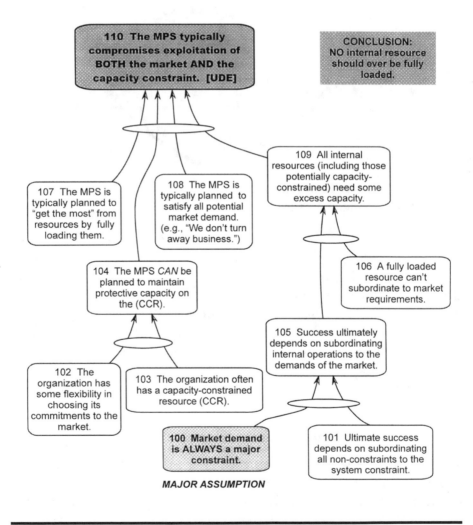

**Figure 10.5    Current Reality Tree: Protective Capacity**

## Demand-Driven Master Production Schedule

Another principle of S-DBR is that the master production schedule should be determined by the company's actual commitments to the market. Those commitments should consider capacity limitations. In other words, commit to your customers based on the limits of your capacity, then create a master production schedule to meet those commitments.

This is quite similar to traditional DBR, but in S-DBR the master production schedule constitutes the "drum," *not* the CCR schedule. In other words, the pace of the entire system is dictated by actual commitments to customers, through the MPS. The limiting factor — potential or real — on the MPS will be the capacity limitation on one resource: the CCR.

## Work Orders Consist of Complete Product Deliveries

Still another S-DBR principle: Every entry in MPS should be a work order for a complete delivery of a product. This means *not* creating a work order for every part in the bill of materials. An S-DBR work order could be deliveries against firm customer orders or (only when absolutely required) deliveries to stock. This principle is highly desirable, but not always supported by MRP.

The perceived disadvantage of having very high-level work orders is that common parts may appear in several separate work orders, yet be needed at about the same time. The concern is the perception of wasted set-up time. But because operators may merge work orders for the same operations, provided the materials are all present at the work center, it's not a real disadvantage. Sometimes, however, production organizations assemble-to-order in an effort to reduce manufacturing lead time. In this situation, work orders for the intermediate assemblies are issued separately from the end-product work orders.

The advantages of equating work orders to customer orders are prevention of stealing and flexibility on the production floor. Look again at Figure 10.1, in which 100 of Product A are due on March 1 and 80 of Product B are due on March 5. Both need part C. In S-DBR, two separate work orders would be issued. The first, for Product A, needs 100 units of C. The second, for Product B, needs 80 units of C. The 100 units would be clearly tied to the work order for Product A. The 80 units would be clearly tied to the work order for Product B. Operators could not divert common C-parts from one work order to another without realizing it.

In the MRP world, the two requirements for part C might have been merged into one work order for 180 units. Producing a consolidated batch of 180 units won't encourage "stealing," but the probability of at least on customer order being late is much higher than it would be if two distinct work orders were used. In S-DBR, with two discrete work orders, the operators of Machines 37 and 38 will see two separate requirements for the same part. Depending on the actual load and priorities, the operators will decide whether to merge the two requirements and save a set-up, or to complete other urgent jobs between these two work orders. To summarize, this feature of S-DBR provides flexibility for operators to reprioritize work to give precedence to the most important or pressing jobs. MRP doesn't provide this flexibility.

In some cases, even using an assemble-to-order policy may not reduce manufacturing lead time enough for the operation to make to order completely. In this case, make-to-stock is required, in spite of its associated risks, which include using a forecast subject to large error and the possibility of accumulating obsolete stock. In a make-to-stock situation, the unconstrained MPS is the list of replenishments to finished goods stock. Changes (refinements, updates) to the unconstrained MPS are based on the capacity limitations imposed by the CCR.

## Balance Market Requirements with CCR Capacity

As previously mentioned, optimistic MPS is an unconstrained schedule — no capacity limitations are considered. The CCR's capacity limits are used to convert the unconstrained MPS into a realistically achievable schedule. In doing so, however, management must fully understand, appreciate, and consider the possible negative impact on marketing.

In S-DBR, exploitation planning is the process of balancing the market's requirements with the capacity of the CCR. In traditional DBR, this is achieved by actually scheduling the CCR and verifying that there's enough time after the CCR finishes a work order to ship it at the required time. In S-DBR, we monitor the total load on the CCR and ensure that it has enough capacity to meet all due dates. The concept of "planned load," which will be addressed later, helps ensure that any new order can be effectively shipped on time.

## One Buffer

S-DBR, uses *only one* buffer — the shipping buffer. For make-to-order environments, the Quoted Lead Time (QLT) should be equal to or somewhat longer than the shipping buffer. This establishes a lower limit for a QLT. Whenever shorter QLTs are desirable to the market (a competitive factor), the QLT can be a tool for capturing more market share. A company can quote a delivery date as early as its current estimation of the shipping buffer, assuming a market order can be immediately converted to a work order.

The shipping buffer is defined as a liberal estimate of the time from the release of raw materials to arrival of the finished product on the shipping dock. It includes set-up and processing times, move and queve times, and a pad for normal (and even excessive) variation. Different products may be assigned different buffer sizes, which provide the option of quoting different lead times.

In S-DBR, the "rope" is the list of material requirements derived when the work order is generated for the MPS. It includes a "don't-start-before" time derived by subtracting the buffer time from the due date of the order. S-DBR strives to have only one work order for the completed product instead of having separate work orders for each level in the bill of materials (as in MRP).

## S-DBR: A Graphic Depiction

Here's a pictorial representation of what we've just described (Figure 10.6). The shipping buffer is the only buffer, and it encompasses the entire production time, plus the required pad for uncertainty and variation. Note that there is no Zone 2 in S-DBR — just a "green" zone and a "red" zone. Note, too, that this depiction is not precisely to scale. The green zone should actually be larger than the red when measured in time.

Materials are released shipping buffer time ahead of the delivery due date. The basic integrity of the master production schedule is ensured by monitoring the dynamic load on the CCR and not allowing it to reach 100%. In fact, somewhere in the neighborhood of 90 to 95% is about as high as the CCR should ever be loaded. It's important to emphasize that these load estimates are based on fairly accurate averages of actual set-up and processing times, not standard times that already include slack.

## Implementing Simplified DBR

Now it's time to see how we go about applying S-DBR. Besides the elimination of all but one buffer, the most prominent difference between traditional DBR and S-DBR is that the activity of the CCR is *not* scheduled. This means that the actual sequence of work-in-process is decided on the production floor

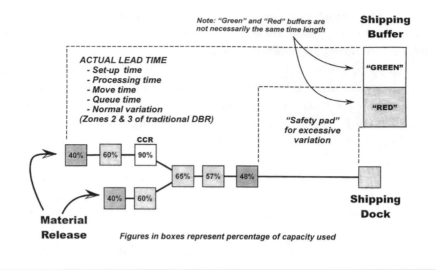

**Figure 10.6   S-DBR: A Graphic Depiction**

in real time. Another significant difference is that initiation of all material release is backed up from the dates when orders are due to be shipped. Since S-DBR is much less concerned with scheduling, it's important to differentiate what must be accomplished in the planning phase from what should happen during execution.

## General Planning and Preparation

1. *Implement the policies required to subordinate to market requirements.*

   ■ Eliminate measurement of local efficiencies. It's crucial to get out of the local efficiency syndrome if the market constraint is to be effectively exploited. This is a three-step process. First, management must embrace the idea, thoroughly rationalized earlier in this book, that measuring local efficiencies actually motivates employee behavior inimical to achievement of the company's goal. Second, this message must be formally communicated throughout the production and information systems departments. Re-education of both managers and hourly employees may be necessary. The new focus should be on Throughput-Based Decision Support (TBDS), as introduced in Chapter 3 and described in detail in Chapter 13.

- Use small production batches. Production employees should not be reluctant to accept the increased number of set-ups that processing smaller batches will require, but reduce process batches only down to a size that will not turn a resource into a bottleneck. In other words, the change in process batch size policy should not create a capacity constraint.
- Transfer work-in-process between stations in batches that are as small as practical. In other words, transfer batches will not likely be the same size as process batches — they'll probably be much smaller. This may not mean transferring in batches of one unit, but it doesn't mean batches of hundreds or thousands, either.
- Give priority to work orders with the earliest due dates. Remember, we're subordinating internal efficiency to customer requirements, one of which we assume to be high delivery date reliability. The exception to this rule is made at a resource that may become a bottleneck because of excessive set-up time.

2. *Establish close coordination between sales/marketing and production.* While this is not, strictly speaking, necessary for successfully applying S-DBR, it *is* necessary to fully exploit both a market constraint and an interactive CCR. Close coordination between sales/marketing and production provides the following advantages:

- Production and sales reach consensus on the optimal product mix — the one that delivers the highest throughput. Sales will then know which products to emphasize.
- Production capacity will not be over-committed. Sales will know what the current load on production capacity is at any given time. Knowing how much excess capacity exists is crucial to using production capacity as a competitive advantage in the marketplace. By coordinating closely with production, sales representatives know what promises they can safely make to customers and what kinds of orders may over-commit production capacity.
- When a CCR becomes active, sales representatives will be able to refine quoted lead times (either upward or downward) to ensure delivery reliability. They'll know when not to promise capacity-consuming product customization, and when to quote longer lead times if the customer really needs such customization. Moreover, knowing when the CCR is nearly fully loaded (or overloaded) allows sales representatives to selectively inhibit the demand for products that consume significant amounts of CCR time. Doing so preserves production's capability to respond to sales' high priority needs.

3. *Identify the CCR.* If the production process is already fully loaded, we'll be looking for an active CCR. If it isn't fully loaded, we'll determine which resource should reach full load first, if demand were to increase. Note that it's possible to influence where the CCR will be in two ways: (a) selective capacity management (purchasing capacity for work centers that should *not* be CCRs), and (b) selective marketing (emphasizing certain products to drive demand distribution to a desired profile, or product mix). It's also important to remember that verifying the CCR is a regular, recurring activity. *Any significant change in either demand or capacity has a high probability of shifting the location of the system's constraint.*

4. *Determine the size of the shipping buffer.* This is a key decision. Products with very different production routings may need shipping buffers of different sizes. The shipping buffer depends on the amount of excess capacity in the system (e.g., less capacity, larger shipping buffer). Since excess capacity varies over time, the adequacy of shipping buffers should be reviewed frequently. However, this is not to say that shipping buffers should be frequently changed. Only significant changes in excess capacity should trigger a change in buffer size. So how do we determine how long the shipping buffer should be? Most production managers have a reasonably good idea what their current manufacturing lead time is for delivering an order. A nice, conservative rule-of-thumb is to start with a shipping buffer that is 75% of the current lead time. As the transition to S-DBR matures and the kinks are worked out, this will probably be too high. The shipping buffer can be decreased incrementally as long as there are no red-line penetrations (holes in the Zone-1 buffer). Pilots use a similar concept in landing an airplane: They don't dive vertically at the runway from 30,000 feet, expecting to make one pullout at the precise time required for a smooth landing. Instead, they reduce their altitude in gradual steps, until they reach the final approach. We want to ease into the right shipping buffer size in the same way, because we don't want the undesirable effects of a late delivery.

5. *Determine the red-line zone.* The concept of a red line, similar to Zone-1 in traditional DBR, is explained in greater detail later (see Chapter 11, "Controlling Uncertainty and Variation: The S-DBR Approach"). This, too, is a parameter that should not change too frequently. Unlike Zone 1 in traditional DBR, the red line is not a fixed ratio of the buffer, so a change in the shipping buffer size doesn't necessarily mean

that the red-line point must also change. If the shipping buffer changes by 50% or more, we should *consider* adjusting the red line.

Once these five steps have been accomplished, general planning and preparation are complete. Now we're ready to execute.

## Short-Term Planning and Execution

Actual application of S-DBR begins from one of two possible starting conditions: Either existing capacity exceeds customer demand (market constraint predominates) or customer demand exceeds current capacity (CCR predominates). Which condition you're in when you begin implementing S-DBR will affect the sequence of actions. Figure 10.7 provides a visual depiction of the entire S-DBR implementation process.

The majority of companies will probably be starting from a market constraint condition (capacity exceeds demand). Those that are experiencing a temporary peak in demand that exceeds capacity would be well advised to delay execution until that peak has dissipated and demand is somewhat less than capacity. If this isn't likely to happen for a while, the procedure that follows will accommodate peak loads/overloads.

A company that is *not* already using DBR to manage its production process undoubtedly has hidden capacity of which it's unaware. The liberation of this hidden capacity is achieved through the implementation of the production policies required to subordinate to market requirements (Step 1 under "General Planning and Preparation," above). If the company already has some excess capacity, these policies will liberate even more. If the company's capacity is overloaded, these policies will reduce the magnitude of the overload — maybe even eliminate it completely, giving the company some excess capacity. In either case, management will have a much clearer, more accurate picture of the true condition of production capacity.

With the new production policies in place, close coordination between sales/marketing and production established, and the shipping buffer and red-line point determined:

1. *Eliminate short-term capacity overload.* This step is performed only when a CCR is overloaded and likely to remain so for some time, or when the production system's instability is so critical that it can't wait until an overload condition dissipates naturally. If this is the case, apply overtime or additional shifts as required to eliminate backlogs,

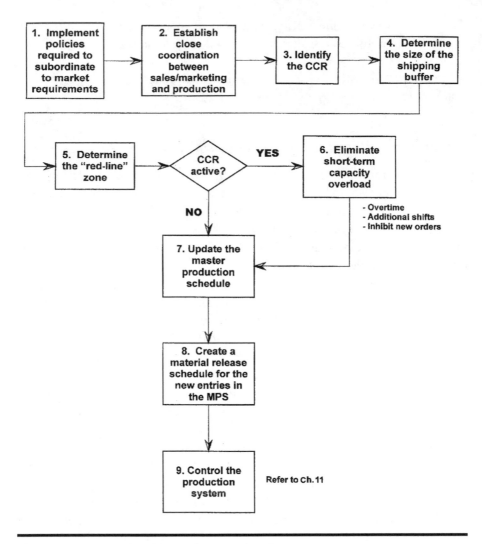

**Figure 10.7  THE S-DBR Implementation Process**

reduce the load on the CCR, or otherwise create some breathing room in production capacity. In extreme cases, specific instructions to sales/marketing to back off temporarily on demand generation may be required. If the CCR is not overloaded, or if company can wait until the overload is reduced, proceed to step 2.

2. *Update the master production schedule.* Do this daily. Take out work orders that have been completed. Add new ones that have arrived

since the last update. If any work order already in the MPS has been canceled, delete it from the MPS and reassign its raw material (or work-in-process) to another work order, if possible. In S-DBR, new orders won't affect existing work orders; their material release and due dates remain the same. If required, re-sequence the MPS according to the order of delivery due date.

3.  *Create a material release schedule for the new entries in the MPS.* Calculate detailed material requirements for each new work order. Check for unassigned materials already on the shop floor and, if found, assign them to the new work order. Release the rest at a time equivalent to the due date minus the shipping buffer. When a quoted lead time is the same as the shipping buffer (i.e., the QLT is fully utilized as a competitive edge), release materials immediately.

4.  *Control the production system.* All that remains is to monitor production operations and intervene as necessary to maintain control of the process and ensure delivery date reliability. Detailed guidance on controlling to make the plan good follows in Chapter 11.

## S-DBR Control

S-DBR control procedures are designed to warn of three conditions:

- Whenever a delivery-due date is at risk.
- When the load on the CCR approaches the limits of stability of the master production schedule (system stability). In other words, when the load on the CCR approaches so close to 100% that the adjusted MPS is likely to be compromised by having to expedite more than once or twice a week, the system is on the verge of losing its stability.
- When the load on non-CCRs becomes too high. That is, when a non-CCR is in danger of becoming an interactive constraint.

Let's explore the control step in a little more detail. As we noted in Chapter 7, the whole purpose of buffers is to smooth out the bumps in production that result from internal variability ("Murphy"), by accommodating in the original production schedule a range of variations that we can regularly anticipate. But we also know that sometimes "Murphy's" capacity to disrupt production can exceed the pre-planned buffer's capability to deal with the disruption.

We also know that external uncertainty can pose an even more serious threat to the integrity of our delivery schedule. Consider, for example, the impact that a large, short-notice order due in a very short time may have on a production process that is nearly fully loaded to begin with. The point is that there are times — sometimes more frequent than we'd care to admit — when waiting until Zone-1 buffer penetration makes it too late to react to the onset of a spike in demand.

So in addition to having a pre-planned buffer, we need an early warning control mechanism that notifies us of an impending overload before it becomes critical — in other words, in time to prevent the overload from developing in the first place. Fortunately, S-DBR provides that control mechanism, and the means to detect emerging problems. Like a geologist's seismometer on the side of an active volcano, the production control indicators provide early warning that an "eruption" is about to occur. Let's see how S-DBR handles the control problem.

## S-DBR Problem Situations

There are two basic assumptions behind S-DBR that are not assumed in traditional DBR:

1. *The market is always a constraint.* Another way of interpreting this assumption is that markets dictate certain requirements that companies must satisfy, or the market will go elsewhere (demand will fade).
2. *An internal capacity-constrained resource (CCR) is generally insensitive to small changes in processing sequence.* In other words, such changes don't usually have much impact on the overall performance of the system.

The first assumption, mentioned earlier, implies that even if you have very large potential market you need to commit yourself to somewhat less than the maximum potential capacity of the constraint, otherwise you run the risk of disappointing your customers to the degree that they'll go elsewhere.*

Suppose our company has 168 hours of capacity a week available (24 hours a day, 7 days). If we allocate all 168 hours to real (firm) orders and we

---

* Consider commercial airlines, for example. When an airline loads up its CCR (seats) to the point that customer service begins to deteriorate, passengers start looking for other airlines to fly.

lose 2 hours on the first day, perhaps to bad quality or breakdown, all subsequent orders will be delayed by 2 hours. The regular shipping buffer should be enough to accommodate this, even though it might be annoying to have all subsequent orders cut into the original buffer time by 2 hours. But if "Murphy" were to visit again on the third day of the week, taking down the CCR for 4 more hours, everything for the rest of the week will now be delayed by 6 hours, creating potentially huge pressure on the downstream operations.

Of course, if we're lucky and 168 hours of work is an average rather than a maximum, we may find a day in which we were able to do 28 hours of planned work in 24 actual hours. But this forces us to hope that the bad fluctuations won't accumulate too much before the good fluctuations will take us back to a normal state. And we all know what Benjamin Franklin said about hope.*

S-DBR buffers the constraint by leaving some excess (protective) capacity, rather than having work-in-process arrive at the CCR early, as traditional DBR does. This provides some flexibility to respond to unanticipated operational disruptions. One situation in which the first assumption doesn't apply is a company with near-monopolistic power. Consider Intel, for instance. The market will forgive Intel when it's late with a new microprocessor or is very slow to respond. Intel can afford the luxury of truly exploiting the internal constraint and subordinate the market's demands, because its competition is not in any real position to threaten its market share.

Now consider the second assumption. If we maintain some protective capacity on our CCR, in most cases small changes in the sequence of work won't matter. We can safely insert late-arriving orders requiring fast turnaround times without disrupting the flow of work through the system. However, in some cases the sequence of work on the constraint must be planned very carefully, and that schedule must be maintained.

## Traditional DBR and S-DBR: Which to Use When?

In Chapter 8 we examined the inner workings of traditional DBR. In this chapter, we learned about simplified DBR and the differences between it and the original. Now let's address the circumstances in which each one should be employed.

---

* "He that lives upon hope, dies fasting." — Benjamin Franklin.

Simplified DBR can be employed in most situations where traditional DBR works, and in most circumstances where DBR isn't used at all. But there *are* certain times when traditional DBR is preferred. Earlier in this chapter, we mentioned two characteristics common to most manufacturing environments:

1. The market demand is always a system constraint, and
2. Internal constraints often experience periods of time where they are *not* actively constraining system performance.

The strengths of S-DBR play particularly well to these characteristics. The first characteristic might really be considered a necessary condition for applying simplified DBR. If this characteristic doesn't apply, the internal constraint is logically the only constraint. If we accept the validity of the Five Focusing Steps as a preferred approach to managing constraints, then we are driven to subordinate market requirements and demand to the exploitation of that resource.

The second characteristic, which we believe applies to the vast majority of the cases, is not strictly a necessary condition for proper application of S-DBR. But it offers a good *reason* to apply it, as the focus and processes in S-DBR don't change when the CCR changes from active to inactive and then active again. Traditional DBR tells us to change the target of our exploitation and subordination as the constraint moves. And when no CCR is active in traditional DBR, the preferred strategy would be to maintain only the shipping buffer, which is what S-DBR does anyway.

However, even when these two characteristics apply, there are times when traditional DBR enjoys pronounced advantages over S-DBR. In those situations, traditional DBR delivers much better results. We'll discuss those instances in a moment.

The most striking difference between the two versions is that in S-DBR no detailed schedule is created for the CCR, even when the CCR is active. Instead, the gross load (planned load) is evaluated to ensure all standing customer orders can be fulfilled by the promised delivery date. Since we need to maintain some protective capacity at the CCR to ensure on-time delivery, controlling planned load provides that capacity without the need for a detailed CCR schedule. Since we see the value in maintaining some protective capacity, and since we know that variability and uncertainty strike our shop floor without warning (often after a schedule has been issued), isn't it sensible to make decisions about the exact sequence of operations in real time?

Let's consider a simple example. Suppose two orders, one for Product A and one for Product B, are supposed to be shipped on the same date. Both products require 8 full hours to process. If we schedule the CCR, we might decide that the CCR will process the Product A work order on Thursday between 8:00 a.m. and 4:00 p.m. And we might schedule the Product B work order to start Friday morning at 8:00 a.m. The sequence of A first, then B, is purely arbitrary in this situation.

Suppose it's now Tuesday morning. The parts for work order B are already queued at the CCR, but those for work order A have been delayed. Good buffer management would, of course, spot the problem and prompt the production manager to expedite work order A, enabling the CCR to start on Thursday morning, as originally planned. Let's assume that the expediting, which included some overtime, was fruitful. But was the expediting really worthwhile?

Under S-DBR the sequence at the CCR is not determined ahead of time, because there's no CCR schedule. So if work order B reaches the CCR first and work order A is somewhat delayed, no expediting is done. The operator at the CCR (or any other resource) is instructed to give priority to the work order with the earliest due date. Since the Product A work order hasn't arrived at the CCR yet, that would be the Product B work order. When the Product A parts finally arrive at the CCR (without expediting), they'll be the next ones processed — probably on Thursday or Friday. Both orders will still most likely make the required delivery date. The flexibility provided to the CCR operator by not being tied to a firm schedule — replacing the CCR schedule with some simple decision rules — enables smooth flow without necessarily requiring extraordinary expediting effort. It's possible that expediting may still really be needed in a case like this, but S-DBR won't demand it when it's not.

From the preceding example, it should be clear that monitoring the load on the CCR only ensures the CCR has enough to do, not the specific sequence of operations. Expediting is done only when one of the orders penetrates the red-line time. And no matter where the work order is at the time of red-line penetration — before or after the CCR — it'll be expedited.

When do we need an explicit, protected schedule for the CCR? There are several instances when a CCR schedule and its protection from "Murphy" are needed. These situations can best be served by traditional DBR.

When an arbitrary sequence of work orders might waste a significant amount of CCR time, careful scheduling of the CCR is important. One factor that may cause this situation is dependent setups — machine set-up time depends not only on what comes next but also what happened before. Take painting, for example. Setting up (cleaning) a paint sprayer is much shorter if the sequence of color changes goes from lighter colors to darker than the other way around. When white follows dark green, a much more thorough cleaning is required.

Traditional DBR is also preferred when the CCR is a group of several different resources that differ in their capabilities and processing times. In such situations a "sequence of opportunity" may result in a less than favorable assignment of resources, which may actually take much more time than a preferred sequence.

When the CCR is involved in two or more operations for the same order, traditional DBR is also a better choice. There are two variations on this theme.

First, a single order may be planned to pass through the CCR several times. In other words, parts coming out of the CCR come back to it again, usually after several other process steps. Consider a textile manufacturer who produces hosiery, for example. In one step, called "pre-boarding," a knitted stocking is stretched over a metal form and heat-treated to impress a foot-and-leg-shape before color dying. After the dying process, the stocking is returned to the work center for "final boarding," which impresses the foot-and-leg shape more permanently. In such a case, a planned sequence of operations can be much better than an arbitrary sequence. But good scheduling software would be necessary to do this job well.

Second, the CCR might be needed for many different parts going to one assembly for the same order. While the actual sequence may not be especially important, it may be advantageous to release materials based on a CCR schedule. In this case S-DBR could still work, but traditional DBR may be better.

S-DBR complements the ideas originally embedded in traditional DBR. In many cases it simplifies implementation, and can be supported by commonly available MRP packages, with only minor modifications (e.g., zeroing all the queue times and inserting only the shipping buffer and the red-line times at the very top of the product routing, as explained in Chapter 9).

In the next chapter, we'll see how S-DBR simplifies buffer management.

# 11 Controlling Uncertainty and Variation: The S-DBR Approach

## Buffers: A Quick Review

Remember that in a make-to-order situation, TOC/DBR uses time buffers — not physical inventory — to protect the production process from variation and uncertainty. And because variation or uncertainty (or both) may exceed the protection capability of a buffer, buffers alone are not sufficient to guarantee success. We need to be able to identify potential buffer overruns in time to respond with corrective action before the system destabilizes.

We've already seen the use of time — the use of liberal estimation of lead time — as a buffer against variation ("Murphy"). Safety or security can be provided by types of buffers other than time, as well. Traditionally, inventory has been used for the same purpose that time is used in TOC — to guard against work stoppage. Raw material inventory protects against material shortages. Work-in-process inventory protects against starvation of work centers. And a finished goods inventory protects required shipping dates against stock-outs. But there are still other types of buffers.

Excess capacity and capabilities protect against variation and uncertainty, in much the same way that inventory does. Duplication of capabilities, especially human resources, allows for better subordination even when the load is quite high. Duplicate capabilities provide more options to expedite by moving idle operators to the most heavily loaded areas. Cash can also be used to overcome unexpected problems. Maintaining more than one supplier for each material protects against problems which may beset a single supplier. Establishing a presence in several different markets can protect against sudden changes in market demand. And, in the final analysis, Lloyds of London can provide insurance — the ultimate financial buffer. All of these buffer a business system against the unexpected in one way or another.

For our purposes, we'll confine our discussion of control to time buffers and excess capacity, which facilitate the ability to react quickly.

## Definition of Control

To ensure that we're all singing from the same sheet of music, let's define "control." Traditionally, control has been defined as comparing actual results with desired results and deciding whether to revise objectives or methods of execution.[1] However, this definition does not lead us to focus on really meaningful results, nor does it lead us to recognize a truly problematic situation, because the real world almost always deviates to some extent from any plan.

For our purposes in S-DBR, we'll define control a little differently: *A reactive mechanism that handles uncertainty by monitoring information that indicates a threatening situation and taking appropriate corrective action before the threat is realized.*

The focus in this definition is established by the specific threats to our planning that may emerge. We analyze potential threats to determine ahead of time: (a) what easily accessible information will point to the emergence of the threat as early as possible, and (b) what actions should be taken to neutralize the emerging threat.

## Objectives of Red-Line Control (Buffer Management)

In S-DBR, we're going to use the term "red-line control" to refer to the somewhat simplified version of buffer management. So whenever you see red-line time or red-line control, remember that we're talking about the state of the buffer. Red-line control, like traditional buffer management, has three objectives.

The first objective is to protect the delivery due date. Red-line control is designed to identify threats to late delivery early enough to prevent compromise of the delivery date. It does this by watching for situations where the buffer is nearly exhausted — or likely to become so — and by providing enough warning before a buffer is exceeded to intervene without excessive disruption to system stability.

The second objective is to warn us that the stability of the system is at risk. Instability is usually caused by the emergence of a new capacity constraint, or CCR. More than one or two red-zone orders appearing simultaneously — orders due in less than the red-line time and not yet completed — is a signal that the protection mechanism is losing its capability to protect the system from the basic threat of missed due dates.

The third objective is to identify the troublemaker — the one link in the chain that has caused the majority of the trouble. By looking for the resource where the majority of the red orders reside, we can determine which resource is becoming capacity constrained.

## How Red-Line Control Works

Here's how red-line control works. A red-line time is established in advance of the delivery due date. This time is equivalent to Zone 1 of the traditional DBR shipping buffer. But there's one significant modification from traditional buffer management. While Zone 1 in traditional buffer management is a fixed ratio of the whole buffer (about one third), the red-line time in S-DBR is a fixed length. This fixed value is much less than the full buffer but not necessarily a fixed ratio. When the shipping buffer changes, red-line time doesn't automatically change.

The red-line time is established by determining how long it takes to expedite a medium-sized order. If this red-line time is too short, late deliveries will occur even if corrective action is taken in response to the red warning. In such cases, the red-line time must be increased. When too many red-line warnings occur, it means either the red-line time is too long, or the shipping buffer isn't long enough for the level of demand on the system, and the system is losing its stability.

How would we know when the red-line time is too long? When many orders regularly penetrate the red-line time zone, but the system seems to be very stable (meaning high confidence that orders will be completed without requiring expediting), the red-line time is probably too long.

However, when this is not the case — when extraordinary efforts are required to keep a red-line penetration from becoming a late delivery — there's a real threat to the stability of the production system. Enlarging the shipping buffer may be one immediate option, but it may not be enough. If the current

CCR is overloaded, or if a new CCR is emerging, enlarging the buffer may be no more than a temporary stopgap. For a permanent solution, additional capacity or a reduction in customer demand will probably be required.

When we find an order that's not ready to ship at the red-line time, we designated it "almost late" and assign it a high priority. Then we locate the order on the shop floor and take specific action (expediting, if required) to speed its processing and prevent late delivery. In some cases, no action may be required, if the last units of the order are at work stations very close to the end of the manufacturing process. However, if this is not the case (if the remaining units can't be completed between the red-line time and the shipping date) we may have to throw manpower at the problem (e.g., overtime, or extra shifts).

As in traditional DBR buffer management, the occurrence of many red-line warnings (the S-DBR equivalent of Zone 1 penetrations) is a sign that the system is destabilizing, probably because of the emergence of a new constraint or bottleneck.

## Red-Line Control for Raw Materials

There's another red line that we have to be concerned about, too. It has to do with the time that we run out of raw materials. The shipping buffer almost never protects against material stock-out. Availability of materials is usually assumed. Since raw material inventory is at the front end of the manufacturing process, and since release of those raw materials is crucial to the success of our exploitation plan for the CCR, stock-outs can't be tolerated.

But the concept of a time buffer is somewhat less appropriate for raw material inventory. While raw material inventory can certainly be converted into average consumption time, this is a very fragile translation that obsolesces over time. While it might be useful to think that we have stock for 2 weeks of average consumption, in reality variable demand may consume that stock in 3 weeks — or 3 days. Consequently, where raw materials are concerned, it's a little easier to manage things, rather than time.

The stock level is first established by determining for how long a period we need to maintain stock. After that, all we need is a warning device to tell us when there's a real threat of stock exhaustion while customer orders continue to arrive.

So in S-DBR, we'll establish a red-line level for raw materials. This is an emergency level below which there is a significant risk that the required material will be exhausted before replenishment can be effected. We can establish the red-line level by determining a liberal estimation of the consumption rate (per day or week) and multiplying that times a realistic number of days (or weeks) that our fastest supplier can deliver a replacement order for considerably more than we would use during that time. Penetration of the red-line level prompts management to generate an emergency resupply order from the fastest, most reliable supplier.

Let's consider an example. Suppose raw material W1 is used in several of our products, with an average consumption rate of 100 units per week. However, we know that sometimes we need as many as 150 units of W1 per week. Our sole supplier for W1 regularly delivers 4 weeks after we re-order but can ship an emergency delivery in a week (at a substantially higher price).

We know that "Murphy" visits our supplier as often as us, so that 1-week emergency delivery might actually take up to a week and a half. We'd better be prepared for a reasonable worst-case scenario: a consumption rate of 150 per week for a week and a half. This means we should at all times hold no less than 225 units of W1 in stock. When the actual stock level drops below this point, we should seriously consider requesting an emergency delivery.

Some knowledgeable readers might claim that it's not likely Murphy will hit twice at the same time, market demand will increase to the maximum, and our suppliers will take more time than usual.

## Red-Line Control: Limitations

Red-line control in production is certainly effective, but it's by no means perfect. It has two limitations worth mentioning. First, in some cases its warning of impending system instability comes too late. While it can prevent many potential problems, it is possible that the onset of a peak, or spike, in demand may occur so quickly that even the red-line control is overwhelmed. Second, red-line control is not very effective at the opposite end of the spectrum — identifying market demand that is too low, or an inventory that is too large.

## Planned Load: An Important Control Information Source

Red-line time is, of course, very useful. But as in traditional buffer management, it's possible that in some cases a red-line warning may come too late to recover before a delivery due date is missed. Fortunately, there are a few other sources of information that can give us even more advanced warning that an overload may occur, well before that peak in demand shows up in the red-line system. One variable, which bears close watching, is planned load.

Planned load is defined as *the total hours required of a resource to complete all work that has been formally released into the system* — and we should focus our attention primarily on the CCR and those resources that may become a CCR. The planned load time window runs from the present (today) to the promised delivery date, and it includes the total work commitment, both currently being processed and in the queue.

Planned load reflects the minimum reasonable time for a new order to be processed without needing expediting, or displacing existing work. When this time approaches the standard quoted lead time (shipping buffer), any subsequent orders accepted may not make delivery due dates on time.

Here's a graphic example of planned load and how we can use it to anticipate an impending overload (Figure 11.1). This is an excerpt from the MICSS simulation,* but any MRP system should be equally capable of reporting the same information.

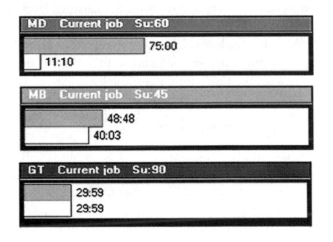

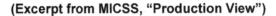

**(Excerpt from MICSS, "Production View")**

**Figure 11.1    Planned Load**

Let's assume that machine D (MD) is our capacity-constrained resource. The shaded bar indicates that the amount of work currently known to be in the schedule is 75 hours. This means that, barring machine breakdown or stock-outs, the internal constraint requires only 75 hours (a little over nine eight-hour work days) to complete all its currently scheduled work.

---

* Management Interactive Case Study Simulation software (MBE Simulations, Ltd. With permission.)

Suppose that our quoted lead time on any order is 120 hours (15 work days). The shipping buffer can't exceed the quoted lead time, otherwise we won't be able to meet our committed delivery date. If we want to promise the shortest possible QLT, we'd better ensure that the QLT is, in fact, the same as the shipping buffer that adequately protects on-time delivery. So if the shipping buffer is 120 hours, we can conclude that we're capable of finishing all the work currently in the system about 6 days before it's due. This tells us that the production system is not very heavily loaded at the moment and can accept more work without risking a missed delivery due date.

However, if more work orders are dropped into the system, the length of the shaded bar (planned load) will increase.* Remember, these are MPS orders. They could be firm orders, with hard delivery dates, or finished stock replenishment orders. When that shaded bar starts to get close to the quoted lead time (120 hours), we can anticipate that we're in danger of an overload. One more order may drive us beyond 120 hours, which means we've scheduled more than 120 hours of work in that amount of time.

We can obtain some other valuable information from this graphic as well. Notice the white bar below each shaded bar. The white bar indicates how many hours of firm work in the schedule reside at the resource indicated. MD has 75 hours of commitments, but only 11 hours is waiting at MD. This means that the rest of the work is still upstream of MD. MB has almost 49 hours of commitments, and about 40 hours of that is waiting at MB. Only about 9 hours of work remain upstream. GT has 30 hours of commitments, and all of it is there at GT. What can we conclude from this?

If we see that the shaded bar and the white bar are consistently the same length, we know that there is no upstream blockage of work flow. If the red bar is big, while the white bar is near zero, it tells us that work may be trapped upstream. (Or it might not be — the trapping problem is only critical when the time associated with the shaded bar gets close to the quoted lead time and that step is not near the end of the process.) When there is an upstream blockage, look for a CCR somewhere upstream — a CCR traps work and starves downstream operations.

The bottom line is that if we understand the meaning of the ratio of planned load to shipping buffer (quoted lead time), we can help the sales force quote better lead times. If we understand the ratio of the planned load to available load, we have a better understanding of the system's internal dependencies.

---

* Although we refer to the colors of these bars as "shaded" and "white." when you run the MICSS simulation, you'll see that planned load is red and the bar indicating queued work is green.

## Limitations of the Planned Load as a Control Information Source

As with red-line control, planned load has couple of shortcomings, too. If there is a large difference in the cycle times of different released orders, it is difficult to determine the point where the load begins to threaten future due-date performance. At an 80% load, we should start to watch the system a little more carefully and definitely not let it go above 90%. So in our preceding Machine D example, with the QLT at 120 hours, we should start to watch the load for increases above about 96 hours.

However, when the QLT is 120 hours for some products and 200 hours for others, assuming the shipping buffer is made equal to the quoted lead time, it can be difficult to know at what point the load threatens due-date performance. In such a case, a planned load of 120 hours can usually be adequate, if we also apply earliest due date priority throughout the system, because a new order to be shipped in 120 hours will have priority over an existing order to be shipped in 180 hours. But we can't be certain that a 120-hour load is always safe. We need a combination of both planned load and red-line control to be sure we don't exceed the CCR's capability to deliver on time.

Another factor that may affect the value of planned load as a control aid is data accuracy. If the routing data are not accurate enough, the threshold for a dangerously high load may not be valid. The planned load is calculated based on the processing time (and set-up time) data written in the scheduling software database. If those data elements are highly inaccurate, the planned load is inaccurate as well. Note that in most companies, processing and set-up times are standard times, meaning the data have been intentionally inflated. Moreover, considering how quickly circumstances change, standard times in a database may become obsolete over time.

But planned load can still be a good indicator, even when it isn't completely accurate. Red-line control, used in conjunction with planned load, can offset these inaccuracies. While planned load is the outcome of formal run times as they appear in the manufacturing database, red-line control is based on a totally different set of data — a characteristic that makes the combination of the two a powerful control mechanism.

# Rough-Cut Capacity as a Control Mechanism

Another potentially useful control indicator is rough-cut capacity. This is a typical variable provided by MRP systems. It provides a general prediction of the average future load on a resource for some time window in the future.

In most MRP applications, rough-cut capacity is expressed in monthly increments, using the MRP time-phased algorithm. Figure 11.2 is an excerpt from the MICSS simulation, which provides rough-cut capacity calculations for shorter intervals.

If the rough-cut capacity indicates near or over 100% for a given window of time, it's a good indication that we could be in for a late delivery sometime during that time window. But don't bet the farm on rough-cut capacity figures, especially when they indicate 100-plus percentage loads. Like planned load, rough-cut capacity is based on standard times from MRP routing files, so take this into account when deciding whether a rough-cut capacity indication seems threatening.

One important benefit of rough-cut capacity is its ability to incorporate known seasonal demands and/or trends. The peaks in an annual sales curve can be included in the capacity loading if they are known with some assurance ahead of time. However, it's not a good idea to put too much stock in a rough-

## Range: | 6 |     ○ Days     ● Months

| Resource | Production | Setup | Break | Total |
|----------|------------|-------|-------|-------|
| GT | 46.2% | 3.6% | 5.6% | 55.4% |
| MA | 24.8% | 4.4% | 3.7% | 32.9% |
| MB | 94.2% | 2.2% | 4.4% | 100.8% |
| MC | 36.7% | 3.8% | 3.5% | 44.0% |
| MD | 46.8% | 2.8% | 4.7% | 54.3% |
| AS | 45.5% | 0.0% | 4.3% | 49.8% |
| PK | 48.5% | 1.3% | 6.6% | 56.4% |

Figure 11.2     **Rough-Cut Capacity**

cut capacity value. Rough-cut capacity uses sales forecast information, which is only a projection — not real load. It also uses other approximate assumptions. Moreover, since it doesn't reflect a detailed plan, it doesn't consider the amount of work-in-process and where it is located on the shop floor, either.

While rough-cut capacity alone isn't sufficient as a control mechanism, in conjunction with load monitoring and red-line control it can reinforce confidence in the validity of the other indicators. For instance, if planned load starts creeping up above 90%, a few more red-line orders start showing up, and rough-cut capacity shows a resource averaging 104% load over the next 3 months, it's a pretty safe bet that the system is overloaded and will present serious problems soon, even if no deliveries have yet been missed.

## Control in S-DBR: Summary

To summarize, the first line of defense in S-DBR is the shipping buffer. We build this into the exploitation plan, and it accommodates most typical deviations resulting from internal variation. The second line of defense is control during execution. For this, we use red-line control and planned load. We monitor the buffer and act immediately when it is penetrated. We depend on planned load to give us advance warning when a problem is likely to occur and to tell us when system stability is breaking down. Rough-cut capacity can give us long-term visibility on the future load, out to the horizon of the information system, but this is a gross estimate only — not usable alone. It can, however, tell us ahead of time when we might expect to see a jump in the planned load.

## Plant ADV200: An S-DBR Simulation

We've covered a lot of ground in discussing S-DBR. Now it's time to see how these new concepts and principles work in a typical manufacturing organization. Let's go back to the MICSS and look at another simulation.

This simulation is Plant ADV200. The situation facing the plant manager is described in detail in Appendix D. Now would be a good time to read through the first part of that appendix. You may follow along on your own personal computer, using the software provided with this book, or refer to the screen images included in Appendix B.

### *ADV200: The Problem*

If you've run the ADV200 simulation according to the "First Run Instructions" (Appendix D), you've probably noticed that on-time delivery to customers was exceptionally good — 100%. But this company is in a hole and continuing to dig. They lose money and sink deeper into debt. The question is, "Why?" Think about what you read in Appendix D and what you observed during the first simulation run. Figures 11.3a and b is a current reality tree that summarizes what you should have observed. If you didn't see these indications, go back and run the simulation again, but this time watch for the content of this tree.

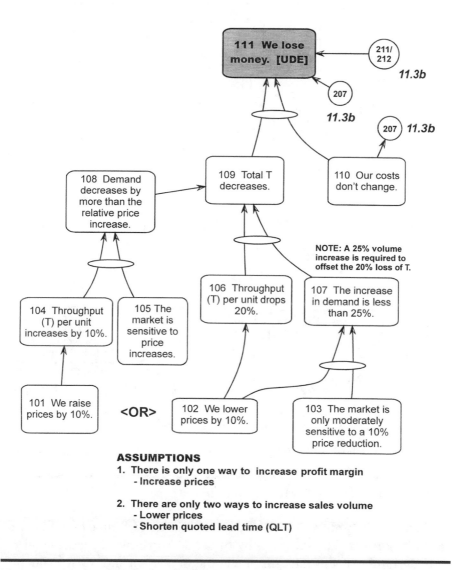

**Figure 11.3a    ADV200 Current Reality Tree #1**

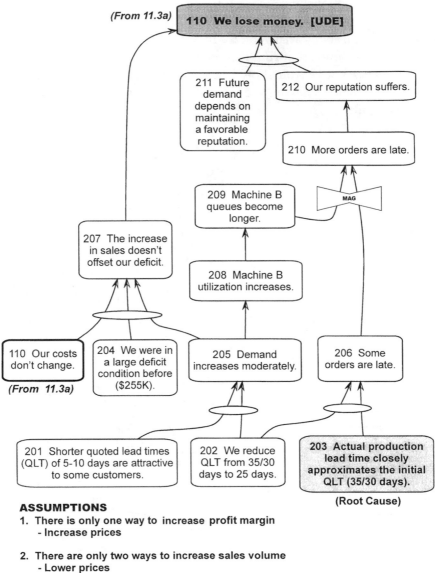

*(From 11.3a)* **110 We lose money. [UDE]**

211 Future demand depends on maintaining a favorable reputation.

212 Our reputation suffers.

210 More orders are late.

209 Machine B queues become longer.

MAG

207 The increase in sales doesn't offset our deficit.

208 Machine B utilization increases.

110 Our costs don't change.

*(From 11.3a)*

204 We were in a large deficit condition before ($255K).

205 Demand increases moderately.

206 Some orders are late.

201 Shorter quoted lead times (QLT) of 5-10 days are attractive to some customers.

202 We reduce QLT from 35/30 days to 25 days.

**203 Actual production lead time closely approximates the initial QLT (35/30 days).**

**(Root Cause)**

**ASSUMPTIONS**

1. There is only one way to increase profit margin
   - Increase prices

2. There are only two ways to increase sales volume
   - Lower prices
   - Shorten quoted lead time (QLT)

**Figure 11.3b   ADV200 Current Reality Tree #1**

Now run the simulation three additional times, each time for a full year. On the first run, reduce the prices by 10%. Make no other changes to polices. Note the results (net profit, cash). Reset the simulation and run it again, this time with all prices increased 10%, and note the results once more. Finally, reset the simulation again and run it a third time. This time don't change any prices, but reduce the quoted lead time on all products to 25 days. After these runs you probably will have witnessed the effects shown in Figures 11.3a and b.*

What can be done to improve ADV200's financial performance? Obviously, this company needs more sales, and it ought to be able to handle them if they were available. If you want proof of this, look at the Machine Utilization status under the Information menu in the Production View. No work center is loaded above about 70% of its capacity. So we ought to be able to accept more sales, but how do we obtain them?

The MICSS environment does not include all the options we would have in the "real world." Some options are foreclosed to us because simulations can't possibly replicate reality completely, so we'll have to work with what we *can* change. At the bottom of the tree are two assumptions about the MICSS simulation and ADV200 in particular:

1. There is only one way to increase profit margin, and that is to raise prices.
2. There are only two ways to increase demand for ADV200's products (sales volume), and those are to lower prices or shorten quoted lead time.

Within the ADV200 realm, these are the only options open to us.

The left side of the tree show why price changes cannot really help. This subject merits a little more discussion. If you ran the simulation with a 10% price reduction, as block 103 (Figure 11.3a) says, you would have expected demand for products to increase. And, of course, it did. Over the course of an entire year with the prices reduced, machine utilization increased and more units were sold, but total revenues decreased and the company lost even more money.

The reason for this apparently contradictory result is that in this MICSS scenario demand doesn't increase enough to offset the effects of the price reduction. For example, when we reduce product prices by 10%, throughput

---

* This is not a typical current reality tree. Such a tree would characterize the situation in the ADV200 Company at the end of the first simulation run, for which none of the marketing, production, or purchasing policies were changed from the default settings. We stipulate that the company is losing money and that the production process isn't fully utilized. Instead, this tree reflects what has happened after the three supplementary runs with the policies changed, as described above. Consequently, each of the three main branches of this tree indicates the unfolding of a different reality.

(marginal contribution to profit) is reduced by considerably more than 10%. When the throughput of a product constitutes about 50% of the regular price, a 10% reduction degrades throughput by 20%. In order to justify a tactic like this, additional customer demand must not only recoup the loss of contribution from a price reduction, but must be significant enough to produce more throughput than we would have had without the price recuction.

For example, if our market demands 1000 units of our product at $100 per unit, our revenue is $100,000. If half the cost of each unit is variable cost, we make $50,000 in throughput on those 1000 units. Now even if we drop the price 10%, to $90 per unit, in an effort to drive up demand, our variable cost doesn't change: it's still $50 per unit, but now we're making only $40,000 on the 1000 units. That's a difference of $10,000 we have to make up before we can even expect to turn more of a profit. At $90 per unit ($40 in throughput), we'd have to sell 250 more units than before — a 25% increase in volume — just to offset the 10% price reduction, and considerably more to make enough additional profit to justify the price reduction in the first place. Will a 10% price reduction generate an additional sales volume (units, not dollars!) of 30% or more? Is it any wonder that price wars are not a good idea? The central branch in Figures 11.3a and b shows the effects of a 10% price reduction.

Another possible outcome is that the increase in demand might exceed our capacity to produce on time, causing us to miss deliveries. This possibility is not reflected in the current reality tree, because a 10% price reduction doesn't actually increase the load enough to exceed capacity. But, if we're lucky enough to realize the 30% increase in sales volume mentioned above (again, units, not dollars), what will this do to the load on our capacity? If we overload it enough, and often enough, we'll disappoint our customers enough to destroy our credibility for reliability. We'll lose those customers and, consequently, sales. So there is a compelling argument not to reduce prices.

## ADV200: The Conflict

If we don't reduce prices, we must find another way to stimulate demand for ADV200's products. In other words, we have to figure out how to add value to our product or service without increasing or reducing prices. One option might be to offer to deliver sooner than our competitors, and the ADV200 simulation does allow us to do this. All other things being equal, customers might value a shorter quoted lead time. It could simplify their planning and help them respond to short-notice changes in their own requirements. But this leads us to another conflict (Figure 11.4) that expands the root cause of the current reality tree (block 203) "Actual production lead time closely approximates the initial quoted lead time." There are two such times: 35 days for products A1 through B2, and 30 days for products C1 and C2.

To improve profitability, we need to increase demand, which we may do by reducing our quoted lead time. But we also must preserve our reputation for delivery reliability. Remember the right side of the current reality tree

**ASSUMPTIONS:**

1. **Promising shorter QLT is sufficient to increase demand**

2. **Shorter QLT have value for customers, and they recognize it**

3. **Customers are aware of promised shorter QLT**

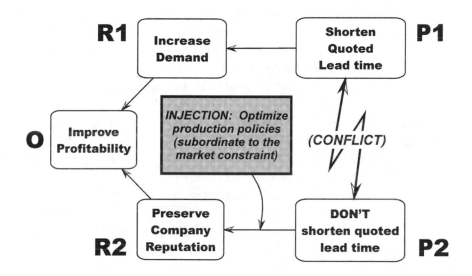

*ASSUMPTIONS:*

4. **We can't shorten QLT without hurting due date performance (now)**

5. **Future due date performance and sales are jeopardized (later)**

Figure 11.4   ADV200 Conflict: Quoted Lead Time

(Figures 11.3a and b)? If we shorten our quoted lead time and our production lead time doesn't change, we can expect to miss delivery due dates. What can we do about *this* dilemma?

Let's look at the situation from a system-level perspective for a moment. Where is ADV200's system constraint at the moment? It's obviously sales (market demand), because the company doesn't have enough demand for its products. This effectively puts the constraint outside the company for the moment, and machine utilization of 70% or less confirms this conclusion. If we expect to apply constraint theory properly, we should do what we can to exploit that constraint (reduce quoted lead times), and subordinate internal management policies in a way that supports this exploitation. In this case, subordination means optimizing production policies, not for maximum internal efficiency, but for the quickest, most reliable delivery possible.

How can we change production policies in ADV200 to subordinate to the market demand constraint? As we've discussed in this and earlier chapters (and experienced in the PRD120 simulation), drum-buffer-rope (DBR) recommends reducing process batches, transferring work-in-process in smaller batches, and giving priority to firm orders (deferring production to finished stock). In particular, S-DBR recommends treating the market as the primary constraint and managing the load on internal resources so as to never create an interactive internal resource constraint.

Go back and look at Figures 6.10a and b for a moment. This is the future reality tree for Plant 120. All eight injections are fully applicable here, even though we didn't really notice any problems with raw material supplied while running ADV200. So, for the time being we can ignore Injections #5 and #6. We may need them in the future, when we succeed in generating so much demand that we experience raw material supply problems.

Isn't it amazing to see how similar solutions can be applied effectively to different core problems in two different scenarios? In Plant 120 we didn't need to shorten the QLT. In fact, we had fixed shipping dates for the whole year. The root causes in Plant 120 (Figure 6.2a, blocks 101 and 104) were *"We strive for efficient use of EACH resource"* and *"We can't separate what's important from what isn't."* But, if you follow the outcomes of those root causes you come to block 110 that says:

*"Actual production lead time is longer than required to deliver on time."*

And that's *very* similar the root problem in ADV200 Current Reality Tree:

> *"Actual production lead time closely approximates the initial quoted lead time."*

No wonder! The initial policies of ADV200 are the direct result of the same generic causes shown in Plant 120.

Revisit in detail Figures 6.10a and b, and Figure 6.11 (Negative Branch #1) in Chapter 6. It's all relevant for ADV200, with one critical addition: We need to add another injection. This injection should read, *"We carefully reduce the quoted lead time to take advantage of the expected reduction of the actual production lead time."*

Let's summarize some basic injections that are fairly generic to the DBR methodology and already tested in the Plant 120 simulation. Those injections should work for us in ADV200 as well.

- Injection 1a. We establish some protective capacity at all resources.
- Injection 1b. We treat set-ups as significant only when they consume protective capacity.
- Injection #2. We install a "control" to detect an incipient bottleneck.
- Injection #3. We act to prevent the emergence of the indicated constraint.
- Injection #4. We reduce batch sizes, plan daily instead of weekly, authorize partial work orders (smaller transfer batches), and give priority to the shortest due dates.
- Injection #5: We reduce our quoted lead time to match our actual production lead time.

## ADV200: Verifying the Proposed Solutions

Will these tactics work? Can they turn the ADV200 Company around? Before we try them in the "real (simulated) world," let's test them logically for sufficiency. Figures 11.5a and b show a future reality tree constructed from these five injections. Read through it and see if the injections lead logically to the desired effects (shorter production lead times and improved profitability).

Now it's time to find out whether we overlooked anything in the future reality tree. Let's apply those injections in the ADV200 scenario and run the simulation again. Refer to Appendix D, and follow the "Second Run Instructions." Here's how these MICSS/ADV200 policy changes match up with the injections:

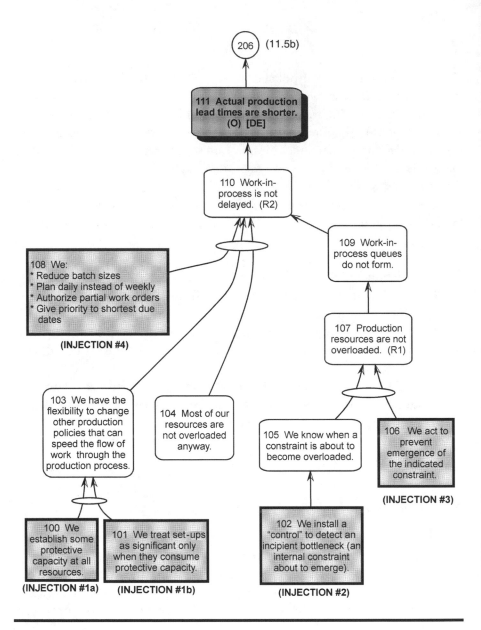

**Figure 11.5a    ADV200 Future Reality Tree #1**

Injection 1a.    Monitor Production View | View Total Load (check the box). Watch for the red bar to increase in length (time). It should not exceed 90% of the Quoted Lead Time (in hours)

Injection 1b.    Production View | Policies | Machine Policy | Dispatch Policy | EDD

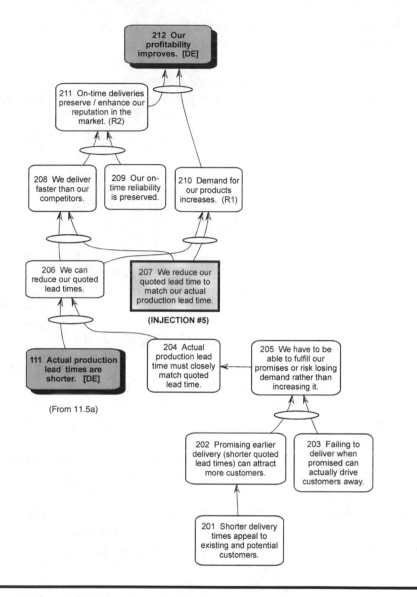

**Figure 11.5b    ADV200 Future Reality Tree #1**

Injection 2.    Production View | Policies | Red Level Policy | 5 days (all products)

Injection 3.    Production View | Policies | Machine Policy | WO Acceptance | Partial WO

Production View | Policies | Work Order Planning | Fixed interval, "1"

Production View | Policies | Work Order Planning | Batch size (as desired, try "30" to begin with)

Injection 4: Marketing View | Policies | Product Parameters | Set quoted lead time to "25" to start, and adjust downward selectively and gradually until the system shows signs of stress (frequent order "red flags")

Injection 5: Production View | Actions | Add extra shift (as required, when order "red flags" appear)

> NOTE: Verify the order "red flags" by pausing the simulation, shifting to the Marketing View, and noting the number of products that display as red. If more than one is red, the need for extra shifts is confirmed.

How did the second run work out? Did you make money? Did you at least lose less money than ADV200 did in 1997? Are these DBR production and marketing policies taking the company in the right direction?

## ADV200: The Second Current Reality Tree

What new problems did you run into? It's highly unlikely that these injections alone provided the silver bullet to make ADV200 easier to manage at a profit. Did you encounter any potholes on the road to profitability? Many users of this simulation do. Figure 11.6 shows some typical undesirable effects that often still remain after applying the first series of injections.

It's not unusual for the increase in demand to begin overwhelming even the improved capacity. In the second simulation run, you probably noticed an increase in the number of order red flags at some point. In some cases, you may have missed delivery dates (due date performance and "Reputation" suffered). You probably found yourself stopping the simulation and applying additional shifts more frequently than you preferred. On the other hand, if none of the indications above occurred, you probably didn't reduce quoted lead time enough to stimulate more sales. Go back and try shorter quoted lead times — after all, we're out to make as much money as we can, aren't we?

In the event that you *did* see more red flags but did nothing to respond to these warnings, you also have seen market demand for your product decline, reflecting the unreliability of your deliveries. This undesirable effect shows up in the sales curve (Marketing View | Information | Sales Summary Graph).

The root cause in this current reality tree is our inability to anticipate an overload condition in time to prevent it from happening. In other words, we

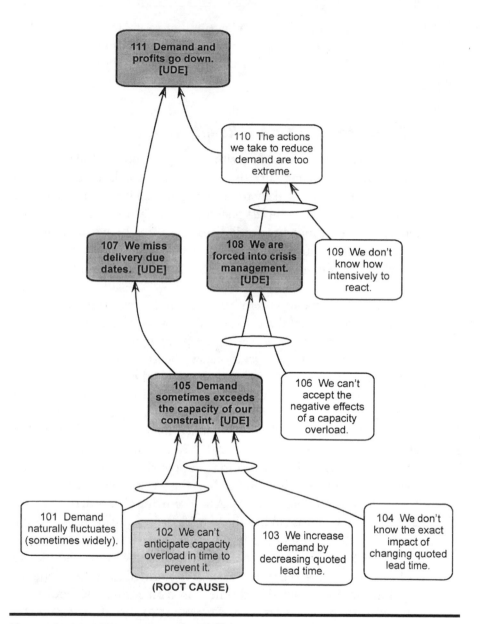

**Figure 11.6   ADV200 Current Reality Tree #2: Anticipating Overload**

don't see the overload happening until several orders become holes in the shipping buffer — 5 days before they're due for delivery those orders appear in dark red in the Master Production Schedule (Production View | Information | Master Production Schedule). That certainly creates management anxiety, and in some cases it may be too late to respond before a couple of orders are delivered late. We need a way to alleviate that root cause (block 102 in Figure 11.6). We also need to figure out how to eliminate some of the crisis management that goes along with frequent penetrations of the shipping buffer.

## ADV200: The Second Future Reality Tree

Figure 11.7 shows a future reality tree with some injections to deal with these new problems that the second current reality tree revealed. If we can find a way to detect an order that is likely to become late well before it reaches the shipping buffer, we can keep buffer penetrations to a minimum by taking less extreme short-term measures earlier. For instance, 2 days of additional shifts 2 weeks before the load on the CCR reaches a point of no return may preclude a whole week of second shifts needed to expedite a number of red-line orders on time.

But in the longer term, no system can "run on the ragged edge" for very long without becoming destabilized. We need a long-term solution to regulate the demand (load) on our resources, to keep them operating with some protective capacity. How can we operationalize the injections in Figure 11.7?

If you recall, earlier in this chapter we discussed the concept of planned load. Based on the amount of each work center's capacity required to produce each product (A1 through C2), the aggregation of all orders in the master production schedule is reflected in the planned load for each work center. This planned load can be seen in the MICSS simulation by selecting the Production View and checking the box in the upper right labeled "View Total Load" (Figure 11.1). Planned load for each of the work centers can be monitored dynamically as the load changes. As more new work orders enter the schedule, the red bars increase in length. As work orders already in the system are processed by different resources, the associated red bars decrease in length.

Each red bar has a number associated with it showing the hours and minutes of work each work center is currently committed to do between now and the expiration of the quoted lead time. Based on a 5-day, 40-hour work week, a quoted lead time of 25 days would represent 200 hours of work center capacity. Each red bar in the "Total Load" view represents the number of hours of a work center's capacity committed to work already confirmed in the schedule (planned load) as of today.

If we know that Machine B is our most heavily loaded resource, we can consider it the capacity-constrained resource (CCR), even if it's not over-loaded at the moment, because this is the work center that will reach maxi-

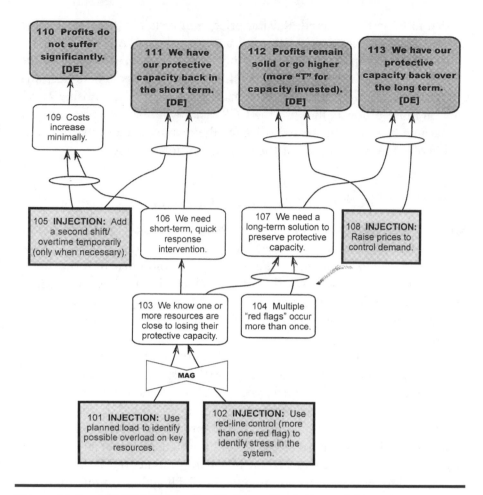

**Figure 11.7     ADV200 Future Reality Tree #2: A Control System**

mum capacity before any other. The rest all have considerably more capacity to spare. So in order to maintain protective capacity throughout the production system, all we need do is watch the planned load on Machine B as it changes dynamically from day to day. With a quoted lead time of 25 days (200 hours), we don't want to see the planned load for Machine B exceed 180 hours (about 90%). As soon as the red bar passes that point and stays there pretty constantly, we should think about applying a few days of additional shifts (short-term injection) to bring the planned load down to something less than 180 hours.

If, after doing this, the planned load at Machine B rises above 180 hours again quickly (or frequently), we need to consider what long term action is needed to tame the demand. Raising prices will certainly discourage some demand, but is it wise to raise all prices across the board? After all, what are we trying to accomplish with the price increase? Of course, we'd like to make more money, but the real motivation with this price increase is to keep the CCR from becoming overloaded. So it makes sense to consider raising prices only on those products that use the CCR. That will liberate some capacity at Machine B, and the increased price for the market demand that remains should offset most, if not all, of the decrease in unit volume.

## ADV200: Effective Exploitation of Capacity

Now, if we want to be really sophisticated about our decision to increase prices, we'll be selective in which prices we increase. Knowing that a price increase will depress demand somewhat, we'd like to get the most benefit for each lost unit of sales. In other words, among the products that use the CCR, which ones give us the *least* throughput per unit, yet use a significant amount of capacity? The simple way to determine this is to calculate the throughput per unit of constraint capacity used to manufacture a unit of each product. Most information systems can provide the entering arguments for this calculation, even if they don't calculate it directly. The MICSS simulation is no exception.

If you go to the Finance View, select the "Information" menu, and open the window labeled "Product Throughput Summary." You'll see the marginal contribution to profit (throughput) for each product, A1 through C2. If you then go to the Production View, select the "Information" menu, and open "All Products Routing," you can determine how many minutes of Machine B time are required to manufacture each product. By dividing those minutes into the throughput for each product, you obtain a dollars-per-minute figure (through-put per unit of CCR time). (Refer to Figure 11.8.) The product with the lowest value is the one for which you should increase the price to depress demand. This will liberate capacity on the CCR, resulting in lower planned loads, which will be visible on the "Total Load" screen as the simulation runs. From Figure 11.8, we can see that the best candidate for liberating Machine B capacity at the least loss in marginal contribution to profit is C1. If we wanted to liberate even more of Machine B's capacity, the next product least detrimental to profit would be A1.

But what if price increases on C1 and A1 depress customer demand so much that ADV200's planned load on Machine B (the CCR) drops well below 90% — say, for example, to 60%? Should we split the difference on the price

| Product | "T" (per unit) | MB Time (CCR) | T/CU ($$/min) | Rank Order |
|---------|---------|---------|---------|---------|
| A1 | $239.96 | :25 min | $ 9.60 | 5 |
| A2 | $169.92 | 0 | ∞ | 1* |
| B1 | $164.96 | :04 min | $ 41.24 | 2 |
| B2 | $214.96 | :12 min | $ 17.91 | 3 |
| C1 | $159.94 | :26 min | $ 6.15 | 6 |
| C2 | $209.94 | :17 min | $ 12.35 | 4 |

\* A2 is a "free" product, meaning it doesn't use the CCR.
Consequently, T/CU has no meaning.

**Figure 11.8    ADV200 Product Prioritization**

increase? Actually, the same computation we performed above can help us here.

If the ADV200 Company has excess capacity to fill, wouldn't it be better to fill it with products that produce a higher marginal contribution to profit (i.e., more throughput)? According to Figure 11.8, A2 is a "free product," meaning that it doesn't consume any of Machine B's capacity. We can increase throughput by selling more of A2, even when Machine B is heavily loaded. But we must be cautious in doing so. Remember the basic rule of emerging constraints? Any significant change in *either* demand *or* capacity can cause another resource to emerge as the system constraint. From among those products that do use Machine B, Product B1 produces the highest throughput per minute of Machine B's time.

And how can we stimulate demand for more of those products (A2 and B1)? Reducing the quoted lead time would be one way that we know works in this particular simulation. So why not do that, just for those two products?*

---

\* Keep in mind that any increase in customer demand at this point might drive Machine B back into an overload condition without warning. It would be advisable to make quoted lead time changes in smaller increments, while watching the effect on planned load, so that it will be obvious when to stop reducing QLT.

Then run the simulation again, using the "Third Run Instructions" from Appendix D. You may be surprised to find that the ADV200 Company can make even more money by selectively emphasizing the right products, even without adding capacity.

However, there are a few other subtleties to draw your attention to. Product C1 is the least profitable *only* as long as Machine B is the CCR. When Machine B is well below 90% of full load — say, 50%, for example — it's not clear anymore that increasing the demand for Product B1 at the expense of C1 is such a good idea. It's possible to depress demand too much with C1 price increases. 2 or 3% at a time (in the simulation) is probably prudent. If the load on Machine B is already very low, we might need to recover some of the lost demand for Product C1, preferably by decreasing the quoted lead time, but possibly by backing off on the price increase a little.

## ADV200: The Third Future Reality Tree

Let's step back a little and look at the big picture of what we've done with the ADV200 Company. The Future Reality Tree shown in Figures 11.9a through 11.9d will be useful in doing this. By applying effective constraint management principles (the Five Focusing Steps and DBR production policies), we reduced actual production lead times as low as possible without risking late deliveries (block 102). By reducing quoted lead times, we increased demand without having to compromise our prices (block 101).

Since there's no way to become more efficient (doing a *better* job of building products), the only ways we can improve profitability are to expand capacity (block 106) or to become more effective (choose the *right* products to emphasize). To decide how to better employ our limited capacity, we rank-ordered products A1 through C2 according to the ratio of the throughput they generated to the CCR capacity they consumed (blocks 111 and 202). Then we selectively raised prices on the products that returned the lowest throughput per minute of CCR time used (block 206). This opened up more capacity on the CCR to produce higher-value products (better T/CU ratio).

This is the essence of S-DBR. We established the market (customer demand) as the major system constraint — the one that always resides in the background, even though it might be temporarily masked by an internal CCR. We established a shipping buffer to protect the integrity of delivery due dates. We monitored the planned load on the CCR (Machine B), doing what was necessary (selective application of additional shifts) to keep it in the 90%

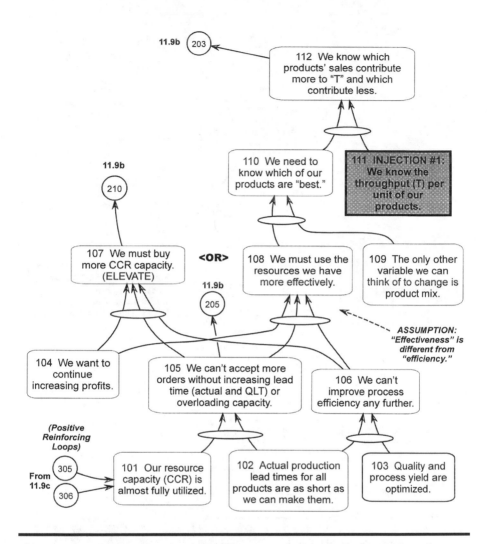

**Figure 11.9a ADV200 Future Reality Tree #3: Manipulating Demand**

range, rather than establishing a formal CCR buffer. And we "tied the rope" to customer demand through the selective application of pricing and quoted lead time tactics to keep the load on the CCR from dipping too low or surging too high.

Manipulating demand using throughout-per-contraint unit to prioritize decisions may cause a different resource to emerge as a CCR. We'll discuss this in more detail later. In reality, we may consider dropping less profitable product lines completely, introducing new products, or opening new geographic markets for our existing new products, or opening new geographic

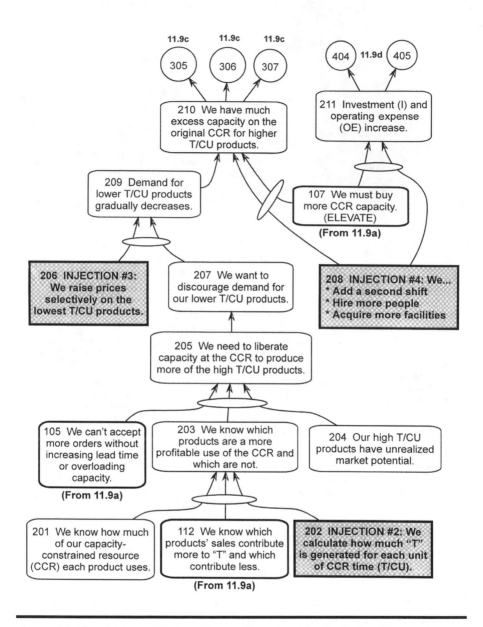

**Figure 11.9b    ADV200 Future Reality Tree #3: Manipulating Demand**

markets for our existing product lines. The ultimate outcome of all these options is more throughput and higher profitability.

At some point, however, we must consider the possibility that we have manipulated demand and reprogrammed our capacity to the point that we've had a significant effect on our external environment, including customer

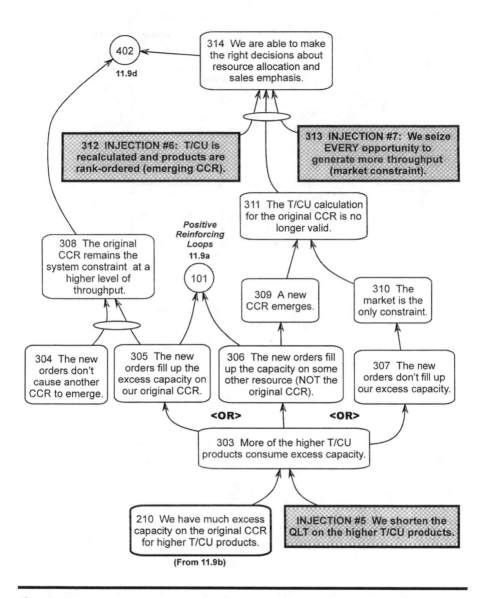

**Figure 11.9c   ADV200 Future Reality Tree #3: Manipulating Demand**

demand. This, in turn, exerts new pressures on our internal resources. One effect is that we may find that just exploiting and subordinating internally are no longer enough. It may be prudent to elevate our capacity — to buy more capital equipment, open new facilities, hire more employees, etc. It's truly amazing how many companies jump straight to this step, without reaping the benefits of good exploitation and subordination first — benefits

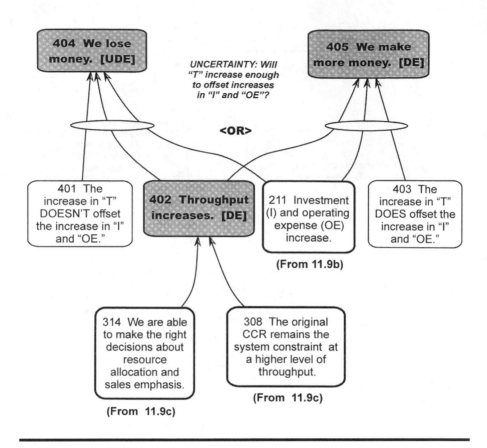

**Figure 11.9d ADV200 Future Reality Tree #3: Manipulating Demand**

that generally don't cost the company much, if any more, in inventory costs or operating expenses. The ADV200 scenario should be sufficient to persuade you that significant swings in the bottom line are possible merely by adjusting the policies that dictate how we use our resources.

## *ADV200: Constraint Shift*

Another key effect to watch for is a shift in the location of the internal capacity-constrained resource (CCR). Anytime we mess around with either capacity or demand, we change the load profile on our internal resources. If we do this continually (which we did in ADV200 by adjusting prices and quoted lead times), eventually a different resource will begin to emerge as a CCR (block 307). This is especially true if we have a "free" product. Remember Figure 11.8? A2 was such a product. It doesn't use Machine B (our CCR

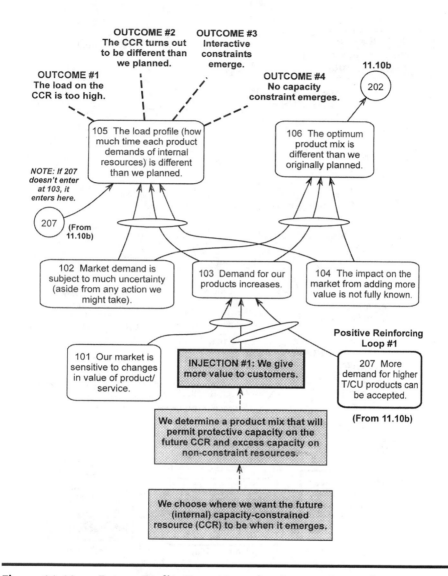

**Figure 11.10a    Future Reality Tree: Managing System Constraint Dynamics**

at the time) at all. Because of this characteristic, we can promise shorter delivery times for A2 without worrying about its effect on Machine B's load. If we *do* that, demand for A2 will subsequently increase. (Try it in another simulation run — you can see it happen in the Sales Summary Graph for A2.) At some point, the increased demand for A2 will start to overload non-

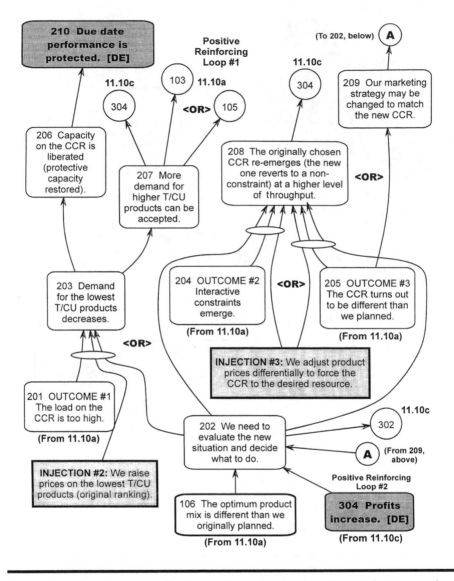

**Figure 11.10b  Future Reality Tree: Managing System Constraint Dynamics**

CCRs (Machine D, specifically) that also support the remaining products, which *do* use the CCR. When this happens, order red flags start appearing more frequently, more short-term expediting is required, and the company starts missing deliveries — in other words, all the indications are that the system is starting to destabilize. But in this case, the problem child is no longer Machine B — it's Machine D! This forces us to change our focus of attention. As a matter of fact, expanding the market for Product B1 will have the same effect on Machine GT and Machine D. One of them, depending on the demand for other products, will emerge as a new constraint.

The principles and procedures for managing the system remain the same constraint-conscious ones we used before. We just refocus them in a different direction.

Recall that back in Chapter 4 (Figure 4.3), we suggested that the theory of constraints provided a strategic framework for managing whole systems. The future reality tree in Figures 11.10a, b, and c represents a strategic view of the application of the five focusing steps, S-DBR, and throughput-based decision support (more on that in Chapter 13). The important lesson to learn from this book so far is that organizations ultimately live or die as complete, tightly integrated systems, not as a collection of loosely associated parts. In integrating the management of system components, the aim of the theory of constraints is to contribute to overall success.

# Reference

1. Fogarty, Blackstone, and Hoffman. *Production & Inventory Management*, 2nd ed., Cincinnati, Ohio, Southwestern Publishing, 1991, 14.

# 12 Managing Excess Capacity

T hroughout most of this book, we've stressed the importance of maintaining excess capacity everywhere in the system, including some at the capacity-constrained resource. We've seen that DBR can actually liberate excess capacity we may not have known about — hidden capacity. Let's assume that we've been able to establish some excess capacity in our manufacturing system. How should we go about managing that newfound capacity? How can we hold on to it? What can we do with it?

Before we talk about what to do with excess capacity, we should probably define it. Take a look at this illustration (Figure 12.1). The horizontal bar represents all the capacity of a particular resource (maybe a constraint, maybe not). This total capacity can be roughly divided into two categories: *productive* and *non-productive*.

"Non-productive" doesn't mean useless — it's not a bad thing. Non-productive only means that this time is not being used to do work that directly generates throughput (producing products for sale). Non-productive time on a resource is (or can be) used for a number of useful purposes. We can do the minimum required set-ups needed for production, perform required maintenance (fix breakdowns), do preventive maintenance (keep functioning equipment operating), or train operators.

Chances are that after these non-productive activities are accounted for, there will still be some unused (available) time on most resources. This is considered excess capacity. Sometimes we fail to see excess capacity because people tend to hide it. Nevertheless, when there is a demand for that capacity, the job usually gets done anyway!

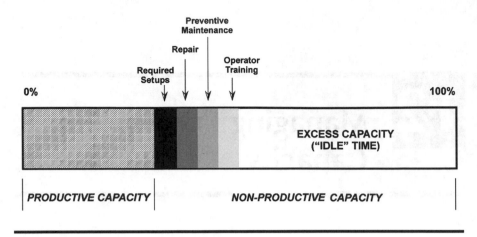

Figure 12.1    Resource Capacity Profile

## Excess Capacity: What Can We Do with It?

What are some of the things we can do with this excess capacity? One thing is discretionary set-ups. These are the additional set-up changes, beyond the absolute minimum required, to produce our products. This would include the added set-up changes that we incur as a result of processing smaller batches. Or, if there's enough excess capacity, we could use some of it to build new products — things we don't produce and sell now. Alternatively, we could try to load our resources a little more, by producing more existing products for sale. This, of course, would require some related activities to stoke up demand for our existing products — sales and marketing efforts, such as reducing quoted lead time or special promotions. Figure 12.2, a future reality tree, shows some of the beneficial outcomes that having excess capacity makes possible.

It's important to note that different resources have differing amounts of excess capacity. A CCR will usually have very little excess capacity. A non-CCR will have considerably more. There will be more options for what to do with the excess capacity at non-CCRs. But it's crucial to remember that *some* protective capacity is required at both the CCR and at non-CCRs.

## Excess Capacity: Protection from What?

Why do we need protective capacity? It's necessary for reasons that we've already discussed: internal variability, unanticipated machine breakdowns,

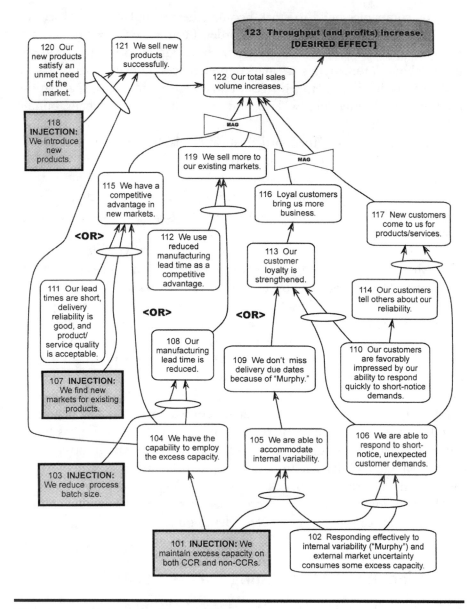

**Figure 12.2  Future Reality Tree: Excess Capacity**

unpredictable rework, and unplanned absence of key personnel. It's also needed to accommodate external uncertainty, which can result from two different causes: unpredictable fluctuating market demand, and inaccurate market forecasts.

Many companies build to stock because their manufacturing processes aren't fast or agile enough to build to order. But the stock level targets are usually determined by forecasts, which are based on historical trends, best-guesses about future trends in market preferences, known or anticipated product introductions, planned sales or marketing campaigns, speculation about what the competition will do, and the reading of crystal balls, bones, and chicken entrails.

The ultimate result of these prognostications is that forecasts are notoriously unreliable. Yet companies routinely treat them as gospel. Why? Because they have no other source of more reliable information. And since they usually load their manufacturing capacity until there is no protective maneuvering room to react, they have to depend on a forecast — which is inevitably wrong to varying degrees.

What happens if you don't have enough excess capacity? Here's an example of what can happen, and you are forced to depend on a sales projection.

In 1998, AT&T decided to try to capture more market share for its budding cellular telephone business. The company introduced, with much public fanfare, it's new *Digital One* rate — a single rate for each minute of cellular phone use, whether local or long distance, when calling anywhere in the U.S. Response was so much greater than AT&T's marketing department anticipated, it overwhelmed the company's installed capacity to provide phone service. The result was thousands of customers, new and existing, who couldn't dial into the AT&T cellular network or had their calls dropped when they did get in. The resulting dissatisfaction with AT&T's service has led to wholesale defections of subscribers to other services, a grassroots class action suit movement, and damage to AT&T's reputation among existing, former, and potential future subscribers.[1]

These are some of the serious consequences that can result from insufficient protective capacity and overdependence on forecasts.

## The Dilemma of Maintaining Excess Capacity

Why is it difficult to maintain excess capacity? The primary reason is that senior management typically sees excess capacity as a waste of money — the glass is neither half-full nor half-empty. You've simply got twice as much glass as you need!

Because of the local efficiency mentality driven by cost-absorption accounting practices, idle resources are seen as incurring cost without producing any revenue. So management traditionally exerts great pressure on production to keep resources as busy as possible. This means that production typically keeps busy by filling idle time (excess capacity) with work that is not immediately needed to satisfy firm revenue-generating orders — in other words, make-to-stock: "We don't have any documented needs to fill right now, so we'll make things for a 'rainy day' and 'look busy' at the same time!" And in doing so, protective capacity (against uncertainty) is squandered — but at least our resources are efficient (if not effective!).

The impact of this cost mentality is not lost on the work force. Identified excess capacity is often trimmed, meaning layoffs! Consequently, employees will usually try to hide their excess capacity by stretching out the time required for any operation, because they don't want to appear to have nothing to do. This effect is known as "Parkinson's Law" — work expands to fill the time allotted for it. The accompanying cause-and-effect tree (Figure 12.3) explains how Parkinson's Law works in a manufacturing environment to guarantee that any excess capacity remains well hidden. Notice that while desired effects result for the work force, a major undesirable effect results for the company.

## The Excess Capacity Conflict

Paraphrasing Shakespeare, to maintain excess capacity, or not to maintain excess capacity — that is the question. This dilemma is expressed in Figure 12.4.

We've already seen what not having enough excess capacity can lead to: longer production lead times; inferior due-date performance; loss of flexibility to customize products, maintain a wide variety of products, or maintain high quality; and a reputation for inadequate customer service (e.g., AT&T, commercial airlines, etc.). Notice that these are the flip-side of everything that excess capacity makes possible, as expressed in the excess capacity future reality tree (Figure 12.2).

## Effects of Various Policies on Actual Production Lead Time

Here's an interesting phenomenon concerning the relationship between various policies and actual production lead time (Figure 12.5). All the factors we concern ourselves with in DBR have a linear effect on manufacturing lead time except one.

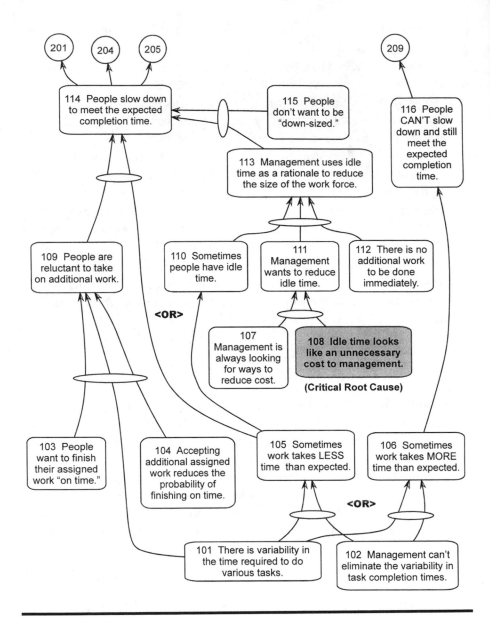

**Figure 12.3a   Parkinson's Law Applied to Excess Capacity**

Scheduling new work orders weekly instead of daily adds a fixed increment to actual lead time. So do large process and transfer batches. And making the saving of set-ups a higher priority than finishing the earliest delivery-due order does the same. Capacity loading alone seems to have a variable effect on actual production lead time. It remains fairly level — and

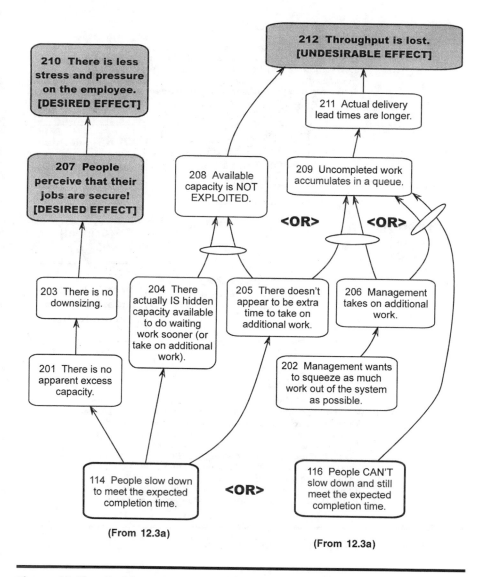

**Figure 12.3b    Parkinson's Law Applied to Excess Capacity**

insignificant — until loading reaches about 80% or more. After that, lead time starts to increase disproportionately and becomes very steep the closer loading approaches 100%.

Scheduling daily translates the curve downward by a fixed amount. The same happens when we employ smaller batches and prioritize by earliest due date. Keeping the loading of capacity below about 90% — which

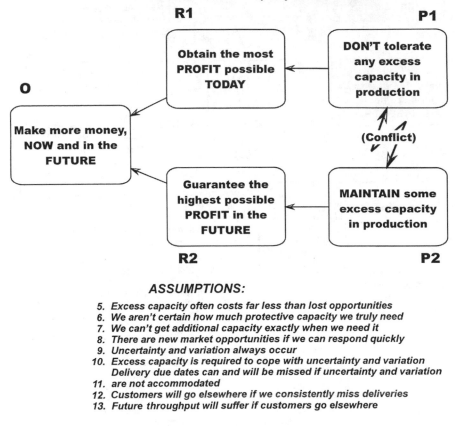

ASSUMPTIONS:

1. *Unused (excess) capacity wastes money*
2. *We can always fill excess capacity with more orders*
3. *We know exactly how much protective (truly needed excess) capacity we need*
4. *We can obtain additional capacity whenever we need it*

**R1** **P1**

Obtain the most PROFIT possible TODAY

DON'T tolerate any excess capacity in production

**O**

Make more money, NOW and in the FUTURE

(Conflict)

Guarantee the highest possible PROFIT in the FUTURE

MAINTAIN some excess capacity in production

**R2** **P2**

ASSUMPTIONS:

5. *Excess capacity often costs far less than lost opportunities*
6. *We aren't certain how much protective capacity we truly need*
7. *We can't get additional capacity exactly when we need it*
8. *There are new market opportunities if we can respond quickly*
9. *Uncertainty and variation always occur*
10. *Excess capacity is required to cope with uncertainty and variation*
11. *Delivery due dates can and will be missed if uncertainty and variation are not accommodated*
12. *Customers will go elsewhere if we consistently miss deliveries*
13. *Future throughput will suffer if customers go elsewhere*

**Figure 12.4   Excess Capacity Conflict**

management certainly has the discretion to do — seems to produce the most positive influence of all.

## Excess Capacity: A New Way to Think about It

In a perfect world, the obvious solution would be to know exactly how much excess capacity is needed to maintain adequate subordination to market requirements. That's not likely to ever happen, but management often acts

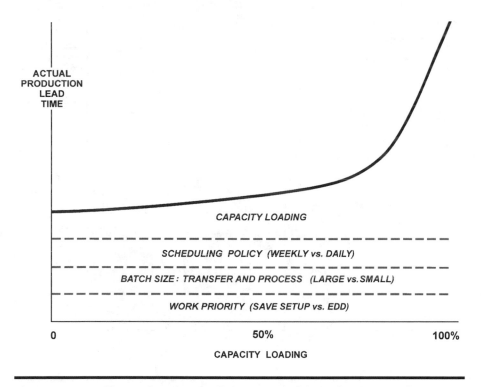

**Figure 12.5    Effects of Various Policies on Actual Production Lead Time**

as if it does. Management's misconception (that they know exactly how much excess capacity is enough) is based on three erroneous assumptions:

1.  That we are able to know *a priori* how much excess capacity is actually needed.
2.  That this excess capacity can be easily manipulated according to our needs.
3.  The only way to solve a dilemma is to find an acceptable compromise.

The way to justify holding onto excess capacity (rather than trimming it, as management cost accounting might suggest doing) is to base the argument on the possibilities for generating more throughput through new business opportunities. Excess capacity makes reduced lead times possible. These can be a competitive weapon upon which sales and marketing can capitalize.

Sometimes the only thing required to be able to offer other benefits to customers is additional capacity. Quite frequently, a supplier will specify a minimum order size. This policy can be justified only when small orders take so much capacity from a resource that it becomes a constraint. The ability

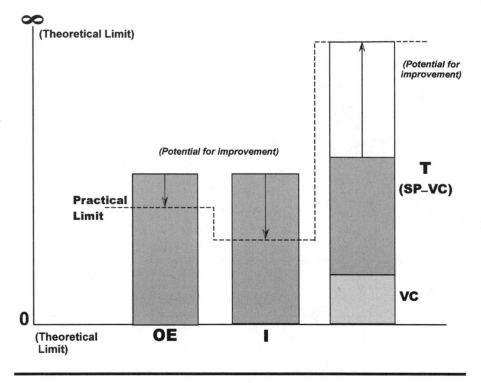

**Figure 12.6    Managing By T, I, and OE**

to accept small orders benefits the customer. It can add many more customers and sales and provides a much better insight into market trends. Customization of certain products can often be achieved with the same materials, and with no more than additional capacity (set-ups). Excess capacity makes it possible to capture additional market segments that a company with out excess capacity cannot attempt to do.

Remember this diagram from Chapter 3 (Figure 12.6)? There is always more opportunity (and more latitude) to increase T than to reduce OE or I. Moreover, you can never be sure to what extent you've compromised your ability to produce current T when you cut OE or I.

## Common Reasons Why Excess Capacity Remains Hidden

Employees aren't the only ones who hide excess capacity. Managers do it, too. Usually it is policy constraints that bury our excess capacity in manufacturing organizations. Such policies include the emphasis on efficiency that drives operations to large process batches. In addition, management realizes a false sense of control from transferring work in the same quantities that it processed. Keeping it all together seems to make it more visible, and thus under better control. Accepting as a way of life the long lead times that come with these policies drives manufacturing to produce to stock or to forecast, rather than striving to produce to order as much as possible, and to stock only when absolutely necessary.

## The Cost Mentality and Excess Capacity

The cost mentality, which is part and parcel of full absorption costing, reinforces the local efficiency syndrome, because products priced on the basis of fully absorbed fixed costs reflect less profit margin. Thus, the only way to achieve better profit margins seems to be cost reduction, which comes from... better efficiency!

Cost mentality also heavily biases consideration of new market opportunities. Suppose we find that a new product, for a new market segment, doesn't appear to cover all the costs of its development. Obviously, objections to continuing development will be raised. Objections can come as late as just before product introduction, after development costs have been committed. Even if the company has enough excess capacity to manufacture the new product, cost concerns may prompt objections to introducing the product. In other words, the company may have productive work for otherwise idle resources to do, instead of having to pay them to do nothing.

However, short-term cost considerations often ignore the real potential advantage: an active presence in more than one market segment. Such a presence can help dampen wild swings in the demand for a company's products that often occur in single or narrow market segments. Producing for more than one market segment buffers the sales curve against the effect of a demand crash in a single segment. The CCR can be better exploited. In summary, strategic advantages are often sacrificed to short-term cost considerations.

Companies typically subordinate everything else — especially customer needs! — to better efficiency of resources that have (and should have) excess capacity. All of the preceding policies derive from the erroneous notion that wasted capacity costs money.

## When Is "Excess" Too Much?

Certainly there are situations where an excess of anything is too much and is truly waste. This really means that an "excess of excess" doesn't add any throughput to the organization. How can we identify such a situation? When our buffer management never finds any "almost late" orders stuck behind a protected resource, we can conclude that we might have excess capacity there. Remember, truly excess capacity exists only when trimming it won't cause any loss of throughput.

There is a striking difference between trimming excess capacity and adding excess capacity to the system. One is usually a lot easier to do than the other, and both decisions come with consequences attached. Remember that capacity comes (and often goes) only in "chunks." Beware of trimming excess capacity, especially when that capacity is people. The human capacity that does remain in the organization will learn a lesson from such "capacity trimming" and make Parkinson's Law alive again.

On the other hand, be careful when you add capacity to your organization. Is there compelling evidence that you need the added capacity? Is that evidence truly valid? Would the additional capacity actually add throughput? Are we losing throughput now because we don't have enough protective capacity?

These are the questions managers have to ask themselves before they rush to add capacity. Our advice is

1. If you're contemplating *cutting* excess capacity, be absolutely sure you won't need it before you commit yourself.
2. If you're thinking about *adding* capacity, be sure (a) you really need it — that the throughput it generates will justify the investment; and (b) you haven't overlooked any "hidden" capacity you might already have.

## How to Prepare for Excess Capacity

Okay, let's assume you're convinced that excess capacity is really an opportunity, not a liability. You're willing to modify the way you're currently doing business to capitalize on this opportunity. You want to change the policies described above. But there are some preliminary steps you must take first. Before eliminating the preceding policy constraints:

1.  Make sure that everyone understands the rationale for doing so —
    especially that excess capacity, or idle time will not be punished (with
    layoffs).
2.  Make certain you know the identity of the current CCR, and the CCR-
    to-be in the near future — that is, where the system constraint is
    likely to move, if your actions cause the constraint to shift.
3.  Be sure the CCR is not overloaded in the process of changing policies.
4.  Ensure that a new CCR is not created by changing the policies, unless
    that is your consciously chosen objective. Sometimes we may want
    to move the constraint from where it is to somewhere else. If this is
    the case, make sure you have a control mechanism in place to identify
    the emergence of a new constraint.
5.  Finally, look for opportunities to use the newly found excess capacity
    for generating more throughout. Few thins are as discouraging as the
    discovery of hidden capacity for which there is no immediate
    demand! However, be sure you have red-line control in place and are
    carefully watching planned load. This allows you to avoid penetration
    of protective capacity and to protect against the emergence of an
    interactive constraint

## How to Expose Excess Capacity

Now that we're ready to handle it, how do we go about revealing the hidden
excess capacity that resides in most manufacturing organizations?

First, the culture of the organization must be changed from cost thinking
to throughput thinking. The key question for everyone should be "How much
'T' did we generate today?" not "How much cost did we save today?" Second,
apply the five focusing steps. Exploit the right resources, and subordinate all
the others. Third, control the right subordination targets: due dates, quality,
and exploitation of the constraint (internal or external). Finally, do only what
is necessary now to meet specified customer needs. Don't build what is not
needed for immediate (or relatively short-term) sale. This applies to both
exploitation and subordination. The only exception: When demand is certain
to exceed capacity by a significant amount in the near future, minimal making
to stock or assembling to order is acceptable.

## Summary

Let's summarize what we've covered in Chapters 10 through 12. First, simplified drum-buffer-rope (S-DBR) is simpler and easier to manage than traditional DBR. Control is critical to the successful application of DBR, and early warning is a prerequisite for control, but buffers are incapable of doing it all.

If we expect to satisfy our customers, every part of the organization must have some excess capacity. Even the CCR needs some excess capacity for protection. Non-CCRs require even more excess capacity to preserve their flexibility to respond to internal variation and external uncertainty, but some excess capacity can be used for other throughput-generating activities. And increasing throughput offers much more potential for improving profitability than reducing costs.

## Reference

1.  Harris, Nicole, "Frustrated Love: As Americans Bond with Cellular Phones, More Fail to Connect," *Wall Street Journal,* Monday, July 19, 1999, p. A1.

# OPTIMIZING DECISIONS

IV

# 13 Throughput-Based Decision Support

We introduced the concept of throughput-based decision support (TBDS) in Chapter 3. Since then, we've talked about using throughput, inventory (or investment), and operating expense in making both day-to-day and long-term operational decisions. But applying TBDS in the real world requires more than a superficial understanding of it. Now it's time to examine the financial concepts of the theory of constraints in a little more detail.

## Management's Problem

The biggest challenge in operational decision making is to resolve the disconnect between the global organizational system and the local operating department or process where the day-to-day work takes place. Organizations succeed as whole systems, not as a collection of loosely connected component processes. But companies are typically divided and subdivided into departments or branches dedicated to one particular function of the whole business. This is typically done to make the larger, more complex system more manageable.

However, when this subdivision takes place, the parts of the system usually lose their system perspective. Visibility of the big picture usually deteriorates — and often disappears. The most they can usually see with any effectiveness is their own area and the process steps immediately upstream and downstream from themselves. The bigger and more complex an organization is, the greater the degree to which this is likely to happen.

Complicating the partitioning of the (system for manageability) is the underlying assumption we discussed first: The efficiency of the whole organization is the sum of the local efficiencies. We now know this assumption is false, but many — perhaps most — companies continue to operate as if it were true. Witness the fact that functional managers are measured and rewarded on how efficiently they manage their own departments, without regard for how well they contribute to the success of the overall organization. In many cases, the interdependencies that determine overall system success are not even clearly delineated or understood.

On the other hand, the success of the global system is measured by a different set of measurements, and these are invariably financial: net profit, return on investment, and cash flow. But while the success of the overall organization is usually assessed financially, many of the measures by which functional managers are evaluated are not financial, or are generally not expressed in financial terms alone. Typical measurement factors may include production volume (units produced), scrap rates (percentages), order fill rates — also referred to as delivery due-date performance (percentages) — sales volume (sometimes in dollars, often in units), test failure/rework rates (percentages), production yield (percentages).

In complex organizations, senior management usually assumes that the sum of the local efficiencies equals the overall organizational efficiency. They also assume that the right yardsticks for local efficiency have been selected, and that maximizing performance against these yardsticks everywhere in the company will automatically produce the best global financial performance. And, finally, they assume that minimizing costs across the whole organization helps maximize profitability.

But as we've seen in the preceding three parts of this book, these are flawed assumptions. Local efficiencies don't really matter, except at the capacity-constrained resource (CCR). There is no logical connection between most non-financial local yardsticks and global financial performance (net profit, return on investment, cash flow), and chasing cost reductions can actually hurt overall system performance. In fact, it may compromise generation of throughput while not making enough difference to justify the effort invested.

## Management's Challenge

To achieve a truly synergistic organization, management has to find a way to predict and accurately measure the effects of local decisions — those made at the functional departmental level — on the global financial performance of the whole company.

For example, what would be the effect on net profit of a decision to restructure the human resources department? How would profit (or cash flow) be affected by a decision to break (or not break) a set-up on a milling machine? What would a decision to forego overtime tomorrow do to the company's return on investment this quarter?

To know with confidence that a local decision truly advances the goal of the company (which we assume for most manufacturing organizations is to make money), we need to understand how such decisions actually impact the global financial performance of the organization — if they do at all. What management needs is a new set of yardsticks that enhances decision making at all levels. These yardsticks should provide a clear, unequivocal connection between local decisions and global performance. They should motivate functional managers to make the right exploitation and subordination decisions — the decisions that improve the whole organization's performance, not just their own department's. And these yardsticks must be simple and easily understood by everyone.

## Traditional Global Measurements

Why aren't the traditional global measurements satisfactory for local decision making? Let's examine them a little more closely.

Net profit is the difference between total revenues and total expenses per period. It's often parsed down to profit margin per unit of product. Return on investment is net profit divided by the money invested to generate it. What could be wrong with these measurements?

These common global financial measurements do an effective job of characterizing the goal of a business organization, but they don't effectively guide local managers to make the right decisions, for either their own level or the whole organization level.

Let's consider an example. If a client demands a 5% price reduction on a very large deal, should we accept it? If an urgent order shows up unexpectedly, should we break an existing set-up or delay the urgent order? Quick, answer these questions: How will the company's net profit and return on investment be affected by those decisions? Will the outcomes be positive or negative? You see, it's not really easy to relate those global financial concepts to daily decisions, is it?

The daily decisions in most business organizations are not directly relatable to the common global financial measurements. Consequently, companies often derive some kind of surrogate, or intermediate measure, to help a local manager make the right decision. Some of these intermediate measures may include profit per unit, cost per unit, efficiency ratios, and variances. These intermediate measures certainly look good, but are they really any better at steering local managers toward the right decisions — the ones that benefit the organization as a whole?

## TOC Global Measurements

The theory of constraints provides an alternative set of financial measurements that will better support both daily local decision making and high-level decisions.* The primary emphasis in constraint management is on generation of throughput.

Throughput is defined as the rate at which an organization generates money.[1] Another way of viewing it is the *added value created by the company*. Mathematically, throughput is represented as total revenue minus the total truly variable expenses. These truly variable expenses mainly include the raw material costs, but other truly variable costs may include sales commissions, warranty repair/replacement costs, or transportation costs. They do not include direct or indirect labor (unless paid by each piece produced), or any other element of overhead.

No so-called fixed expenses are included in variable costs. If the expense is incurred by unit of time (hourly, daily, weekly, monthly, quarterly, etc.), it is not considered to vary with the number of units sold.

It should also be noted that throughput constitutes new money coming into the company, usually as a consequence of the sale of finished product to an external customer. Transfer pricing associated with the exchange of components internally (between departments or divisions of the company) is not included in throughput.

The other two unique TOC financial measures represent the cost of generating throughput: inventory (or investment) and operating expense.

---

* More detailed treatments of the financial accounting details of throughput, inventory, and operating expense can be found in a number of other books on the subject, including
Corbett, Thomas., *Throughput Accounting*, Great Barrington, MA: The North River Press, 1998.
Noreen, Eric, John Mackey, and Debra Smith. *The Theory of Constraints and Its Implications for Management Accounting*, Great Barrington, MA: The North River Press, 1995.
Smith, Debra, *The Measurement Nightmare: How the Theory of Constraints Can Resolve Conflicting Strategies, Policies, and Measures*, Boca Raton, FL: St. Lucie Press, 2000.

Inventory/investment represents all the money the system invests in assets and materials that are used to make the products or produce the services the system intends to sell.[1] Operating expense is the money the organization spends to turn Inventory into throughput.[1]

Another way of looking at these three measures:

- Throughput is all the money coming into the company
- Inventory, or investment is all the money tied up in the company in tangible assets
- Operating expense is all the money going out of the company

## Link between TOC and Traditional Global Financial Measurements

The relationship between TOC financial measures and traditional global financial measure is simple. Net profit is throughput minus operating expense. Throughput (T), in turn, is equivalent to total sales revenue minus total variable costs. The definition of T does not include direct labor (or indirect labor, either), unless compensation is paid by the piece. Note that operating expenses (OE) — all fixed costs — are deducted *after* the throughput is calculated, not simultaneously with it. Return on investment is net profit divided by inventory (I). Many decisions, both local and high level, have an impact on throughput.

It's critical to never forget that T relates to revenue and is measured in dollars (or to other monetary units). Although T is closely related to physical output, there is an important distinction between the two. Output is in physical units of some kind. Throughput is the financial value of the output. For example, which would you rather have, a pound of gold or a pound of feathers? It's the financial value of the output that matters, not its physical measurement.

Output is the volume of product or service produced, expressed in non-monetary units, for example, tons or units of product. Throughput is the financial value of a certain volume of output. It is always expressed in monetary terms, whether dollars, pounds sterling, francs, deutschmarks, shekels, drachmas, rials, rupees, or pesos.*

---

* This definition of throughput applies to for-profit companies only — companies whose goal is to make money. Therefore, as a measure of success in achieving this goal, throughput must be expressed in goal-units, i.e., financial terms. Organizations that are not for-profit can still use T, I, and OE to assess their success, but in those cases T must be expressed and measured in other than monetary terms.

# How T, I, and OE Support Daily Decisions

Let's see how T, I, and OE might be used by a functional manager to assist in making the right operational decisions. We'll consider one of the examples cited earlier:

> *A client demands a 5% price reduction on a very large purchase. Should we accept?*

From our knowledge of the definitions of T, I, and OE, it seems clear that such a price reduction has an impact on T. It does not, however, affect I or OE. Those costs are already committed. So in order to know whether the decision to accept the order at the reduced price is a good one, we must calculate its impact on T. This impact is considered over some period of time (weekly, monthly, quarterly, etc.).

The first of two primary considerations is the impact on throughput in the short term. Will the total revenue from the reduced price be less than the total of the truly variable costs of producing the order? Will we lose T in the short term by accepting the order? Will we have to forego a more lucrative order because a CCR is already fully loaded? If the answer is "yes," we should probably reject the order, but there is an exception to this rule. It's possible to win the battle, but lose the war. If, by taking less throughput now, we realize much higher T in the future — more than enough to offset the short-term loss in T — we should accept the order at the reduced price. Remember, the goal is to make more money *now and in the future*.

This naturally brings us to the second consideration: the impact on throughput in the long term. Will we be held to this lower price again in the future? Will other customers receive the same favorable treatment? If the answer to these questions is "yes," then we should definitely reject the offer. If we'll be forced to give others — or everyone — the same price reduction, the answer should be to reject the offer, as throughput will probably suffer in the long run. As you can see, effective assessment of decision options can require a longer-term perspective.

To summarize, we can state a general rule: Even with a price reduction, if the total revenue from an order exceeds the total of the variable costs of producing it, we should accept the order, as long as no other customer receives a price reduction because of this decision.

The only exception to this rule occurs when we have a capacity-constrained resource, and we can tap a market for a product that offers a better return (more T) for the same amount of the CCR's time as the offer in question. In other words, we may be constrained and under those

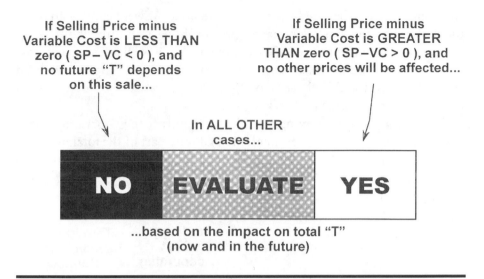

**Figure 13.1    Price Reduction: "To give or not to give? That is the question..."**

circumstances there may be better choices that will bring in more total T. We'll discuss this particular decision rule in more detail in a moment.

Here's a graphical way to look at it (Figure 13.1). If the selling price for the order minus the variable costs of producing it is less than zero, and no future T depends on this sale, the answer is to reject the order. If the selling price minus the variable cost of producing it is greater than zero, and no other prices will be affected, the answer should be to accept the order. In all other cases, evaluate the impact on total throughput more thoroughly.

## Calculating the Financial Impact

Now, one of the most important questions to consider is whether traditional financial rules, which are based on product costing, give a different answer than one would obtain using throughput-based decision support (TBDS). In virtually all cases, the answers would be quantitatively different, though in some cases they would lean in the same direction (i.e., toward "accept"or "reject"). But in some cases TBDS would produce an "accept"answer when traditional management (cost) accounting would say "reject." And traditional accounting would be wrong.

The reason that cost accounting produces a different answer is that traditional product costs include many more than just the truly variable ones. Under traditional accounting rules, a 5% price reduction may completely wipe out the profit margin. In such cases, the usual answer would be to reject the deal, even though it might have a positive impact on throughput.

Consider a simple but specific example. Let's say we have a product that sells for $88 per unit. Variable cost is $45 per unit. Fixed company overhead (including direct and indirect labor) is $6000 per week. The forecast sales demand is for 150 units per week.

Traditional cost accounting would say, "Subtract the $45 variable cost from the unit selling price (revenue), then allocate part of the total overhead against each unit of product forecast to be sold ($6000 divided by 150 = $40 per unit). Subtract the $40 of overhead allocated to each unit, and the gross profit per unit is $3.00." (See Figure 13.2.)

|  | Traditional Cost Accounting | Throughput-Based Decision Support |
|---|---|---|
| **REVENUE** | **$ 88.00** | **$ 88.00** |
| **VARIABLE COST** | **$ 45.00** | **$ 45.00** |
| **OVERHEAD ALLOCATION** | **$ 40.00** | **N / A** |
| **GROSS PROFIT** | **$ 3.00** | **N / A** |
| **THROUGHPUT** | **N / A** | **$ 43.00** |

**Figure 13.2    Differences between Traditional Cost Accounting and TBDS**

Throughput-based decision support would say, "Subtract the $45 variable cost from the unit selling price, and the throughput is $43.00 per unit." However, remember throughput is *not* the same as net profit. What happens to the overhead costs in TBDS? Hold that thought — we'll see the answer to that question in just a minute.

Let's say that the market currently demands 150 units of the product per week, and our new customer wants 50 more than that at the 5% reduced price. If we have the capacity to deliver this order without buying more machines or adding employees or overtime, will we make or lose money on the order?

First, let's compute the answer using traditional accounting procedures (Figure 13.3). If we grant the 5% price reduction, our new selling price is

| | |
|---|---|
| **SELLING PRICE** | **$ 83.60** |
| **VARIABLE COST** | **$ 45.00** |
| **OVERHEAD** | **$ 40.00** |
| **PROFIT PER UNIT** | **< - $ 1.40>** |
| **No. of Unit in the New Order** | **x 50** |
| **LOSS on the New Order** | **< $ 70.00>** |

**Figure 13.3    The Traditional Accounting Answer**

$83.60. Variable cost doesn't change — it remains at $45. Overhead allocation doesn't change, either — it's still $40.* If we subtract these two from $83.60, we get *minus* $1.40. Multiplied by the 50 additional units we'd be selling at the reduced price, we come up with a $70.00 loss! Definitely, we'd reject this order!

Now let's see what the difference is if we calculate the answer using throughput accounting procedures (Figure 13.4). If we subtract the $45 variable cost from the new reduced price of $83.60, we find that our throughput-per-unit is $38.60. We know we have a current market demand for 150 per week at $88 each, and we won't be obligated to reduce the price on those deliveries. Our new customer wants another 50 per week at $83.60. Our total T for existing demand is $6450 ($88 – $45 = $43, and $43 × 150 = $6450). Our total T for the potential new order is $1930 ($83.60 – $45 = $38.60, and $38.60 × 50 = $1930). So the combined projected T for both is $8380.

Now, remember that fixed overhead is $6000 per week, and we don't spend any more for additional machines, people, or overtime, because we already have the capacity to produce those additional 50 units. So, since we incur no additional operating expense, if we *don't* accept the order, our current net profit (T minus OE) doesn't change. It's only $6450 – $6000, or $450.

But if we *do* accept the order, our projected net profit will be $8380 – $6000, or +$2380! In other words, we forego $1930 in additional profit if we

---

* Even though production quantities have been increased, the allocation procedure will not likely adjust the overhead frequently — maybe not until next year.

| | |
|---|---|
| SELLING PRICE | $ 83.60 |
| VARIABLE COST | - $ 45.00 |
| Throughput per Unit | + $ 38.60 |
| Current Market Demand | 150 per week |
| Potential New Order | 50 per week |
| "T" for Existing Demand<br>150 x $43.00 | $ 6,450.00 |
| "T" for Potential New Order<br>50 x $38.60 | $ 1,930.00 |
| TOTAL PROJECTED "T" | $ 8,380.00 |
| LESS FIXED OVERHEAD<br>(Operating Expense) | - $ 6,000.00 |
| NET PROFIT | $ 2,380.00 |
| INCREASE IN PROFIT | 430% |

**Figure 13.4   The TBDS Answer**

base our decision on traditional cost accounting! Or, another way to look at it: We "pass" on an opportunity to increase our profit by *more than four times!*

The only significant difference in the two calculations is that in one case, we allocated a part of fixed expenses to every unit of product sold. In the other case, we treated fixed costs separately — we calculated all the throughput (revenue minus variable costs) first, and then subtracted the fixed cost. By allocating fixed overhead to units of product, we lose sight of the question: "Did we incur any more real out-of-pocket costs by accepting the order?" We just assumed we did, but we did not. And it led us to the wrong decision!

So let's briefly summarize. Traditional cost accounting tells us not to accept the order, because we'll lose $70 on it. TBDS says, "Take the order," because we make $1930 more than we're already making without incurring any additional operating expense. In other words, the change in T minus the change in OE is a *positive* $1930.

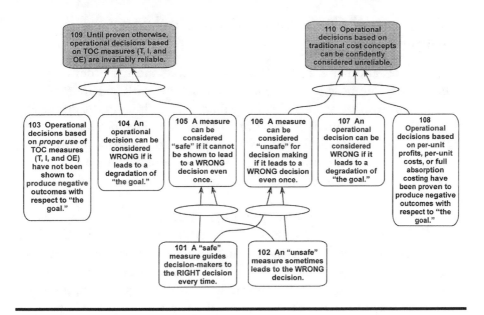

**Figure 13.5    The Logic of Measurements**

## The Logic of Measurements

The cause-and-effect tree in Figure 13.5 succinctly states our conclusion. This tree does not suggest that cost accounting is always wrong and TBDS accounting is always right. Rather, it's intended to convey the ideas that, if the goal is to make more money, now and in the future:

1.  Traditional cost accounting, if performed faithfully as its proponents prescribe (i.e., no distortion or misapplication of the method), often delivers answers that suggest the wrong course of action.
2.  If performed faithfully, as its proponents prescribe (i.e., no distortion or misapplication of the method), TBDS has not yet been shown to deliver answers that suggest the wrong course of action. This is not to say that it can't happen in the future, just that it has not happened yet.

Both TBDS and cost accounting can be subverted (meaning deliberately distorted) or misapplied (accidentally) in ways that produce wrong decisions. But properly applied (as the logic tree specifies) TBDS is safer for decision making than traditional cost accounting.

## How T, I, and OE Support Daily Decisions: Another Example

Let's consider another example. We'll assume that another order comes in unexpectedly. Suppose that an expensive machine, with considerable set-up time, is now processing a very large batch. Everything in this order will eventually be sold, but it is not urgently needed right now. Should the shop foreman break the current set-up and start working on the new, urgent order? Keep in mind that this will cause another set-up to be done later to finish the remainder of the batch on which the machine is currently working.

This is strictly an operational decision, isn't it? Or does it have a financial component? There is no relevance to throughput here, is there? But there certainly is a cost issue — an additional set-up on an expensive machine costs us money! This should be the overriding consideration, shouldn't it? Marketing should just do its best not to lose the urgent sale, even though it will be late (because we don't want to break the set-up), right? Wrong!

Why is this approach wrong? Let's look at the real costs of an additional set-up on an expensive machine. The first is labor. Set-ups are done by direct labor people. These people are on the payroll, and they are paid by the hour, not by the set-up. They'll be paid whether or not they do the set-up, so no additional direct labor costs are incurred.

Second, there's the time of the expensive machine. At the time we're considering doing the set-up change, the machine is not producing anything for immediate sale. The costs of raw materials for the products it's working on have already been incurred, but there is — as yet — no customer (and no immediate prospect of revenue) for these products. They'll be going into finished stock inventory. So, if the machine is not actively generating money for the company at the moment, no money is lost if the machine stops producing products for which there is no immediate customer and is engaged in a set-up.

Third, there's the material lost in the set-up change. This is a potential real cost — the *only* real cost, so far. Sometimes the materials on the machine must be scrapped if the set-up is broken in mid-run. Sometimes the set-up operation itself consumes materials that are intended to be scrapped, usually by having to test whether the set-up is good. The value of these lost materials is a real cost.

Of the factors just mentioned, only the loss of scrapped materials in the set-up change may really generate additional expenses. As long as there is excess capacity (both people and machines) no added cost is incurred by stopping a machine for a set-up change. We're already paying for labor (by the hour), whether they're producing, setting up, or on a break. We've already paid for the machine (or are paying for it over time), whether it produces or not. If the machine and people are being paid but are not producing anything, no extra real cost is incurred.

The only real loss may be an opportunity loss: Other revenue that is potentially lost as a result of the set-up change. But this is not the case, because the machine was not building to a firm order to begin with — it was building to stock (stock that was not requested by any customer). However, *not* changing the set-up risks losing a paying customer to a competitor (if we can't deliver when the customer needs it). The throughput value of that order constitutes an opportunity loss — real money we won't take in if we retain the set-up.

## Using T, I, and OE in Making Daily Decisions

Let's see how we would apply the concepts of throughput, inventory, and operating expense to daily decisions.

The first question we would ask is the most important one: Is the machine on which we propose to break the set-up the constraint of the whole organization? The only two possible answers to this questions are "yes" or "no." Suppose the answer is "no." In this case, we can assume that the machine has some excess capacity — by definition, non-constraints do. This means that if we do one more set-up on this machine, the time for that set-up comes from that excess capacity — which has already been paid for. No extra expenses are incurred, except possibly for materials that might have to be scrapped as a result of the set-up change.

But in this case (when the answer is "no") we have an urgent order — a situation in which more T can be generated if we respond right away. If we don't respond right away, the T may be lost. We know that the extra set-up does not impact any future T in any significant way. There will still be time to return to building the original order (excess capacity). We might still incur some minimal expenses (lost materials that are not included in the total variable cost), but these will probably be negligible.

So, the common-sense decision rule compares additional T expected from the urgent order to the cost of scrapped materials. If the change in T minus the cost of scrapped materials is positive, we should break the set-up to fulfill the urgent order.

Now let's see what happens if the machine in question is a capacity-constrained resource (CCR). In other words, it is now working on a job for which there is a firm order. In this case the additional set-up comes out of time that will otherwise be used to create revenue-generating products. The time lost to the additional set-up will cause a delay in delivering the product on which the CCR was originally working. Or, it's possible that the delay of the current order may be enough to prompt the customer to cancel it completely. At the very least, we can assume that the customer will not be happy about the delay. But it gets worse. The additional set-up delays *all* subsequent orders in the CCR schedule. After such delays, it's difficult for a CCR with little or no protective capacity to make up for that lost time. *All* the customers whose orders are delayed will be dissatisfied. And, if the CCR becomes backlogged, we might be forced to decline a future order because we don't have the ability to complete it in time. The risk here is to throughput that has yet to be realized — future T.

Obviously, the ideal solution is to manage our resources so we never get into the undesirable position of having to choose between customers. But sometimes, despite our best efforts, we may find ourselves in that position anyway. If that happens, the question we need to ask ourselves is: "Will we realize more T from the urgent new order than the T we would lose from delaying the existing order?"

There are two ways we can lose throughput from delaying the existing order. One is time is lost in setting up the CCR and producing that urgent new order. The second is potential delay and/or cancellation of the existing order.

Here are some basic TOC-oriented guidelines for operating decisions:

1.  Producing firm orders on time generates throughput for the whole company now.
2.  Producing to forecast or to stock does not generate T for certain. There's no way to know how long finished goods will remain in stock, or whether they will ever be sold. Will they become obsolete and have to be scrapped (or sold below cost)? Moreover, in some cases, producing to stock can actually block generation of T (production of firm orders, for which there is a paying customer now).
3.  Loading the CCR with real T-producing work improves the utilization of limited capacity, because CCRs limit T for the whole organization.

## How to Load the CCR and Maximize T without Increasing OE and I

Here's a recommended strategy for loading a CCR and maximizing T without increasing OE and I.

First, seek out as much demand as the CCR can handle. Remember to maintain *some* protective capacity on the CCR. Second, when the CCR cannot fulfill all of the demand, choose the option that provides the higher total T across all product lines. In other words, in the same way that we depressed demand in the Plant 200 case study for products that contribute less throughput but use significant amounts of the CCR's time, consider deferring/delaying lower T products in favor of higher T products, and always produce to order before producing to stock, even if it means breaking a set-up to do so.

Since the common denominator among different products is the CCR time that each requires for production, follow this general rule. Compare products by the ratio of the throughput they generate per unit to the CCR each unit consumes. Prioritize both sales efforts for products and the operations that produce them by this ratio. The product with the higher T per unit of the CCR's time is manufactured first. We refer to this as the "throughput-per-constraint-unit"(T/CU) rule.

## Throughput-per-Constraint Unit Rule: An Example

Let's look at an example of this rule for prioritizing efforts. Assume we're capacity constrained, and we have two opportunities for regular, recurring monthly production. The first option is to produce and sell an order that generates $10,000 and consumes 10 hours of the CCR's daily capacity. The second option is to sell our least profitable product. Each unit of this product generates $1000 of T for 1.5 hours of the CCR's daily capacity, but we have a virtually unlimited market for this product. We can't do both of these jobs this month, so which one should we choose?

Let's calculate the first option. Dividing $10,000 by 10 hours, we find that this option generates $1000 for every hour of the CCR's daily capacity. We could also have divided the total throughput for the order by the number of minutes required to produce the whole order. This would have given us a dollars-per-minute ratio, which is equivalent to dollars-per-hour.

To calculate the second option, we divide $1000 by 1.5 hours, which gives us $666.67 for every hour of the CCR's time. The decision is clear: The first option is preferable, as long as choosing this option does not adversely affect any other throughput in the future. The unlimited nature of the market is irrelevant — our constraint makes it impossible for us to capitalize on that. The best we can do is compare the relative values of different uses of the same amount of the CCR's time.

This preceding analysis presumes the following assumptions to be valid. First, the CCR is a true constraint at the time. It can be loaded to its full capacity for throughput-generating production. Second, there is only one CCR. If there is more than one CCR (an interactive constraint situation), we can't effectively manage production to maximize throughput. Third, the decision we're about to make will not cause the constraint to shift to some other resource.

## When No CCR Exists: Decision Rules

What if no internal constraint is active? The rules change in this case. If we're not internally constrained, any order promising positive T can be considered a blessing — go for it! Since excess capacity exists everywhere, take advantage of it. Use it to provide added value to customers for which they would gladly pay, such as customized products, faster delivery, or new or different products or services.

Total Quality Management and Just-in-Time guidelines are potentially useful, as long as we subordinate effectively to the market constraint. Where TQM is concerned, don't necessarily try to improve everywhere. Target those improvements from which customers will see benefit. These can be assumed to protect or enhance future T. Target those improvements that will contribute directly to T by permitting an increase in selling price or a decrease in variable cost. For example, reduce scrap and rework, improve reliability (reduce warranty repair/replacement). Don't use Just-in-Time principles to justify improved cost performance. The rationale for JIT is faster, more reliable delivery.

And watch carefully for resources that might become capacity constrained as demand and production loads change.

## How Do Big Decisions Differ from Small Ones?

There are some differences in the rules of thumb between big decisions and small ones. A big decision may cause a significant change in operating expense and inventory as well as in throughput. This would be the case anytime the decision requires an elevation of capacity to meet a higher demand (actual or anticipated).

Any elevation of capacity brings with it the potential to shift the system constraint to a new location. It may move to a different internal resource, in which case a new T/CU priority must be calculated immediately, or exploitation will be compromised. Or it may push the constraint outside the company altogether, perhaps into the market, in which case the old exploitation and subordination actions will become invalid.

Keep in mind that two different time windows apply to T/CU. One is obviously short: an hour or a minute in the T/CU calculation. But the long term must be considered as well. With some decisions, large volumes over a longer period may offset the disadvantages of a low T/CU. For example, a long-term contract for a product with a T/CU of $5.50 per minute may produce a million dollars in throughput over the course of a year, filling CCR capacity during off-peak periods. Ad hoc orders for a product with a T/CU of $30 per minute may produce a total T of only $100,000 in the same period of time. Considering T/CU alone can result in a poor decision.

Remember the logic of measurements tree (Figure 13.5)? The phrase "proper application" raises its ugly head again. Even TBDS can be misapplied! T/CU is a good rule of thumb, but it becomes better when it's considered along with long-term throughput.

A general rule can be applied to big decisions. This rule can be applied to small decisions as well, but it is particularly useful in situations where the T/CU rule has limited applicability. The general rule is to evaluate the change in throughput compared with the change in operating expense. In "yes" or "no" decisions, choose "yes" if the change in throughput minus the change in operating expense ($\Delta T - \Delta OE$) is greater than zero. In either–or decisions, choose the option with the greater positive difference between $\Delta T$ and $\Delta OE$. Another way of saying this is the expected addition to the company's profit is the change in global T minus the change in overall OE. Let's call this the "Change in Profit Rule."

But just calculating the difference between the change in throughput and the change in operating expense isn't enough. We can't ignore return on investment (ROI), either. Consider this example. Let's say you have the option of buying one of two automated processes for your plant. Both of them produce the same volume of the same kind of products, and they both cost the same to operate. This means that under the same market demand circumstances, the profit that can be generated from each process will be the same. But process A may cost $300,000 to buy, while process B may be $750,000. All other things being equal (they never really are, but this is only an example!), process A will provide the better return on investment. So an additional consideration, which we call the "Change in ROI Rule," suggests that the change in profit ($\Delta T - \Delta OE$) be divided by the change in the investment required ($\Delta I$). In the preceding example — an *either–or* decision — the same profit divided by two significantly different required investments shows that one choice is clearly superior (a higher ratio) to the other. So, besides $\Delta T - \Delta OE$ being positive, $\Delta T - \Delta OE$ divided by $\Delta I$ must also be acceptable for the company's circumstances (Figure 13.6).

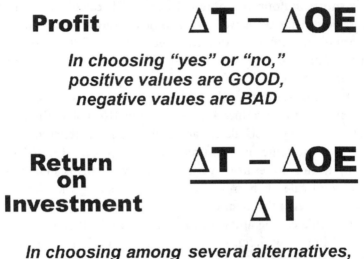

**Figure 13.6    Rules for Changes in Profit and Investment**

## How to Determine $\Delta T$

To determine $\Delta T$, compute the difference between the predicted new T and the current level of T. Since a CCR may limit the potential maximum T that a decision can generate, it's necessary to know whether an internal constraint currently exists. If an internal constraint *doesn't* exist, we'll need to know whether a CCR will *emerge* as a result of the decision.

Here's a typical example of this kind of situation. In a metropolitan area, 40% of the homes subscribe to cable television. The rest use either satellite systems or receive UHF/VHF broadcast signals. The cable company decides to offer internet service through its existing installed cable network; 80% of the company's existing customers sign up for this service. But once the word circulates that cable internet service increases the speed of upload and download by a factor of ten without monopolizing a second phone line, 50% of the households that don't already have cable TV service now request it be installed. Because this unanticipated demand immediately overloads the cable company's installation teams, their decision to offer the internet service creates a capacity constraint (maintenance teams). Depending on how big the population base is, this CCR may require quite some time for relief.

If a CCR does not emerge, the original product priority (by T alone) remains effective. If a CCR does emerge, a new product priority (using T/CU) must be established immediately, because it's probable that the previous rank-order of best products (based on T alone) will no longer be valid. If an internal constraint already exists, we need to know if the decision will cause it to shift to a different resource. If it *does not* shift to a different resource, the original product priority (using T/CU) remains effective. But if it *does* shift to a different resource, a new product priority (using T/CU) must be established, for the same reasons. If the original CCR remains where it has been, and no new one emerges, computing $\Delta T$ is relatively easy, and only a new product priority is required. Figure 13.7 shows a simple decision chart to illustrate this process.

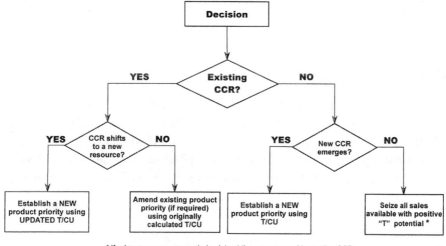

**Figure 13.7   The Impact of a Big Decision on the Product Priority Scheme**

If there is no CCR currently active, we can safely increase the load, assuming that the additional load generates additional T. We should be aware that at some point this increase may turn a non-constraint into a CCR. But as long as the emerging CCR was not fully loaded to begin with, this extra load does not force us to give up producing other products (other T generators). Once the emerging CCR is fully loaded (up to its required protective capacity), any additional orders beyond that level will require us to trade off other orders. A new T/CU priority scheme computation will be required.

## How to Determine $\Delta$OE and $\Delta$I

Now we have to determine the change in operating expense and investment. Most significant additional expenses come from buying additional capacity. Examples of this might be hiring more employees (OE), adding shifts (OE), using overtime (OE), or buying more equipment (I).

If capacity expansion proves to be necessary, the first places to consider are resources that are close to becoming constraints, or non-constraints that may become constraints if their capacity is not enhanced soon. Remember that subcontracting production work is usually done to satisfy specific customer obligations. As such, it should be considered a variable cost of throughput, not a fixed OE increase.*

## The TOC Decision Rule

In summary, remember that $\Delta$T − $\Delta$OE should be greater than zero. This rule is simpler to apply than any other, even when it may be difficult to assess $\Delta$T and $\Delta$OE. Also remember that the constraint, whether it's a CCR or a market constraint, limits the maximum T possible. Another way to look at it: T is only generated by the constraint, while the rest of the system generates OE — not T.

## Reference

1. Goldratt, Eliyahu, M., *The Haystack Syndrome, Sifting Information Out of the Data Ocean*, Croton-on-Hudson, NY, The North River Press, 1990.

---

* Subcontracting an overhead or support function is a different matter, however. Since overhead and support functions are considered fixed costs, subcontracting them should be classified as an operating expense.

# 14 Drum-Buffer-Rope (DBR) and Enterprise Resource Planning (ERP)

Now that we've examined S-DBR, a more simplified, easier-to-manage version of the original drum-buffer-rope, it's time to see how it fits with the latest development in information technology, Enterprise Resource Planning (ERP), and with concepts that bridge more than one system, such as supply chain management.

## Think "E," Manage "E": Management in the ERP Era

The new management buzzword these days seems to be "enterprise," meaning "whole business." This is not a new concept to those who have been preaching and practicing systems thinking, or the systems approach, for years. But the idea of managing completely integrated systems is new to some people. However, as companies recognize the importance of managing whole systems in an integrated way, rather than isolated departments or divisions, they begin searching for a way to grapple with the integration problem.

Given that we're in what has been called the "information age", it's not surprising that senior management grasps at information technology to solve the integration problem. But information is a two-edged sword. We can't make effective decisions without it, but our decision processes can stagnate with too much of it.

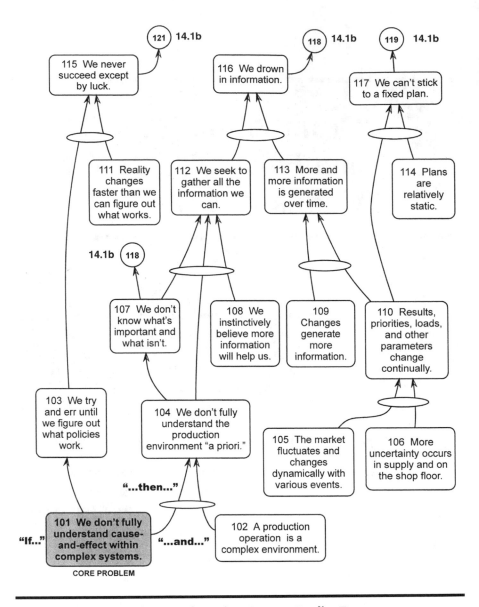

**Figure 14.1a    Generic Manufacturing Current Reality Tree**

Remember this current reality tree (Figure 14.1)? This is the tree you saw in the introduction to this book. It started with the core problem: (101) We don't fully understand cause-and-effect in complex systems. This eventually led to the two undesirable effects: Somehow we survive (barely), or We don't survive.

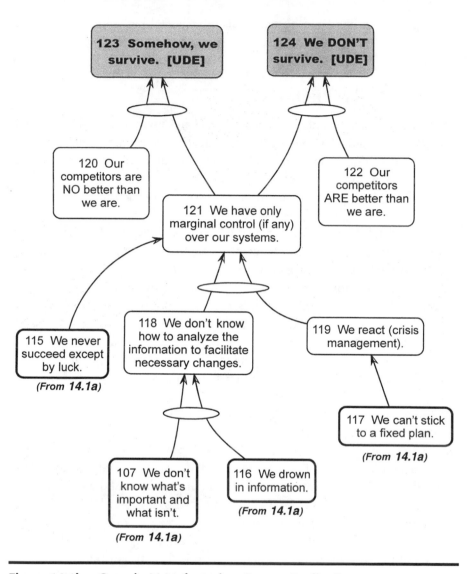

**Figure 14.1b   Generic Manufacturing Current Reality Tree**

But there's another contributing root cause in the middle of this tree that leads to indecision or wrong decisions: (108) We instinctively believe that more information will help us. This is a typical assumption most senior managers make — that more information will help — and it often leads to the false conclusion that technology is the solution. However, the reality is that information technology is only as good as the data that go into it (garbage in, garbage out), and a state-of-the-art information system is no substitute for intelligent, enlightened human decision makers! Let's consider the situation at SMPRO, Ltd.

## Case Study: SMPRO, Inc.

When Bob came back after 2 intensive weeks in Singapore, he was sure that the rest of the staff at SMPRO (Smart Protection Inc.), the company where he served as vice-president for marketing and sales, would applaud him. An order for $3 million was not a common occurrence. All of SMPRO sales during the past year totaled $28 million, and the forecast for the following year pointed — with cautious optimism — to $31 million. The agreement with Singapore's Security Department had not been included in the forecast, since nobody believed the company stood a real chance to win the contract.

SMPRO sells elaborate alarm systems, meant to protect sensitive buildings from the introduction of firearms, as well as from any kind of break-in. The company plans the general system. Some of the components are produced at the company's central plant, and the rest of the security system is manufactured by subcontractors.

Before the staff meeting Bob updated Ron, the SMPRO operations manager, on the new requirements introduced by Singapore, particularly the tight schedule for the delivery of the initial system.

Ron went pale. "There's not a chance in hell! The initial system consists of 60% of the final product. I don't have capacity to do that within 2 months. Have you gone crazy? You need to advise Singapore of that immediately! The engineering planning hasn't even been started, and it will take them at least 2 months to do that. Furthermore, I'm not sure we have all the components. When I tell you that the initial system can only be completed under pressure in 6 months, you'd better believe me."

Ann, the vice-president of finance, wasn't at all happy with the 4% discount that Bob had been forced to allow right before the contract was signed. "This whole contract is crazy. The important thing is selling, eh? And it doesn't matter that we lose money here?"

Those two reactions made it clear to Bob that the coming meeting would not be very pleasant. From the top of the world to the bottom of the sewer in about a minute and a half ....

The truth was, Ron's and Ann's reactions didn't take Bob completely by surprise. The same thing had happened in the Los Angeles contract, Bob recalled, but today everybody is happy about that sale, which had brought three additional sales in California. Why can't these people learn a lesson from that? Bob still hoped that John, president of SMPRO, would support him. John was the one who had suggested that Bob go to Singapore for 2 weeks to see if there was any chance of getting the contract, and then push it the best way he could.

His presentation during the meeting was received without interruption. Morty, vice-president of engineering, started reading the paperwork about the changes that Singapore wanted to introduce into the system. Ann sat quietly, but the cynical smile on her face looked threatening. Arthur, the logistics manager, sat next to Ron, and they exchanged glances. Bob finished his presentation.

**John:** "I understand the contract is signed, there is no way out of it. Am I right?"

That was not exactly the response Bob had expected.

**Bob:** (defensively) "You gave me complete authority to sign, and I did. I think it is a great sale."

**John:** "Yes, and now all we have to do is deliver the system. Let's start with the development issues. I understand there is a lot to be done in engineering."

**Ann:** "One minute — before we start talking about what to do, we need some financial background. This system requires a lot of work, and I don't have all the details, but Ron and Arthur said that we had extra capacity. When we bid for the contract, it was already clear that it wasn't such a big deal.

Now there's a new situation. Ten days ago another contract came in, and this changes the whole picture. What I want to make sure here is that our losses won't be significant. Please, gentlemen, no extra hours, no night shifts, and no emergency air deliveries of electronic cards. No subcontracting, which kills us with prices every time we need something urgent. The Singapore contract isn't specific about when we will be penalized for late delivery, so I suggest we take advantage of it and install as late as possible — the main thing is to do it as cheaply as possible."

**Bob:** (annoyed) "What?! We could lose our reputation entirely acting like this!"

**Ann:** "Show me a way to quantify reputation financially, and I'll be willing to talk about it. Until then, save as much money as possible on this contract."

**John:** "Okay, okay. Before we make any decisions about jeopardizing our reputation, let's see what problems we'll have in building the system on time in the first place."

**Morty**: "I can speak for engineering. I believe the plans alone will take 2 months. Things will be a little crowded during the next 2 weeks, but we'll be able to manage afterward."

**Ron**: "In order to meet the schedule, I should start producing right now. By the way, Ann, do you really think you have any idea of what's going on in production right now? The contract with Techno that we got last week doesn't have anything to do with this Singapore deal. This is a totally different production line. Don't mix up my jobs.

Anyhow, we're talking about a large system here, with many intermediate products and with enormous pressure on the testing. There is nothing we can do about it. It takes time. I can start some of it without engineering. There are several standard subsystems in the overall system, but in 2 or 3 weeks I'll need finalized plans. Otherwise we'll surely need night shifts if we don't want to be too late. And I still don't know anything about the purchasing requirements."

**John**: "Morty, what will happen if your people stop what they are doing now and work on the Singapore system? Will you be able to present Ron with some plans in 3 weeks?"

**Morty**: (angrily) "John, you do this all the time — you keep doing this to me! You can't treat development engineers as if they were machines. If I divert people from what they're doing now, it takes them several days to get into another system, and it takes much more time to go back to the first system again. It's a terrible mess. It lowers the morale of my people to zero.

And another thing — who says that what they're doing now is not urgent? Don't forget that Ron's production planning is based on a schedule I provide him. There's no way we can work without planning. Development resources are expensive, and they should be treated with respect, not moved around every time there's a new sale. Why can't we have overall planning that works properly? People would like to know what they're working on and when."

**Arthur**: "As far as purchasing is concerned, I can't tell you whether we have all the items or not. We'll have to run a detailed plan and then check, but I understand this won't happen for at least another week. At a quick glance, we probably have most of the elements. We ordered them for the project in Mexico, which was canceled. But I'm not sure we have everything.

Moreover, Morty's guys sometimes come up with demands for non-standard circuit cards, and then we have a big problem. I understand they have trouble getting into the purchasing system and checking whether the specific item exists at all in our catalog. If I don't have it in the catalog, it may take months to find a reliable supplier and make a purchase."

**John:** "You know what? It has become clear to me we really need an ERP system, where all the different information systems are linked together. That way Bob would have known that the initial system consists of 60% of the work. Ann would have known that there is extra capacity. Morty would have known about every circuit card, whether it existed in our catalog or not, and whether purchasing had it in stock. Ron and Arthur would, of course, have gained from the knowledge about marketing priorities, etc. The problem is that such a system costs hundreds of thousands of dollars at the very least. Is there any way to quantify the benefit such a system could bring to a company like ours?"

---

Let's examine the SMPRO situation. What seems to be the trouble with SMPRO? Is it the information system, or is it something else? In other words, without addressing another problem, would enhancing the information system add any real value? What managerial problems occurred?

What information system (IS) problems occurred? While not really the core problem, some information is missing. It would be nice to have more online information regarding the availability of material, but this is really just a nice-to-have feature. The missing information could be obtained if everybody recognized what's important and found the needed data. So what went wrong with the Singapore contract?

The overriding complaint is the time issue. Bob promised an early delivery without knowing whether engineering and production could make good on such a promise. Would a better information system have solved the problem? In reality, the information system can have value only after the managerial problem is solved.

## Case Study Discussion Questions

1. Is there a management/leadership problem on top of the information problem? If so, what's the nature of it?
2. Is there a problem in the SMPRO organizational culture? For discussion purposes, consider the definition of organizational culture to be

*The set of basic assumptions that are shared by the members of the orga-
nization, that are perceived as self evident and which dictate the values of
the members and guide their behavior.*[1]

## Problems Related to Information at SMPRO

There are clearly some information-related problems within SMPRO. For
one thing, Ann had no idea how much capacity was available, yet she asser-
tively demanded no overtime, additional shifts, or subcontracting.

Bob didn't know (and never did when negotiating the contract) how
much capacity is required to finish the initial system. He discounted the
production manager's warning about the total time needed to complete the
project. This job was basically customization of a common core system, yet
the sales manager was sent off to bid on a system without production knowing
the scope of the effort required to deliver it.

Ron, Morty, and Arthur didn't know whether all the materials were available.
This is really the most important missing information issue. Morty didn't know
what the overall system priorities were, because no master plan was available.
However, this is not really information issue — it's a managerial deficiency.

### SMPRO Management Problems

Each of these managers saw the problem from his or her own local perspective
only! Bob didn't seem to recognize that maybe there would be a problem in
delivering on time. Ann didn't care about capacity or reputation, just because
she couldn't evaluate them financially. Ron, Morty, and Arthur knew and
recognized the problems among them (these functions work closely together
in daily operations), but they completely ignored the marketing and finance
perspectives.

John didn't take control in a situation of confusion among his subordinates. Though it's clear that the various functions of the organization
(finance, engineering, production, sales) are not synchronized, John didn't
demonstrate firm leadership in solving the problem. He seemed to think that
an ERP system is the solution to all their problems.

Ann was not aware that the cost of a night shift should be compared with
the damage resulting from refraining from a night shift. She was ready to
recommend management action based on the cost just because the damage
is not measurable.

And Ron indicated that there may be a capacity shortage (a CCR?) in testing.

## ERP Implementation: Basic Assumptions

In the SMPRO case, John (the CEO) sees Enterprise Resource Planning (ERP) as the solution to the company's problems. He's not alone. A lot of companies are grasping at the same straw.

All companies engaged in adopting an ERP system are proceeding on the basis of three key assumptions:

1.  Integration and synchronization are good for the organization. More than that, they are necessary for superior performance. (It makes one wonder how we got along without them for so long!)
2.  There is a lot of resident knowledge within the company about how the new information system procedures and capabilities will work and how they support the overall business strategy. Management knows how the IS parameters and customization should be tuned to fully support the business strategy, and the technicians who do the actual work know what management is after, and they know how to force the ERP system to do what management wants.*
3.  Managers at the local level (departments, branches, sections, etc.) are aware of their need for integrating information, and are motivated to use it if they have access.

But are these assumptions valid?

## The Second ERP Assumption

Let's consider the second one. Internal capabilities of the ERP system and customization and parameter setting by the technical staff usually drive organizations toward new processes and procedures. Top management should be asking the following questions:

---

* In most cases ERP systems force changes in the processes from the way management would prefer that they be. Whether the changes are good or bad, and whether the ERP system can be manipulated to do what is good for the business, depends on critical analysis of both management and technical perspectives.

- Are new procedures for using the ERP completely aligned with the company's business strategy?
- If the strategy is to fully satisfy a customer's request for special customization, will the ERP system support that strategy?
- If the strategy is mass production of standard items, can the ERP system be tuned to do just that?
- Once enhanced, will the processes for using ERP really support market requirements (or are they targeted at efficient internal operations?)

One of the most devastating pitfalls in an ERP implementation by technicians (rather than by management) is focusing on the wrong strategic target (task efficiency, rather than mission effectiveness).

Does the actual process of using the ERP system allow for the growth of the business that corporate leadership envisions? Knowing what areas are supposed to grow is of utmost importance for an effective ERP implementation. Trying to provide all options to grow — to be all things to all people — may make the system cumbersome and choke its ability to grow in the areas that matter the most. Imposing too narrow a scope for growth will necessitate troublesome, radical changes in the near future.

Do local managers (and senior executives, for that matter) comprehend the cause-and-effect at work within their organizations sufficiently to know what the impact will be if key variables of the ERP system are changed? Suppose production batch size is cut from 240 to 120 — do all the local managers fully understand the impacts on the flow of materials to their own areas? Suppose MRP lead times are cut in half. Does the marketing manager know what impact this will have on his department?

Do people understand the impact of batch size, MRP lead times, assemble-to-order, and Just-in-Time purchasing policies on the bottom line of the organization? In most cases, the answer is "no."

These issues are related, yet most decision makers see only one immediate effect from such policies. Take batch size, for example. If batch sizes are reduced, total set-up time will increase, but manufacturing lead time will decrease. A lead time reduction may provide a favorable competitive edge, but only if sales really capitalizes on that capability by offering it to a customer. On the other hand, as set-up time increases, it ties up more capacity. In some cases, it can even cause a bottleneck to emerge. If the excess capacity on even one resource shrinks too much, manufacturing lead time will increase by much more than the time saved in reducing batch sizes. Moreover, reduced batch sizes have a collateral impact on purchasing departments, as inventory levels may be reduced, too.

But decision makers don't normally recognize these lateral effects. Usually, all they know is that increased batch sizes equates to reduced lead times, but higher cost-per-unit. They rarely appreciate the need to control the change, and they aren't truly aware of the longer-term effects on the bottom line — which is the real issue!

All of which begs the question, "What will ERP do to address these knowledge gaps?" The answer is "probably nothing." Information systems are not a substitute for an intimate understanding of the cause-and-effect within an interdependent system. They can heap astronomical amounts of data on decision makers, but the decision makers themselves must know how to separate out what's important from what's not. As Goldratt observed, real information is the answer to the question asked.[1] Everything else is merely data. Lacking an effective knowledge of cause-and-effect, which Deming referred to as *profound knowledge,*[2] management is like running in the dark — you may get where you're going, but you also may kill yourself. And an ERP system has the potential for creating more problems than it solves. Triumph is not inherent in the sword… it's in the swordsman.

## The Third ERP Assumption

Now let's test the third assumption. Do local managers (department heads, etc.) know enough to discern what information external to their own areas is useful or necessary for improving their decision making, so their decisions support what's best for the global system, not just their departments? Much of effective learning requires knowing what questions to ask.

The emphasis here is on understanding the cause-and-effect of something that resides in an area other than our own. The preceding (second) assumption emphasized understanding the ramifications of a decision or policy in *our own* area of the system.

In fact, can we safely assume that local managers are willing or motivated to act in the best interest of the global system, rather than for their own local benefit? What motivation is there for them to do so? Do the current performance measurements support good global decisions by local managers? Does the organizational culture value global thinkers?

Put yourself in the shoes of Bob, the vice president of marketing and sales for SMPRO, Inc. Suppose you know that operations will have a very difficult time in expediting the initial system, and the probability is high that it won't be in Singapore on time. Would that cause you to give up on the contract? Isn't it likely that the deciding factor for you is the nice bonus you're going to receive from the $7 million you added to sales revenues? After all, this is how you're measured, isn't it?

## Why ERP?

A variety of reasons are usually offered to justify adopting a major system like ERP. One is that the current information system is falling apart, usually meaning that it fails frequently, or it's unequal to the task of new, expanded data management requirements, or it's difficult to maintain (data accuracy, system reliability, recovery). Another rationale was that ERP systems were supposed to solve the Y2K problem, "…and we have to solve that problem anyway, so now's the time to upgrade to a bigger system." A third justification is speed, sophistication, and the latest advancement in technology. And finally, "old reliable" — everybody else is doing it!

But are there valid reasons to go to an ERP system? The real reasons for going to an ERP system should be

- It eliminates a devastating obstacle to improving the business.
- It provides a way for every part of the organization to see the entire business, or enterprise, not just part of it.
- It supports the notion of a new integrated management within the organization's culture.
- It can be used to improve exploitation of the system's contraint(s).
- It can be used to improve subordination of the rest of the system to the constraint(s).

In short, the effort to integrate is central to all new management approaches. ERP should be used to bring more business to the organization, thus having a significant effect on the bottom line.

## TOC Support in an ERP System

In order to be able to apply the theory of constraints, and in particular, in an organization using ERP, the ERP system should support exploitation of the constraint, wherever it may be. It should also support subordination of non-constraints and TOC control methods and techniques. And it should support TOC management accounting principles, specifically the use of throughput, inventory (or investment), and operating expense as discrete financial variables. And it should contribute to a new work culture that considers the organization as a whole system.

## Improving Subordination to the Market: Designing Key ERP Processes

Once the decision to proceed with an ERP system is made, the challenge for TOC practitioners is how to use ERP to the best advantage. In other words, how can it be used to achieve an operational advantage over competitors? Can we use it to react faster to the market? To offer additional products or services? To improve quality? To improve other factors that impact customer satisfaction?

If we can achieve these advantages with the help of an ERP system, how can we use that operational advantage to sell more? How can we realize higher prices for all products and/or services?

Remember that one of the basic assumptions of S-DBR is that market demand is always a system constraint. If this is a valid assumption (and we submit that it is), effective application of constraint management requires that we subordinate our internal operations to the needs of the market. So the central question we must answer is, "How do we configure the ERP system to support a managerial decision process that subordinates internal operations to the market?" If we're not prepared to answer that question, ERP will not live up to its potential.

## Customizing the ERP System: Critical Questions

Before we can make full use of an ERP system to support constraint management, ten key questions require answers.

1.  What is the current constraint to achieving significant operational advantage today?
2.  If information is not a factor in elevating the constraint, why do we need an ERP system? And even if it is instrumental in elevating the constraint, are all the other interdependent parts of the elevation strategy ready as well?

3. How can integrated information help maintain an operational advantage?
4. Where should the system constraint be after the improvements we intend to make? Where would it naturally go? Is this where we want it to be?
5. Are all the critical data elements required for operational processes well defined?
6. Are all management information requirements well defined? If not, what are those requirements?
7. Are the organization's decision-making processes clear and well supported by information? If not, what aspects need repair?
8. Are control processes well supported?
9. Does the information system contain data and processing that are not absolutely needed? If so, get rid of it! Where manufacturing management is concerned, there is no virtue in collecting and tracking information just because we have the capability to do so!
10. Is the new global system design well accepted and agreed upon by those who will be called upon to use it to maximum organizational benefit? Or has it just been imposed on the rank-and-file?

## Supply Chain Management

There has been much discussion recently in professional management circles about the concept of a supply chain, and the potential benefit in managing it. This is perhaps the ultimate in systems thinking.

The supply chain includes all processes from the basic materials to the end consumer. For example, the supply chain for that bag of potato chips you eat at home would include the farmer and all the activities he goes through to grow the potatoes; the wholesale distributor that acquires the farmer's potatoes and supplies them to food processing companies; the potato chip factory that slices, bakes, and bags the potatoes into 17 different flavors and shapes (regular and ruffled); the retail distributor who moves the chips from the factory to the point of purchase; and the retail store that sells you that bag of barbecued mesquite-flavored chips in time for the pro football double-header on Sunday.

This supply chain is composed of independent organizations of varying size and complexity. It's important to remember that while ERP is often touted as a supply-chain management tool, in reality it is an integrating system for just one link in the supply chain — in the potato chip example, that link is the potato chip factory.

An ERP system can only provide support to the interfaces with the links of the supply chain that immediately precede and follow. In the potato chip example, ERP support beyond the system boundaries of the factory is limited to the retail distribution purchasing manager and the manager in charge of the wholesale distributor's shipments.

The concept of supply chain management is based on the assumption that the whole chain can achieve more than the independent links alone can by acting as one system. This is a valid concept in theory. In fact, it's one of the three basic assumptions of the theory of constraints, and we apply it conscientiously *within* the boundaries of our system.

But achieving this improved performance by managing the entire supply chain is easier said than done. A "win–win" arrangement is required for all parties involved in the supply chain. Achieving this becomes extremely difficult when the chain is composed of independent organizations with different objectives. Each link in the chain tends to emphasize its own local efficiency. Imagine telling your raw material suppliers that they'll have to subordinate their profits (and dividends to their stockholders) in the interest of exploiting your market!

An effective supply chain is truly possible only if a global and objective ERP can be operated for the whole chain, and exploitation and subordination achieved across component organizations (all the links in the chain). Of course, for a single global, objective ERP system to be effective, policies that reinforce and enhance integration must drive management planning. There must be consensus support for such policies and trust among the links of the chain for the policies to work. Even with such a consensus, each link in the chain must fully *understand* the new rules of engagement, and the new management system configuration must be *perceived* as a "win–win" arrangement for everyone involved.

Let's say that you, within your own organization, have effectively exploited and subordinated to the market, but your suppliers haven't. Maybe they don't even understand the concepts of exploitation and subordination. Their failure to subordinate to your needs compromises, to some degree, your ability to subordinate to your market. So as long as any one component in the supply chain has difficulty exploiting and subordinating properly — or won't do it — how can anyone expect a whole supply chain to be managed effectively?

The conclusion here is simple. It may never be possible to effectively manage a whole supply chain. But once you have embarked on TOC/DBR, it is certainly in your best interest that both your customers and suppliers do the same.

## Supply Chain Management: An Example

For example, let's assume that you are operating on a TOC basis. You're applying DBR and exploiting market demand (i.e., your customer's needs). You're subordinating your internal operations to those customer needs. But your suppliers are not using TOC. They're maximizing their own internal efficiencies, sacrificing service to you, and creating a different constraint for you. In doing so, they're compromising your ability to exploit your market and compromising your ability to subordinate your operations to your customers' needs.

Suppose your supplier is only willing to accept orders for at least 1000 units of a certain material. Your supplier imposes this requirement because 1000 is a minimum batch representing one shift of work on a certain expensive work center, which is not a CCR for your supplier. For you, the 1000 units represent 6 months of sales of your end products that use that material. You're forced to hold a very large raw material inventory, just because your supplier is acting from a cost world mentality. Even worse, because of the supplier's large batches and high level of work-in-process, the lead time for such a minimum batch is 3 months — and even that time is not very reliable! Isn't it in your best interest to make your supplier aware that it is possible to make even more money by using DBR, and to be able to process many more smaller orders much faster?

In a situation like this, how effectively do you think your supply chain can ever be managed? The moral of this story is that managing a whole supply chain may be a pipe dream. The best you can probably hope for is to do your best to persuade the immediate upstream and downstream links in your supply chain to adopt a constraint management approach to business. But in the meantime, effectively manage your own constraints, on your own. If you can't optimize the meta-system, do the best you can to optimize your own system.

## Conclusion: Lessons Learned

This concludes *Manufacturing at Warp Speed*. To wrap up this book, let's review the major lessons of the last 14 chapters:

1. Companies live or die as integrated systems, not as a collection of isolated processes.
2. The performance of complex systems is limited by very few factors at any given time — maybe only one. This is the system constraint.
3. Third, striving to achieve local efficiencies inevitably suboptimizes or compromises the performance of the whole organization.
4. Constraints can be either external or internal. Within these major categories, they can be either:

   ■ A physical constraint: A resource (CCR) or material, or
   ■ A policy. Policy constraints may include

   Vendor/supplier: No reliable vendor (quality of service/product, or excessive delivery time).

   Financial: (Example: "We will not consider a new product introduction if it does not generate an internal rate-of-return greater than 20%.")

   Market: (Lead time, price, choice of products offered).

   Knowledge/competence.

   Knowledge: We don't know how to do something we need to do.

   Competence: Our people are not qualified to do something we need to have done.

5. Market demand is always a constraint — usually to future profitability, sometimes to current profitability.
6. Uncertainty and variability will undo the best efforts to balance a system.
7. The five focusing steps can be used:

   ■ Tactically, to manage today's constraint, and
   ■ Strategically, to manage tomorrow's constraint.

8. Throughput, inventory (or investment) and operating expense can bridge the gap between local decisions and the global measures of success.
9. No system can ever be loaded to its full capacity for long without eventually compromising system performance.

Now may be a good time to go back to the introduction and review our four expectations of what you should have realized from reading this book. Did this book meet those expectations for you? How about *your* expectations?

You have in your hands the tools to improve your organization. Whether you succeed or fail in applying what you've learned here depends on four related factors:

- Your understanding of the messages in this book
- Your motivation to see your system improve
- Your ability to influence change within your organization, and
- Your willingness to accept accountability for action.

Good luck!

# References

1. Goldratt, Eliyahu M., *The Haystack Syndrome: Sifting Information Out of the Data Ocean*, Croton-on-Hudson, NY, The North River Press, 1990, 6.
2. Deming, W. Edwards, *The New Economics for Industry, Government, and Education*, Cambridge, MA, MIT Center for Advanced Engineering Study, 1993.

# Appendix A: The Dice Game

T he Dice Game is intended to demonstrate the impact of variability, or what Goldratt has referred to as "statistical fluctuations," on dependent events. In any complex system, some components depend on others for their inputs. Since each component experiences variability in some form, the effects of variation are compounded in sequences of two or more components, or events. And variation, like "tolerance backlash," can accumulate over an extended sequence of events.

## The Situation

To demonstrate how variation can accumulate within a complex system, we're going to simulate a manufacturing operation using dice and poker chips (Figure A.1). As in any gambling casino, there is no chance or luck involved — only statistical probability.

There are six work centers in this manufacturing operation. Work centers are composed of one operator and one machine each, represented in this game by one person and one die. Work centers are arranged in a single sequential line.

In addition to the six work centers, there is a raw material inventory, composed of 100 poker chips. The color of the chips is immaterial to the game. As the game goes on, finished goods will accumulate at the output end of the process. For the purpose of the game, we'll assume that finished goods are sold (i.e., converted to throughput) as soon as they come off the assembly line. If there are more than six people participating in the game, others may be assigned as the raw material manager and the finished inventory manager.

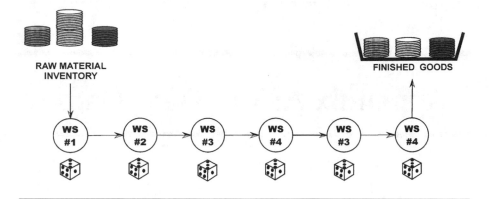

**Figure A.1   Dice Game Layout**

Between each work center there is small pile of chips that constitute work-in-process.

## Objective

The purpose of the Dice Game is threefold:

- To demonstrate the impact of variability on a complex system
- To understand the compounding effect of variability on a system composed of dependent events
- To appreciate the value of constraint management, particularly the first three of the five focusing steps, in successfully managing variability in an environment of dependent events

## The Poker Chip Production Process

Each work station has one six-sided die. These dice represent the machines. Each work station operator will roll his or her own die once per day. The value showing on the die after the roll represents that day's production output at that machine.

Between each machine will be a pile of work-in-process. This is partially finished material that was completed by the preceding step in the process the day before. Each iteration of the game will be comprised of 10 rolls of the dice, or 10 days. This is equivalent to 2 work weeks.

## The Challenge

Your job will be to manage the production process as conservatively as possible. To manage effectively and efficiently, you'll be trying to maximize net profit and return on investment. The formulas for net profit and return on investment are shown in Figure A.2. For the purposes of this game, we're going to disregard operating expense — we'll assume it's constant and has already been paid. This means that to manage effectively (maximize net profit), you'll have to maximize throughput. In order to manage efficiently, you'll have to minimize work-in-process. So your 10-day production objective is

$$\text{Net Profit = Throughput } - \text{ Operating Expense}$$

$$\text{NP = T} - \text{OE}$$

$$\frac{\text{Return on}}{\text{Investment}} = \frac{\text{Throughput} - \text{Operating Expense}}{\text{Inventory}}$$

$$\text{ROI } = \frac{\text{T} - \text{OE}}{\text{I}}$$

**Figure A.2    Net Profit and ROI Formulas**

- Produce as many finished good poker chips as you can, while you…
- Maintain as little work-in-process as you can

## Ground Rules

These are the rules you'll be required to follow. Pay close attention — everybody manages to screw up these procedures at least once!

- One roll of the dice represents 1 day's output — an 8-hour shift.
- Everybody must roll the dice AT EXACTLY THE SAME TIME — after all, you're ALL on the same 8-hour shift.

- The first production work station is what we call the gating operation. It draws material from the unlimited (more or less) supply of raw material controlled by the Raw Material Manager.
- All other work stations may draw work ONLY from the work-in-process pile immediately between them and the preceding work station.

  Each operator may only draw from what was passed on by the preceding station on the previous roll of the dice!!!

  Pay special attention to this — it's where most of the screw-ups occur. You MAY NOT WAIT for the preceding station to roll and move chips if your incoming WIP pile is less than you need to cover the day's roll!

- We'll assume that the process has already been up and running, and stabilized, meaning that some work-in-process is already in the system (from the preceding week).
- Establish the starting WIP level of four chips between each of the work stations. This number represents the average of all faces of a die (3.5), rounded up to the nearest whole number.

## Production Worksheet

No self-respecting manufacturing operation can survive very long without data! So that we can properly evaluate how we're doing, there's a production worksheet for each work center to fill out each day, with each roll of the dice (Figure A.3).

Notice that there are 10 numbered rows, one for each day of the exercise. The second column indicates the planned output for each day. Since the average of the 6 faces of the die is 3.5, we'll use that as a daily target. Each work center operator should enter "3.5" in each block of column 2.

The total of the daily averages will be 35 in 10 days. Enter "35" in the block labeled "2-week data." Put the same number in the block labeled "[7] Expected Shipments", at the bottom of the page. As each work center rolls its die for each day of the exercise:

- Record the value of the roll in column 3.
- Then record the number of chips actually moved to the next person's work-in-process pile

| [1]<br>ROLL<br>(Day) | [2]<br>Expected<br>Value | [3]<br>Actual<br>Roll | [4]<br>Pieces<br>Moved | [5]<br>Efficiency<br>[4] / [3] x 100 | [6]<br>Effectiveness<br>[4] / [2] x 100 |
|---|---|---|---|---|---|
| 1 | | | | | |
| 2 | | | | | |
| 3 | | | | | |
| 4 | | | | | |
| 5 | | | | | |
| 6 | | | | | |
| 7 | | | | | |
| 8 | | | | | |
| 9 | | | | | |
| 10 | | | | | |
| 2-Week<br>Total | | | | | |
| | (Total) | (Total) | (Total) | | |

| [7]<br>Expected<br>Shipments<br>(Objective) | [8]<br>Actual<br>Shipments | [9]<br>Shipments<br>Past Due | [10]<br>Work-in-<br>Process<br>Inventory |
|---|---|---|---|
| | | | |
| (Total from<br>Column 2) | (Total from<br>Column 4) | [8] minus [7] | (Total between<br>all stations) |

**Figure A.3   Production Worksheet**

- For now, disregard the last two columns — we'll calculate those figures after the exercise

When all 10 days are over, total up the first 3 columns, and fill out blocks 8, 9, and 10.

# Instructions

1. Synchronize each roll of the dice — everybody should roll at the same time.
2. Record the value for each roll of the dice in column 3.
3. Count out the pieces to be moved. This number should equal the value rolled, if there are that many available in your WIP pile. If there are not enough to equal the value rolled on the die, count all that are available.
4. Move the counted chips to the next person's WIP pile. Everybody should move their counted chips at exactly the same time.
5. Record the number you actually moved in column 4.
6. When everyone has done this and is ready to go on, repeat this process until the 10th day (roll) is completed.

> *Remember:* People at work stations 2 through 6 may *not* use chips passed to them on the same roll (day) that they are currently working. You may only pass on chips *completed the preceding day (roll of the dice),* even if that means they can't move as many as the number they rolled!

# Performance Reporting

After the 10th roll, participants should complete the Production Worksheet and calculate the "Efficiency" and "Effectiveness" (columns 5 and 6).

The game coordinator then asks for a report on their efficiencies and "browbeats" a little bit those whose efficiencies are less than 90%. Tell them they'll have to do better than that, or they won't get bonuses at the end of the year.

The game coordinator points out that the efficiency and effectiveness figures are comparable to those measured in the real world, even if the values aren't the same.

The game coordinator fills out a transparency version of the "Team Totals" chart (Figure A.4). In the "PLAN" column, enter:

- "35" for "Output"
- "20" for "WIP"

Poll each team for their results, and enter the figures in the "Actual" column. Analyze the data:

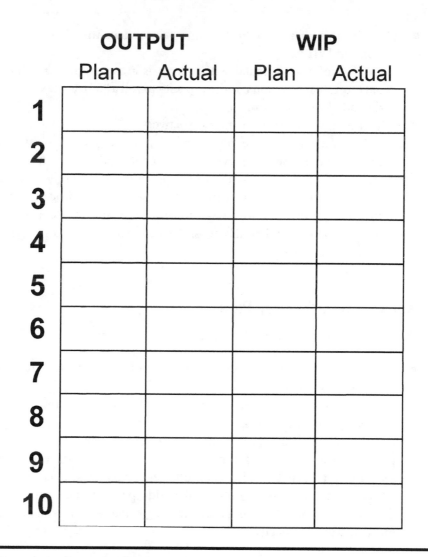

| | OUTPUT | | WIP | |
|---|---|---|---|---|
| | Plan | Actual | Plan | Actual |
| 1 | | | | |
| 2 | | | | |
| 3 | | | | |
| 4 | | | | |
| 5 | | | | |
| 6 | | | | |
| 7 | | | | |
| 8 | | | | |
| 9 | | | | |
| 10 | | | | |

**Figure A.4   Team Totals**

- How many made the objective (35)?
   [ANS: None, though some may come close]
- How many ended up with more WIP in the system than they started with?
   [ANS: Most, if not all]
- Was there a bottleneck in your system? Where was it?
   [ANS: Normal response is for people to point to the work center where the most chips have accumulated]

- If we did this again, would the same person have the biggest pile of unfinished WIP?

  [ANS: No. No particular work center is a constraint. The line is balanced (each person has the capacity to roll a "6"). Only variation degraded that performance.]

- Why didn't everyone meet their objective?

  [ANS: Variation in the rolling of each die degraded individual performance. Because every work center after the first one depended on the production of the previous work center, individual variation accumulated in the final step of the process. Thus, the average of the entire six-step process is always less than the average of the individual steps. This is why nobody reached 35 (without cheating!).]

## Lessons Learned (First Pass)

The lessons to be learned from this iteration of the game:

- The mean of a series of dependent events will always be less than the mean of each event.
- In a series of dependent events, variation of each step accumulates at the last step of the process.
- Because all the work centers had equivalent (balanced) capacities, performance deteriorated from the average value of the die (3.5). Had the line not been balanced (i.e., different capacities at each work center, as usually happens in the real world), performance would have deteriorated from the average of the least-capable work center (i.e., most restricted capacity).

This is why the system can't produce any more than the weakest link in the chain of dependent events, adjusted downward for variation.

## Directions for the Second Pass

Now run the production process for another 10 days, but make the following changes:

- Collect the standard dice from each work station

- Return all poker chips to the raw material inventory
- Distribute six unbalanced dice

*NOTE: Unbalanced dice are available from most game stores. They come in tubes of six dice each. The dice vary in the numbers of their sides. Most sets have dice with 4, 6, 8, 10, 12, and 20 sides. On the 10-sided die, a zero is interpreted as "10." On the 10-, 12-, and 20-sided dice, 9s and 6s are usually differentiated with a small dot in the normal decimal point position. The tetrahedron die is read a little differently. Each exposed face shows the same number closest to the surface of the table. This is true no matter which side is down. When you read your die value after each roll, read that number closest to the tabletop.*

- Place the 20-sided die at work station #1
- Place the 4-sided die (tetrahedron) at either work station 3 or 4
- Place the 12-sided die at work station #6
- Distribute the rest of the dice randomly to the remaining positions

## Ground Rules (Second Pass)

This time there's an easily identified constraint. It's the tetrahedron die, in position 3 or 4. The objective is still the same: Maximize throughput, and minimize WIP.

The new production objective, however, will be the average of the constraint's performance range: 2.5 per day. The new starting level for WIP will be 3 between each workstation. Work center operators may discuss strategy among themselves for 5 minutes before starting the game. They are free to challenge the way production was run in the past (the first pass). Operators may change ANY policy or rule EXCEPT:

- They MAY NOT move machines (sequence of dice)
- They MAY NOT change the STARTING WIP (neither its quantity nor its location)
- They MAY NOT add shifts (i.e., roll any die more than once per day)

Operators should make a note of the policies they change, and be ready to explain what they did and why after this run. Be sure they fill out their Production Worksheets as on the first pass.

## *Performance Reporting*

After the 10th roll, direct participants to complete the Production Worksheet, as before. They may disregard "Efficiency" and "Effectiveness" (columns 5 and 6). That point has already been made.

The game coordinator fills out a transparency version of the "Team Totals" chart (Figure A.4). Enter in the "PLAN" column:

- "25" for "Output"
- "15" for "WIP"

The game coordinator polls each team for their results, and enter the figures in the "Actual" column. Analyze the data:

- How many made the objective (25)?
   [ANS: None, though some may come close. REASON: variation (same as the first pass).]
- How many ended up with more WIP in the system than they started with?
   [ANS: Some, maybe, but most will be at, near, or below the starting value.]
- What policies did you change to manage better? What happened as a result of those changes?
   [ANS: Most will have limited material release to the rate at which the constraint (tetrahedron die) performed. This is equivalent to tying a "rope" to the "drum" (tetrahedron).]
- Was there ever a time when the bottleneck was starved for work?
   [ANS: Most, if not all, will have noticed that the tetrahedron die was starved at least once, especially early in the game, meaning it rolled a value higher than the number of WIP chips available to move. Some may have anticipated this problem and allowed a buffer to accumulate in front of the tetrahedron die.]

## *Lessons Learned (Second Pass)*

- The system is more predictable when a definable constraint is identified and managed.

- There are fewer things to keep your eye on when managing by constraints, and you know where to look at all times.
- t's not possible to operate smoothly (less WIP, higher on-time delivery) and still be efficient everywhere in the system.
- What they've done so far is to:

  IDENTIFY the constraint (the tetrahedron)
  EXPLOIT the constraint (ensure it's not starved)
  SUBORDINATE non-constraints (not use them when not needed to keep the constraint from starvation)

- No more money (I, OE) was spent. All that was done was to change the policies used to guide our operations.

# Third Pass (Optional)

Once the constraint has been identified, exploited, and everything else has been subordinated, no more improvement in throughput is likely without spending more money. The only other way to increase throughput is to ELEVATE, which means to expand capacity. This inevitably means an increase in operating expense (overtime, additional shifts), or investment (capital equipment, facilities).

## *Ground Rules (Third Pass)*

The rules will be exactly the same as the second run, with one exception: Work centers will be allowed to ELEVATE. In this case, elevation will be limited to adding shifts, since there are no more dice to distribute.

The production team may add shifts anywhere in the system at any time. However, as in the real world, these additional shifts will cost more money (OE). Each work center must keep track of how many extra shifts it runs. At the end of the third pass, deduct ONE CHIP from finished stock for each extra shift performed at any location (not just the constraint) before the output is totaled. This will constitute the added cost of the extra shifts.

Work centers may take a few minutes to discuss elevation tactics, then proceed with the final run. Keep track of data on the Production Worksheets the same way, noting extra dice rolls (additional shifts). Be sure to maintain synchronization of rolls, or the passing of dice will break down.

## Performance Reporting

After the 10th roll, work centers should complete the Production Worksheet. The game coordinator fills out a transparency version of the "Team Totals" slide. Enter in the "PLAN" column:

- "25" for "Output"
- "15" for "WIP"

Ensure that any chip deductions from finished goods have been made for any added shifts. The game coordinator then polls each team for its results and enters the figures in the "Actual" column. Analyze the data:

- How many made the objective (25)?
  [ANS: Most, because the added shift option allowed them to make up for variation. Some will exceed the objective.]
- How many ended up with more WIP in the system than they started with?
  [ANS: Most should be at or near the starting value. Some may be slightly above.]
- Did anyone notice anything different about this run?
  [ANS: The constraint should have shifted from the tetrahedron (if shifts were added there) to the 6-sided die.]
- Was there ever a time the bottleneck was starved for work?
  [ANS: Again, sometimes, maybe, at the beginning. Very quickly, however, they learn to protect the tetrahedron with WIP. But after they add shifts there, they may forget to increase the buffer size, or not increase it enough.]
- What policies were changed to manage better? What happened as a result of those changes?
  [ANS: Adding shifts at the tetrahedron required a larger buffer of WIP in front of it to prevent starvation. When the constraint shifted to the 6-sided die, a buffer is now required in front of that die to prevent its starvation. The buffer in front of the tetrahedron can be disregarded (as long as the second shift remains in effect there), and the release of materials can be higher at the gating operation to compensate. The WIP should be allowed to accumulate in front of the 6-sided die until the desired buffer level is reached.]

# Lessons Learned - Summary

What can we conclude from the dice game?

- First, the system optimum is not the sum of the local optima (efficiencies). There's no way to make each work station fully efficient anyway.
- Variation and dependency affect all systems.
- If we try to balance a manufacturing process (same capacity everywhere), it isn't going to remain balanced for very long, because of variation and dependency.
- Measuring and managing complex systems by local efficiencies are not only a waste of time, but actually can hurt the system's overall effectiveness.
- Knowing where the system constraint lies and exploiting it gives us greater control over the system, with less confusion.
- Subordinating the non-constraints to the exploitation of the constraint maximizes system performance without additional investment or operating expense. In other words, effective solutions to constraint, variation, and dependency problems need not cost a lot of money.
- Success depends on being able to differentiate between the critical few and the trivial many.
- And, perhaps most important of all, any change you make to the capacity of your system has significant potential to move the constraint.

# Appendix B: The Management Interactive Case Study Simulator (MICSS)

Concepts aren't very useful unless we can apply them. Especially when we're learning new concepts, trying to apply them in a real-world environment carries risks with it. One risk is that the real-world environment has many variables, some of them uncontrollable. In some cases variation in these factors, and even the uncertainty of the external environment, can confound results. Usually this is temporary, but it can be enough to compromise the learning experience for new concepts. Another risk is the impact of failure. Trying new concepts learned in the classroom on a real system could result in system failures due to inexperience, and a real manufacturing system may not be able to tolerate learning failures very well.

Novice diamond cutters don't practice their very first cuts on real diamonds. They try to perfect their skills on stones that will split like diamonds but don't have much value, so that failures during the learning process won't impose "high levels of regret" on the diamond merchant. Similarly, we're going to afford readers the opportunity to try out these new concepts in the relatively safe environment of a simulation. So have a ball — try different things and don't worry about the outcome. With this simulation, you can always reset and start over.

The software that accompanies this text is called the Management Interactive Case Study Simulator (MICSS), or "mikes." This simulation software walks a fine line between approximating the complexity of the real world and being simple enough so that users can master it relatively quickly. The net result for the first-time user is that it seems somewhat overwhelming. And that's not bad, because the real world sometimes overloads the senses, too! So, to that extent the MICSS is a reasonably accurate representation of reality on which to learn.

## A "Walking Tour" Through the MICSS

This appendix is intended to provide readers with a reasonable overview of MICSS and how it functions. A more detailed guided tutorial, with screen views in color, is available on the compact disk that accompanies this book. Let's take a look at the MICSS. If you haven't loaded it onto your computer, please do so now. The software runs on any IBM-compatible personal computer with a color display monitor and a pointing–tracking device (mouse or touch pad).

When you activate the *micss.exe* file (or double-click on the MICSS icon), the first screen that opens has an information box on it. Click the mouse cursor on the "OK" button in the lower right corner. An "Open Session" box appears with a selection of files displayed. For this navigational tour of the MICSS, double-click on the file labeled *adv200.mcb*. This opens the simulation to an information page labeled "Marketing View" (Figure B.1), and we're ready to start the tour.

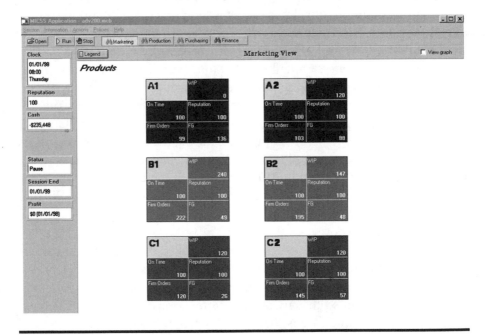

**Figure B.1    Marketing View**

## Functional Views

The MICSS might be considered an Enterprise Resource Planning (ERP) software in microcosm. It certainly isn't as complex as the big commercial ERP packages, but it does have similar functions. Like "big ERP," MICSS has interconnected modules that integrate four of the many functions that a company needs to operate. These functions are Marketing, Production, Purchasing, and Finance.

### View Buttons

As you look at the task bar near the top of the screen, you can see four buttons with these same names:

Marketing View
Production View
Purchasing View
Finance View

As you click on each of these buttons in turn, you'll see that the workspace display changes. We'll examine each of these views in detail in a moment, but for now, please reset the display to the Marketing View.

### Status Band

Notice that the title "Marketing View" appears in the band just above the workspace. Other indications also appear in this area, too. Right now, you can see a button that says "Legend" and a status box labeled "View graph." Other status indicators (invisible for now) will periodically appear in this area as the simulation runs.

### Menu Bar

Just above the view buttons is a Menu Bar. The Menu Bar has selections entitled "Session," "Information," "Actions," "Policies," and "Help." All of these menu entries have pull-down menus associated with them. The first and last buttons on this bar — "Session" and "Help" — contain the same pull-down menus, regardless of which functional view you select. However, the contents of the pull-down menus for the other three buttons

— "Information," "Actions," and "Policies" — change depending on which view you select. We'll examine some of these pull-down menus in more detail, too, in a moment, and we'll leave the rest for you to explore on your own.

## Simulation Status

Along the left side of the screen is a vertical status bar with several windows labeled:

Clock. Tells you what date/hour/day the simulation is on

Reputation. Shows the on-time delivery record, totaled for all products for the past 6-month period (adjusts each month)

Cash. Indicates how much cash is on hand in the company's bank account (more on this later)

Status. Tells whether the simulation is currently running, paused, or ended

Session End. Shows the date on which the current simulation scenario will terminate

Profit. Show current profit status for the year, as of the beginning of the current month

The information in these windows always remains visible, no matter what view you select. The values in these windows are updated in simulator time as they change.

## Marketing View

Let's look at the Marketing View a little more closely. In the workspace, you can see six boxes subdivided into six blocks each. All of these boxes contain similar information. Each box represents one of the six products the ADV200 company makes. The products are labeled "A1" through "C2." Beside each product name is a block labeled "WIP," which shows the number of units of that product currently being built on the production floor.

In the next row are two delivery status blocks. The one marked "On Time" indicates the percentage of orders for this product that have been shipped on time so far this month. The simulation always assumes 100% on-time delivery, until a delivery is missed, at which time the percentage is adjusted downward. The "Reputation" block shows a 6-month rolling total for each product. As each month passes, the previous month is added to the total and the oldest month is dropped out of the computation.

In the bottom row of each box we see "Firm Orders" and "FG." "Firm Orders" represents the number of units the company is obligated to deliver to a customer to fill a firm order. This figure changes continually as the simulation runs, decreasing as finished products are delivered and increasing as new orders come in. "FG" is the number of finished goods in inventory that can be immediately applied toward the firm orders. Notice, for example, that product B1 has firm orders for 222 units. There are only 49 units in finished goods to apply against these requirements, which is why there are 240 in some stage of production ("WIP"). When those 240 are completed, 173 will be added to the 49 in finished goods and shipped to meet the market demand for 222. The remaining 67 completed B1s will go into finished inventory.

## Marketing Information

On the menu bar in the Marketing View, click on "Information." A pull-down menu will appear (Figure B.2). This pull-down menu has 10 entries:

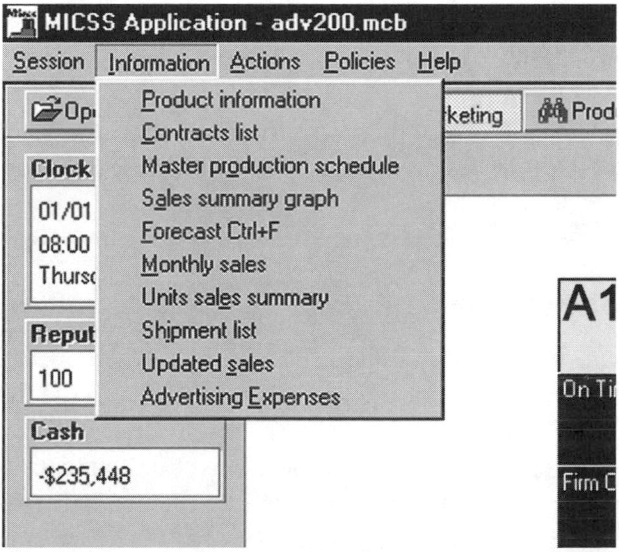

**Figure B.2    Marketing View | Information**

*Production information.* Shows basic information for each of the six products.

*Contracts list.* No long-term contracts in this particular scenario, but if there were, the recurring delivery schedules would appear here.

*Master production schedule.* This is a duplicate of the same entry in the Production View. We'll wait until then to examine it.

*Sales summary graph.* Shows the sales curve for last year. More on this below.

*Forecast Ctrl+F.* Besides the current production/order status, this feature shows how many units of each product are expected to be sold for the future time period you select, up to 12 months. (When using this feature, keep in mind that forecasts are best guesses, and they are considerably less accurate the further into the future they are projected.

*Monthly sales.* Shows the units and dollar value of sales for each product for the preceding 2 months. Updates monthly.

*Units sales summary.* Shows the average number of units sold each month for the preceding year.

*Shipment list.* Indicates what firm orders (and units of product associated with each) must be shipped, and their required shipping dates. Since this plant builds only to order, only firm orders are shown.

*Updated sales.* A more detailed picture of the current year's and month's activity. If you stop the simulation in mid-month and look at this window, it will give you up-to-the-minute status.

You can select each one of these in turn, click on it, and see the information provided. For now, let's look at just one feature: the *Sales summary graph* (Figure B3).

## Sales Summary Graph

Notice that sales are valued in dollars, not in units. When opened, this graph reflects total sales revenues for the past year. You can also use the small pull-down menu in this graph to break down the revenue trend by each individual product. Notice that when you do so, the Y-axis scale changes. Some of these products are subject to wide swings in market demand. Two of them (the "C" products) appear to have a seasonal peak between June and September. Remember, this is historical data for the preceding year. It promises nothing about *this* year.

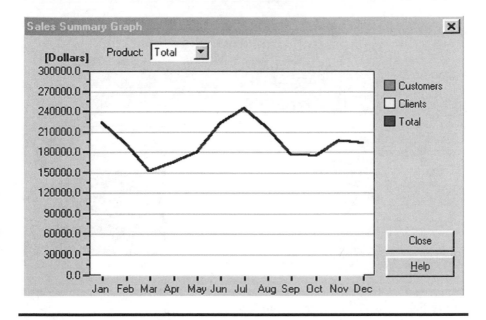

**Figure B.3    Marketing View | Information | Sales Summary Graph**

Close the *Sales summary graph* and select the menu button labeled "Policies" (Figure B.4). Then, in the pull-down menu, click on "Product Parameters." The window shown in Figure B.5 appears.

### Product Parameters

This window indicates the quoted lead time (QLT) for an order of each product and the price-per-unit. As you can see, you will have the latitude to change these values. And the market will respond *inversely* to your changes! If you increase QLT or price, you can count on a decrease in orders for your products. If you decrease them, you can expect an increase in orders. The sensitivity of the market to changes in these parameters is not certain (at least it won't be obvious to you without some trial and error).

The QLTs are all in work days. There are 5 days to a work week, so the 35 days shown here represent 7 calendar weeks. Note that the lead times for products C1 and C2 are only 30 days. ADV200's managers had to promise shorter delivery times to match the competition. Prices are all in dollars.

Safety stock, indicated in units of product, allows marketing people to specify the number of finished products, above and beyond firm customer requirements, that should be maintained in finished goods inventory. Safety

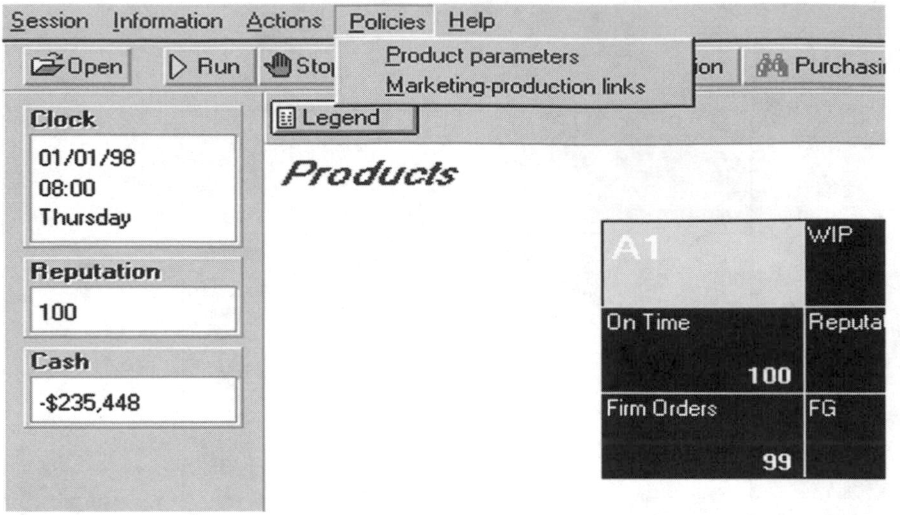

**Figure B.4**    Marketing View | Policies

**Edit Product Parameters**

| | Quoted Lead Time | Price | Safety Stock | Red Line Time |
|---|---|---|---|---|
| A1 | 35 | 350 | 0 | 0 |
| A2 | 35 | 400 | 0 | 0 |
| B1 | 35 | 275 | 0 | 0 |
| B2 | 35 | 325 | 0 | 0 |
| C1 | 30 | 350 | 0 | 0 |
| C2 | 30 | 400 | 0 | 0 |

OK    Cancel    Help

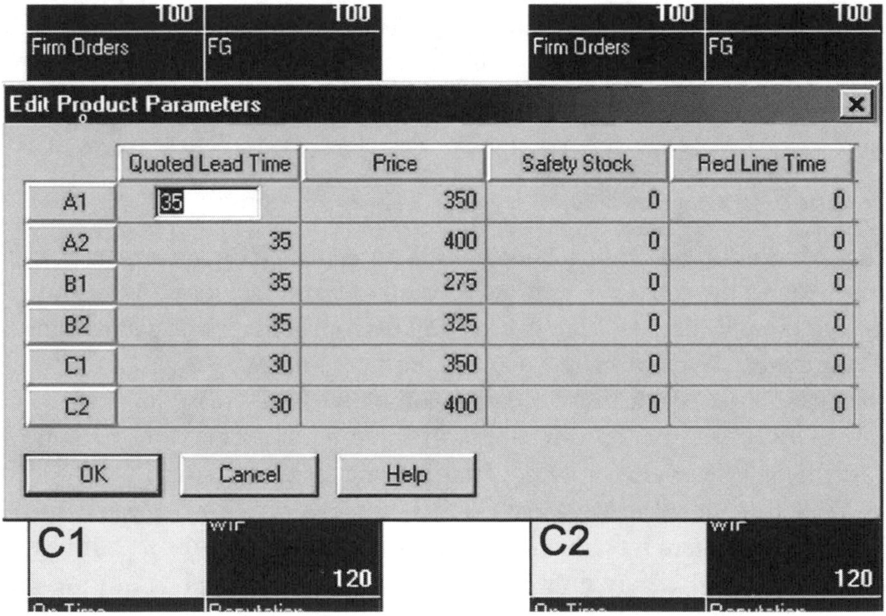

**Figure B.5**    Marketing View | Policies | Product Parameters

stock protects the plant from delays on the shop floor, since these units may be shipped in place of work that is still on the manufacturing floor. Red-line time, indicated in work days, is a warning mechanism that colors the product identifier in red when an order is within that number of days of the required shipping date, but not enough finished goods exist yet to fill the order completely. Neither of these functions is currently used in this scenario.

## Help

Before we go on to the next view, select the "Help" button on the Menu Bar and click on it. Then click on "Contents." The Help menu (Figure B.6) appears. You may explore the "Help" contents at your leisure. However, it's worth noting that as you go through the simulation, you can pause at any time, select the "Help" button in a particular window and display more detailed information on that window. Try this by activating (in the Marketing View) "Policies," then "Product parameters." Then press the "Help" button on that window.

## Production View

Now select and click on the "Production" button. The Production View appears (Figure B.7). What you see before you is a physical layout of the production floor. Each of the simulation's colored rectangles* represents a work center. Some work centers may have only one machine and operator. Other work centers may have two or more. In this scenario the work centers named "GT" (for gating operation) and "PK" (for packaging) each have two machines. All the rest have just one each. Each of the six products passes through most of these machines during manufacturing. Some products use them all.

Between the gating operation and the packaging operation, there are four machines (MA, MB, MC, and MD) and an assembly operation (AS). Each of the machines in the various work centers can provide current (changing as the simulation progresses) status on its activity. Let's take a closer look at MA, for example.

---

\* Refer to the simulation software to see the actual colors.

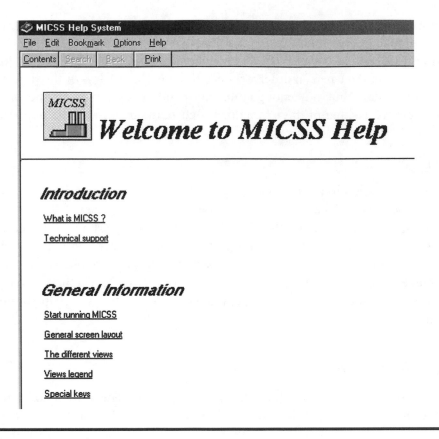

**Figure B.6    Help Menu**

## *Machine MA*

In the band at the top of the MA box, we see the machine name (MA), the words "Save Set-ups," and "Su: 120." "Save Set-ups" refers to the operating policy of that machine, which will be discussed in more detail in a moment. "Su: 120" indicates that this machine requires 120 minutes to change Set-ups between different products.

The block labeled "Status" indicated whether the machine is operating or not, and if not, why not. Possible indications here are "Idle," "Prod." (producing), and "Break" (breakdown). When a machine is broken down, the information system automatically notifies the maintenance department, which dispatches a repair team to fix it. You, as the simulator operator, don't need to worry about directing repair.

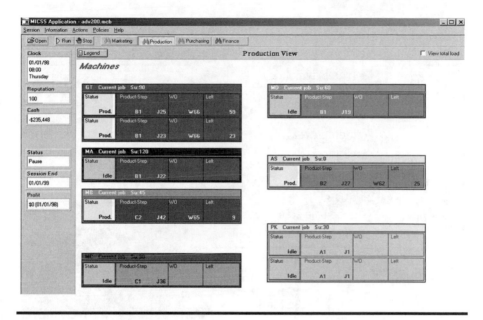

**Figure B.7    Production View**

The "Product-Step" block shows on which product that particular machine is currently set up to work. MA is currently setup to produce B1, but it's idle, meaning that there is no work-in-progress currently waiting to be done. If a work order for A2 arrived at MA, the machine status would change from "Idle" to "Setup" for 2 hours before the status would change to "Prod." for A2. "Step" indicates the designated task a machine is currently performing on the product. Since each of these are multifunctional machines, they are capable of doing more than one task (e.g., grinding and de-burring).

"WO" indicates the work order number on which a machine is currently working. As we look at MA, it's not working on any work order at the moment. However, you can see that both GT machines, the immediately preceding operation, are producing for Work Order #66.

"Left" indicates how many units of a particular work order remain to be done on that particular machine. MB, for example, shows 9 units of C2 left to do before WO #65 is completed at that work center.

## Production Information

Let's look at the "Information" pull-down menu for the Production View (Figure B.8). Notice that the contents are different from the Information menu in the Marketing View. There are nine selections on this menu:

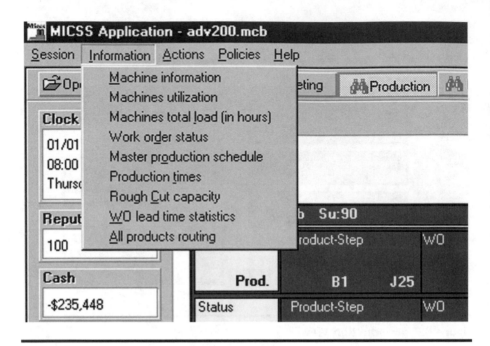

**Figure B.8    Production View | Information**

*Machine information* - This window shows, for each product, what tasks it performs for that product and how long each task takes per part. It also indicates two key operating policies, which will be discussed later.

*Machines utilization* - Shows the percentage of work time that each machine spent in various conditions for the preceding 2 calendar months (Figure B.9). This is a 2-month rolling window. As you can see, any machine can be actively producing ("Prod."), in set-up, broken ("Break"), or idle. Notice that depending on market demand changes, the profile for each machine can change significantly from month to month.

*Machines total load (in hours)* - This window gives two interesting bits of information. "Time to finish existing WO" is another way of saying how many hours of work that machine is obligated to do on all work orders currently in the system between now and the quoted lead time (since these are all firm orders). "Time to finish available work" indicates how long it should take to finish all the committed work that is actually queued at the machine. For example, Machine C has 46 hours and 30 minutes of its time committed to producing products over the next 6 to 7 weeks, but only 20 hours worth of that work is currently waiting at MC to be done.

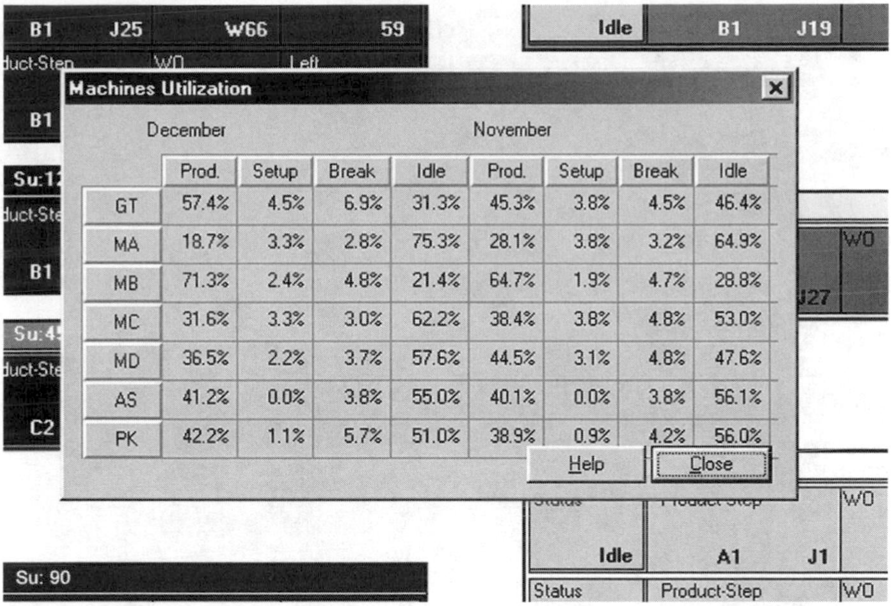

| B1 | J25 | W66 | | 59 | | Idle | B1 | J19 |

duct-Step WO Left

**Machines Utilization** ☒

|  | December | | | | November | | | |
|---|---|---|---|---|---|---|---|---|
|  | Prod. | Setup | Break | Idle | Prod. | Setup | Break | Idle |
| GT | 57.4% | 4.5% | 6.9% | 31.3% | 45.3% | 3.8% | 4.5% | 46.4% |
| MA | 18.7% | 3.3% | 2.8% | 75.3% | 28.1% | 3.8% | 3.2% | 64.9% |
| MB | 71.3% | 2.4% | 4.8% | 21.4% | 64.7% | 1.9% | 4.7% | 28.8% |
| MC | 31.6% | 3.3% | 3.0% | 62.2% | 38.4% | 3.8% | 4.8% | 53.0% |
| MD | 36.5% | 2.2% | 3.7% | 57.6% | 44.5% | 3.1% | 4.8% | 47.6% |
| AS | 41.2% | 0.0% | 3.8% | 55.0% | 40.1% | 0.0% | 3.8% | 56.1% |
| PK | 42.2% | 1.1% | 5.7% | 51.0% | 38.9% | 0.9% | 4.2% | 56.0% |

Help    Close

Idle    A1    J1

Status    Product-Step    WO

Su: 90

**Figure B.9    Production View | Information | Machines Utilization**

*Work order status* - This window shows the flow of work-in-process through the manufacturing floor, by work order and product (Figure B.10). This is not a physical layout. Rather, it's the logical flow. Currently, this window shows the flow for Work Order #62, which is comprised of product B2. Notice that one work center, AS, is a different color from all the rest (fuchsia, rather than yellow, but you must be looking at the computer screen to see colors). This indicates that WO #62 is located at this work center alone. The four small numbered boxes at each corner of the work center provide even more detailed information about the production status. The number at the upper left corner denotes the number of units yet to be processed. The lower left number shows how many units can be processed with the current inventory queued at the machine. The lower right number shows the units completed. The top right number isn't used at this time. Use the "Help" button to find out what these numbers represent.

*Master production schedule* - This window shows the entire master production schedule for all known orders (Figure B.11). It can be sorted in a variety of ways. By highlighting a particular work order and clicking on the "Show WO" button, a hyperlink to the *Work order status* for that work order is automatically activated. Any work order can be quickly located on the production floor.

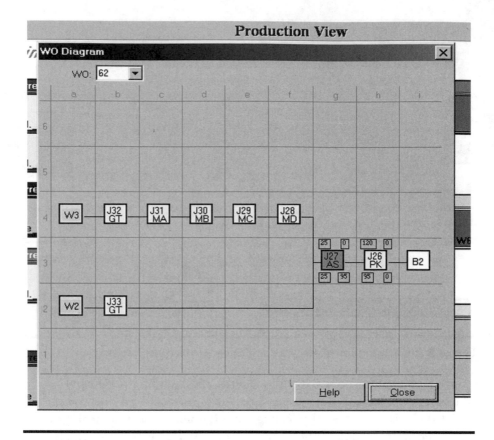

**Figure B.10    Production View | Information | Work Order Status**

*Production times* - Shows the total pure processing time in minutes for each product.

*Rough Cut capacity* - Shows the number of units of each product expected to be produced during a future time window, which the simulation operator can select. Also, the predicted activity profiles of each work center are also indicated for the same period of time. These are estimates, based on historical trends.

*WO lead time statistics* - Shows the average time from release of an order into production until completion of the finished order. In other words, on average, it takes 163 hours for a unit of A1 to make its way from the material release point to the shipping dock. Standard deviations for these averages are also provided for each product.

*All products routing* - This window provides logical routing for all products, but the simulation operator must scroll up and down to see them all (Figure B.12). Each product flow diagram shows the raw materials

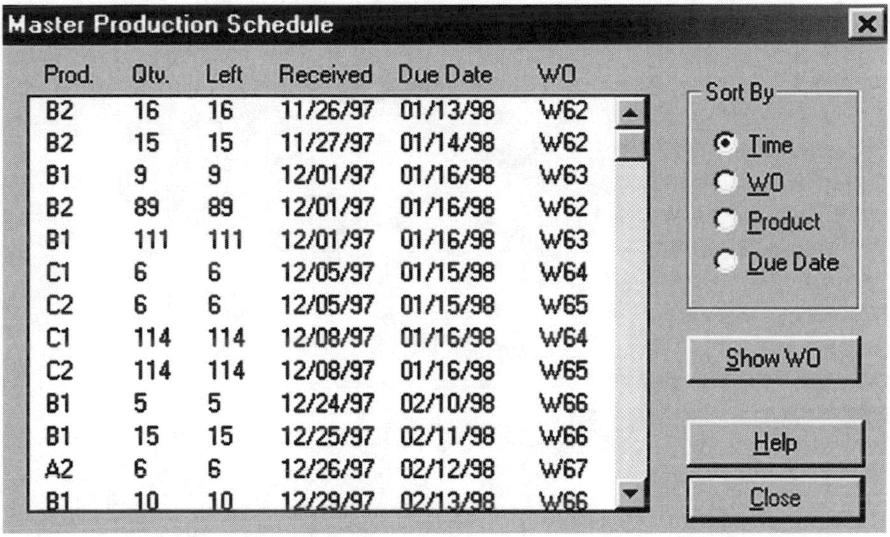

| Prod. | Qtv. | Left | Received | Due Date | WO |
|-------|------|------|----------|----------|-----|
| B2 | 16 | 16 | 11/26/97 | 01/13/98 | W62 |
| B2 | 15 | 15 | 11/27/97 | 01/14/98 | W62 |
| B1 | 9 | 9 | 12/01/97 | 01/16/98 | W63 |
| B2 | 89 | 89 | 12/01/97 | 01/16/98 | W62 |
| B1 | 111 | 111 | 12/01/97 | 01/16/98 | W63 |
| C1 | 6 | 6 | 12/05/97 | 01/15/98 | W64 |
| C2 | 6 | 6 | 12/05/97 | 01/15/98 | W65 |
| C1 | 114 | 114 | 12/08/97 | 01/16/98 | W64 |
| C2 | 114 | 114 | 12/08/97 | 01/16/98 | W65 |
| B1 | 5 | 5 | 12/24/97 | 02/10/98 | W66 |
| B1 | 15 | 15 | 12/25/97 | 02/11/98 | W66 |
| A2 | 6 | 6 | 12/26/97 | 02/12/98 | W67 |
| B1 | 10 | 10 | 12/29/97 | 02/13/98 | W66 |

**Master Production Schedule**

Sort By
- Time
- WO
- Product
- Due Date

Show WO

Help

Close

**Figure B.11    Production View | Information | Master Production Schedule**

required (W1, W2, or W3) and each work center employed in producing the product. The work center blocks indicate the resource name, the task designation (a "J" number), and the number of minutes required to perform that task on one unit of work-in-process.

## Production Policies

Close the "All products routing" window, and click on "Policies" (on the Menu Bar in the Production View). The pull-down window in Figure B.13 appears. There are five menu entries under "Policies."

## Raw Material Release

Three options are available.

"Immediate Release" commands materials to be introduced to the production floor as soon as a new customer order appears in the master production schedule (Figure B.14).
"MRP" commands material to be released using a manufacturing resource planning (MRP) schedule (Figure B.15). As you can see, this mode allows the user to set whatever task lead time may be desired.

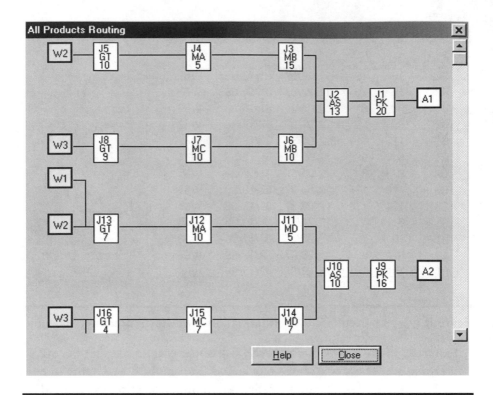

**Figure B.12     Production View | Information | All Products Routing**

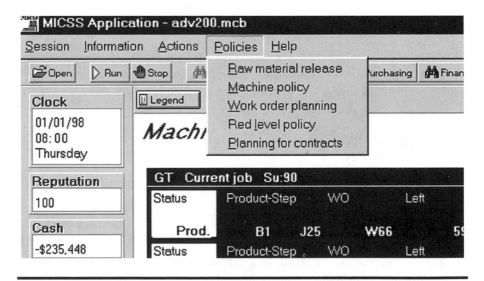

**Figure B.13     Production View | Policies**

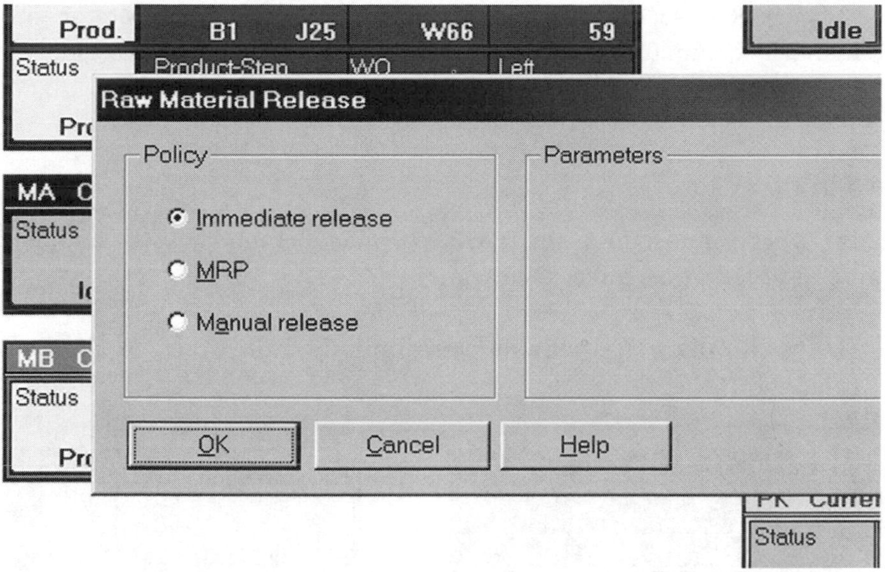

**Figure B.14    Production View | Policies | Raw Material Release | Immediate**

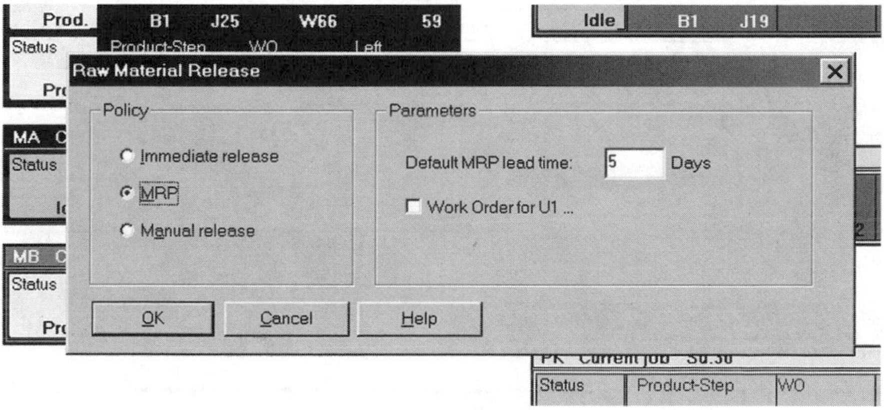

**Figure B.15    Production View | Policies | Raw Material Release | MRP**

"Manual Release," when selected, requires the simulation operator to manually command material release for each order in the master production schedule.

## Machine Policy

This is a very important menu. It tells machine operators how to handle the work-in-process that comes their way.

"Dispatch Policy" has four different options from which to choose (Figure B.16).

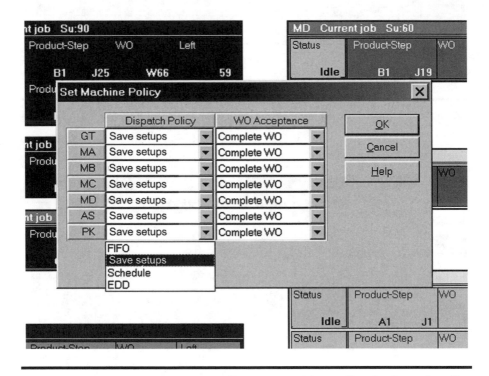

**Figure B.16   Production View | Policies | Machine Policy | Dispatch Policy**

"FIFO" (first-in, first-out) means that the machine operator will automatically choose the next order to work on based on which order arrived at the work center first.

"Save Set-ups" means that the machine operator will do whatever is possible to avoid changing a set-up on the machine. If there are three orders waiting to be processed, and two of them require the same set-up, the operator will do both before breaking the set-up to do the remaining order, even if the same set-up orders are not due immediately.

"Schedule" means that the simulator user must schedule the work for each order manually.

"EDD" (earliest due date) means that every time an order is completed, the operator will look to see which order in the queue is due for delivery first. If there are several with different delivery due dates, the operator will begin work on the one due first, even if that requires breaking the existing set-up to do so.

"WO Acceptance" has two different options from which you may choose (Figure B.17).

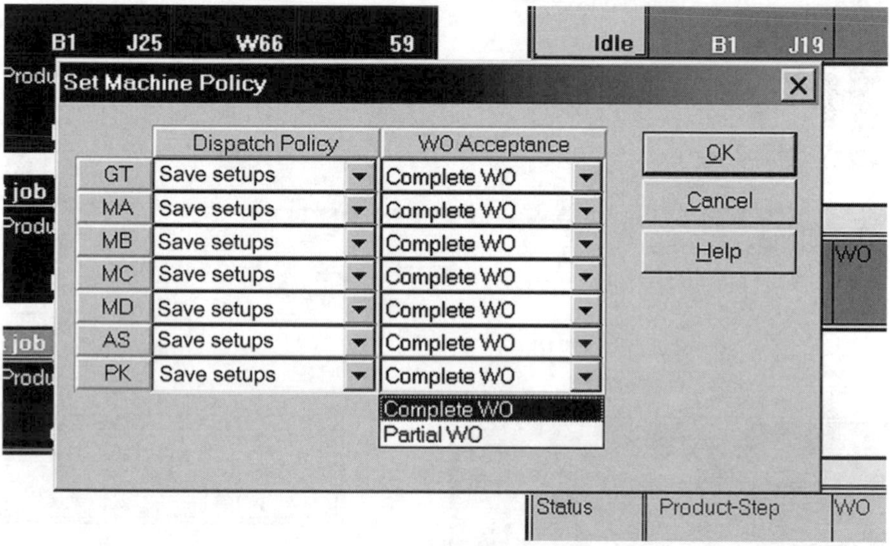

**Figure B.17    Production View | Policies | Machine Policy | WO Acceptance**

"Complete WO" means that the machine operator will not start processing a work order until all the parts for that order are present at his or her work center. Even if the operator is processing under an "EDD" policy, work will not commence on the next order due for delivery unless all the items in that order are physically present at the work center.

"Partial WO" means that if any part of a work order is present at the work center, the operator will commence work on that order in accordance with the directions established under "Dispatch Policy."

## Work Order Planning

This menu establishes some important criteria for production planning (Figure B.18).

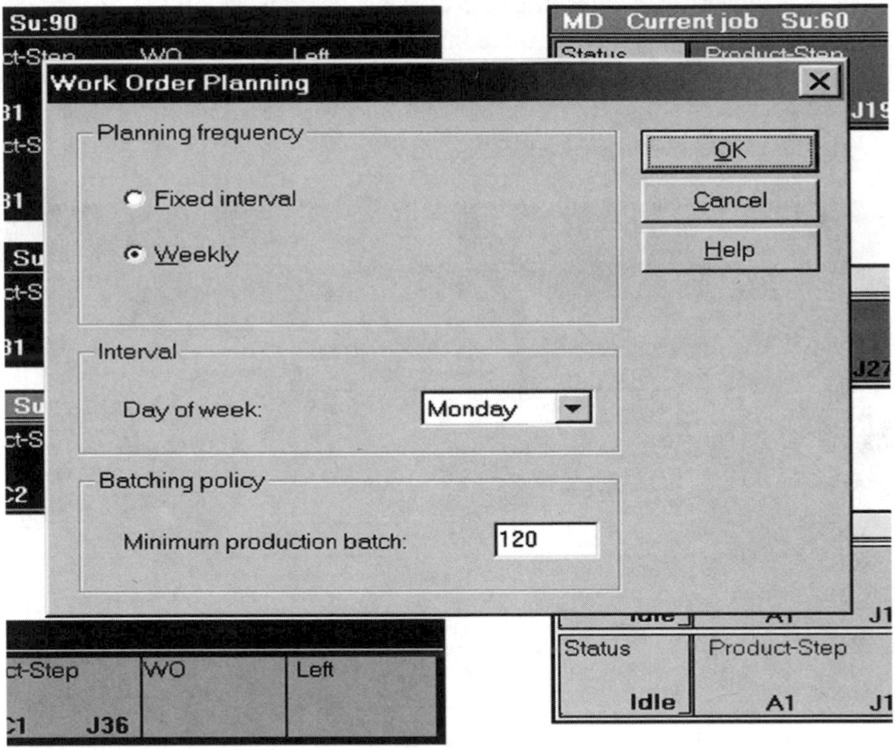

**Figure B.18    Production View | Policies | Work Order Planning | Planning Frequency (Weekly)**

"Planning Frequency" determines how often the master production schedule will be updated.

"Weekly" means any new orders that arrive will be held until the next scheduling day and incorporated into the schedule only once each week. The "Interval" in this case shows the day of the week on which the schedule is updated.

"Fixed Interval" (Figure B.19) means that schedule updating occurs at specific elapsed time intervals. In this case, the "Interval" window shows the number of days between schedule updates.

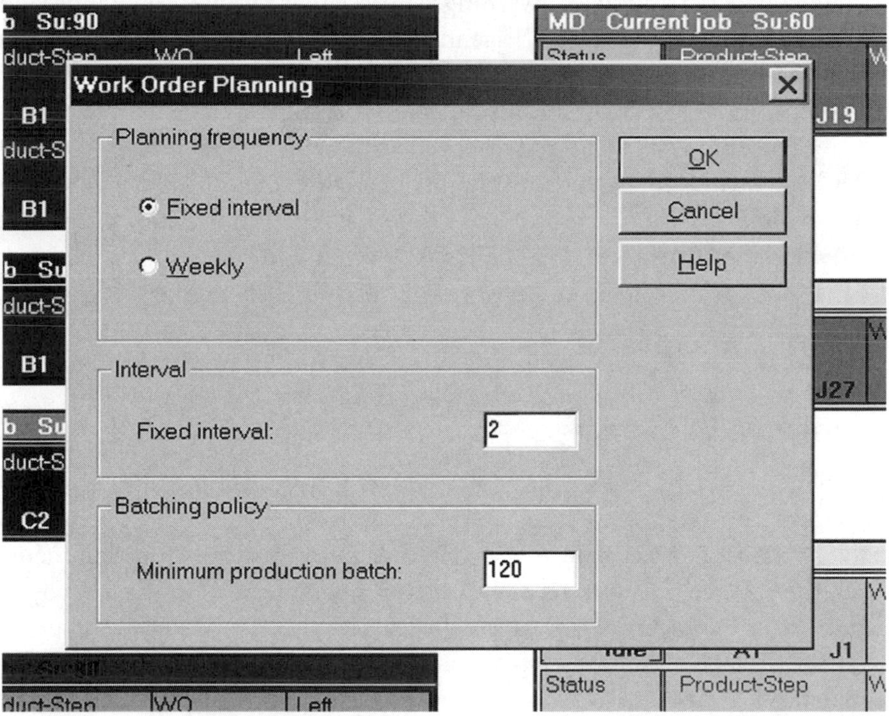

**Figure B.19   Production View | Policies | Work Order Planning | Planning Frequency (Fixed Interval)**

"Batching Policy" imposes batch size (numbers of units that will be processed) in the planning mechanism (Figure B.19). A work order will contain at least "Minimum Production Batch." For example, the value shown in Figure B.19 is "120." If there are firm orders for 70 units, the work order will still be released for 120 units. The 50 units not assigned to firm customer orders will be sent to finished stock, where they will be assigned to any subsequent customer order. This is a way of building finished inventory for immediate shipment when a customer order comes in.

## Red Level Policy

This window offers you the opportunity to receive a warning from the computer when any order is within a specified number of days of its required delivery date. You can set whatever number of days you like for each product. When activated, a "red level" warning flag (a small red box) will appear in the Status Band, near the word "Legend." This is the same feature that appears under Marketing Policies *(Marketing View | Policies | Product Parameters)*. However, this screen includes one additional feature. When the box at the left of "Red-line level policy" is checked, any work center receiving a "red order" will switch to it after finishing its current order, no matter what the dispatch policy is. Furthermore, "red orders" will be immediately processed, even when the "Complete WO" policy is selected and only part of the work order resides at the site. In other words, if "Red-line level policy" is checked, red orders will be expedited.

## Planning for Contracts

This window allows you to start work orders for recurring deliveries under long-term contracts a specified number of days before each incremental delivery is due. For example, the "44" in the "Days to start before shipment" block means that if a contract calls for monthly deliveries on the last day of each month, the materials for each delivery would be released 44 days prior, or approximately 2 months (remember, these are *work* days, not *calendar* days) ahead of time.

### Production View (View Total Load)

Close out the *Production | Policies* windows for now. Before moving on to the next view, click on the small box in the upper right corner of the screen (in the Status Band) labeled "View Total Load." The Production View now looks a little different (Figure B.20).

This screen provides some useful information. Each work center is represented by two horizontal status bars, one red and one green (you need the computer to see the colors). The red bar is on top. Notice that there are times, in hours and minutes, beside each colored bar. The red bar indicates the number of hours of committed to work reflected in the master production

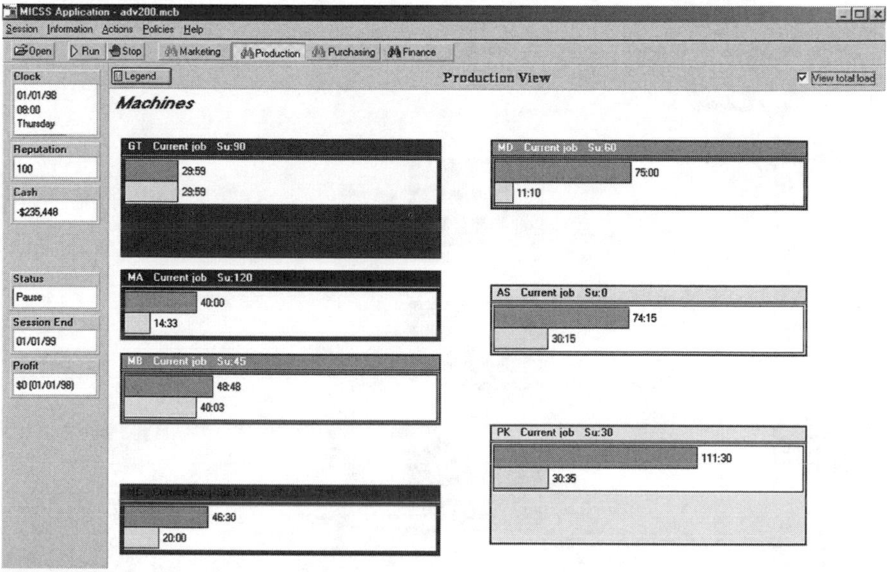

**Figure B.20    Production View | View Total Load**

schedule. The green bar indicates how many hours worth of that work are currently queued at the work center. This information is the same as that found in the Information pull-down menu *(Production | Information | Machine total load [in hours])*, but shown in a dynamic graphic mode.

For example, look at work center MD. Its red bar indicates that 75 hours of this work center's capacity is committed to known requirements in the MPS. But only 11 hours and 10 minutes (the green bar) of that 75 hours' work is physically there at MD. Notice that the two bars are of equal length at work center GT. Remember, this is the "gating operation," and we have an "immediate" material release policy set in the MICSS. So as soon as an order shows up in the MPS, material is automatically released to the GT work center. Planned load will always equal queue size for this work center, under these conditions.

## Purchasing View

Now click on *Purchasing* in the task bar. This will display the *Purchasing View*. The workspace now shows the three raw materials — W1, W2, and W3 — used in the six products, A1 through C2 (Figure B.21).

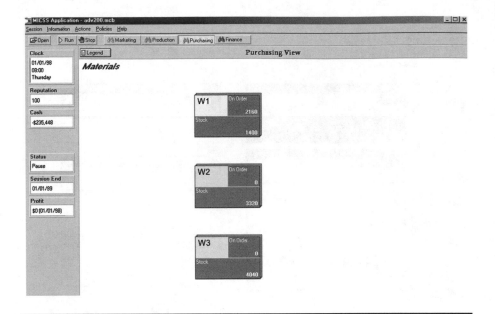

**Figure B.21    Purchasing View**

Each block representing a raw material shows the name in the upper left corner, the number of raw material units on order in the upper right corner, and the number in stock below. You can see that stocks of W2 and W3 are quite high (3320 and 4040, respectively), so there are no open orders for those materials. W1, on the other hand, shows only 1400 in stock, and 2160 more on order.

## Purchasing Information

If you pull down the "Information" menu in the *Purchasing View,* you'll see seven entries (Figure B.22):

    Material information
    Consumed units graph
    Suppliers average lead time
    Purchasing forecast
    Consumption summary
    Measurements summary
    Open orders from vendors

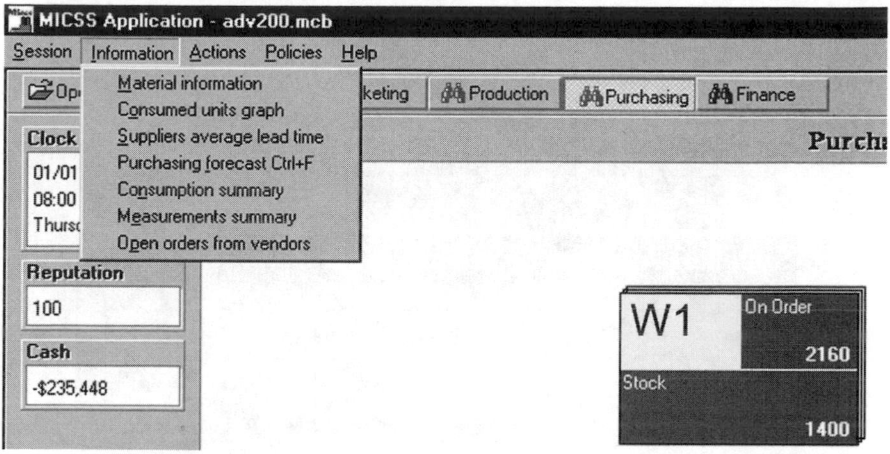

**Figure B.22    Purchasing View | Information**

Each of these provides detailed information on inventories and consumption records. They're fairly self-explanatory. You may study them in more detail at your convenience. Notice that "Open Orders from Vendors" reflects the pending order for 2160 units of W1.

For now, let's just look at one — Suppliers Average Lead Time (Figure B.23). One supplier (shown in the row numbered "1") averages slightly over 48 days to deliver an order. The other supplier (shown in the row numbered "2") indicates zero, but all this really means is that we've never ordered anything from that supplier, so it has no track record.

## Purchasing Actions

Pull down the "Actions" menu, and you'll see two entries (Figure B.24):

## Order

This window gives you the capability of manually inserting an order for any of the raw materials.

## Suppliers

This window (Figure B.25) gives you some detailed information on the two suppliers, "Abc" and "Fast" (labeled "1" and "2", respectively). The "Abc"

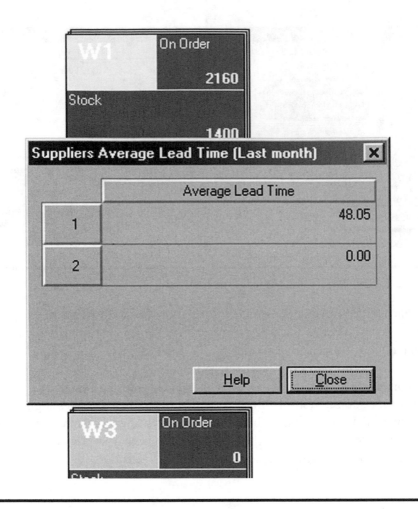

**Figure B.23    Purchasing View | Information | Suppliers Average Lead Time**

supplier charges $50 to ship an order ("S.C.") and quotes a lead time of 44 days. This supplier charges $60, $70, and $40 per unit for W1, W2, and W3, respectively.

The "Fast" supplier charges $25 to ship an order, quotes a lead time of only 3 days, and charges $65, $75, and $44 per unit for W1, W2, and W3, respectively.

Notice that the "Abc" supplier's line shows a "(C)" beside each of the prices. This indicates that "Abc" is the current supplier of choice for the ADV200 Company for each of the raw materials. You have the option of changing primary suppliers, or ordering manually from the other supplier without changing your default supplier. Notice too, that "Abc's" quoted lead time is 4 *days less* than its actual average delivery performance here. There's

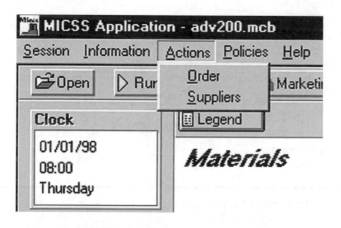

**Figure B.24** **Purchasing View | Actions**

| | Name | S.C | QLT | W1 | W2 | W3 |
|---|---|---|---|---|---|---|
| 1 | Abc | 50 | 44 | (C) 60 | (C) 70 | (C) 40 |
| 2 | Fast | 25 | 3 | 65 | 75 | 44 |

OK   Cancel   Help   To change current supplier click with the mouse on the table cell which intersect the material and new supplier.

**Figure B.25** **Purchasing View | Actions | Suppliers**

a message in this piece of information: "Murphy" strikes suppliers as well as ADV200. In the MICSS program, it's possible for raw materials to be delivered as many as 26 working days beyond the quoted lead time!

## Purchasing Policies

Now close the "Actions" menu and pull down the "Policies" menu (Figure B.26). There's only one entry in this menu:

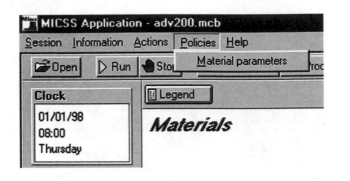

**Figure B.26    Purchasing View | Policies**

## Material Parameters

Figure B.27 shows the maximum stock levels and re-order points for each raw material. When a raw material's stock level drop below 3000, an order is automatically generated to replenish the stock all the way to the maximum of 5000. The column labeled "Red Line Level" shows the stock level at which the computer will display a material red flag on the Status Band in any functional view. In the example depicted in Figure B.27, that flag would appear when the stock level drops below 80 units. You have the option of setting any value you choose in these blocks, or different red line levels for each raw material, if you like.

| Edit Material Parameters | | | ⊠ |
|---|---|---|---|
| | Max Level | Order Level | Red Line Level |
| W1 | 5000 | 3000 | 80 |
| W2 | 5000 | 3000 | 80 |
| W3 | 5000 | 3000 | 80 |

**Figure B.27    Purchasing View | Policies | Material Parameters**

## *Finance View*

Now select the "Finance" button on the task bar. This view displays the annual Profit and Loss (P&L) Statement from the preceding year (Figure B.28). As

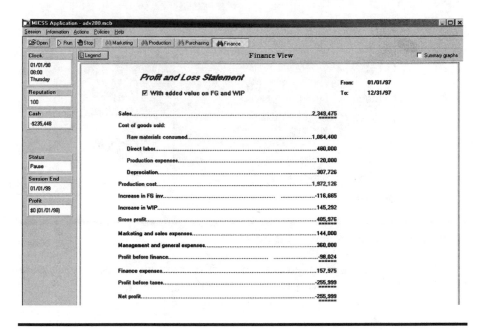

**Figure B.28   Finance View**

the simulation runs, the P&L Statement is updated on the first day of each calendar month, reflecting year-to-date numbers.

One characteristic you'll notice very quickly is that there are no "Actions" or "Policies" associated with those pull-down menus. Only the "Information" menu has any entries in it. (In the real world, this is not likely to be the case, but these issues have been factored out of this simulation.)

### Finance Information.

When you pull down the "Information" menu, the following entries appear (Figure B.29):

Product cost analysis
Contract cost analysis
Current year report
Last year report
Marginal profits summary
Products throughput summary
Contracts throughput summary
EVA measurement

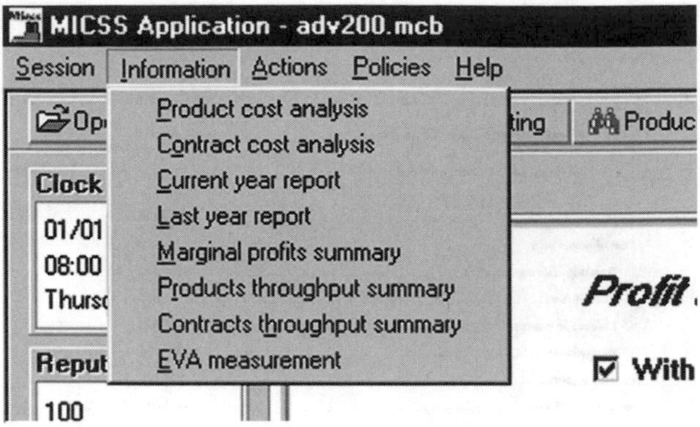

**Figure B.29   Finance View | Information**

While we won't go into detail on most of these menu entries here (you're free to examine them at your leisure), we will mention two of them.

## Product Cost Analysis

This window (Figure B.30) shows, for each product, material costs, direct labor, and overhead (indirect costs). These costs are subtracted from the per-unit selling price to give profit-per-unit, in dollars and as a percentage of the selling price. As you adjust selling prices (in *Marketing View | Policies | Product Parameters*), the dollar and percentage values of profit will change in these windows.

## Product Throughput Summary

This window (Figure B.31) is of particular interest to practitioners of the theory of constraints, because it displays the throughput-per-unit for each of the products, A1 through C2. These values reflect the difference between selling price and raw material cost alone. Traditional cost-oriented people may not find much of use in this window.

# Session

The last item we'll visit on this walking tour is the "Session" pull-down menu in the Menu Bar (Figure B.32). Three of the entries on this menu are worth mentioning.

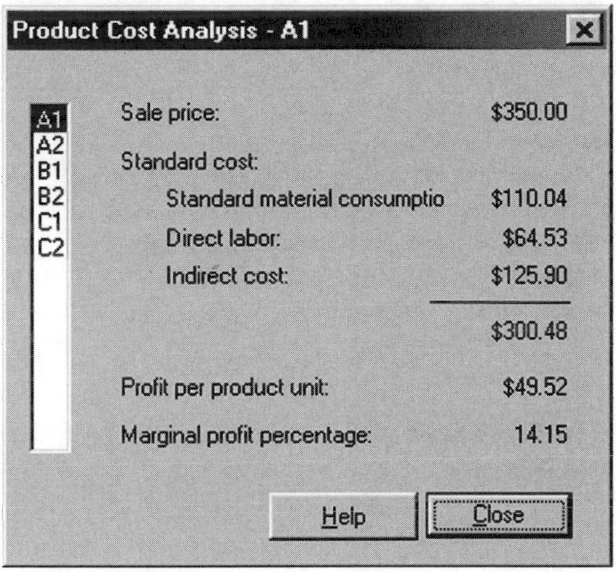

**Figure B.30   Finance View | Information | Product Cost Analysis**

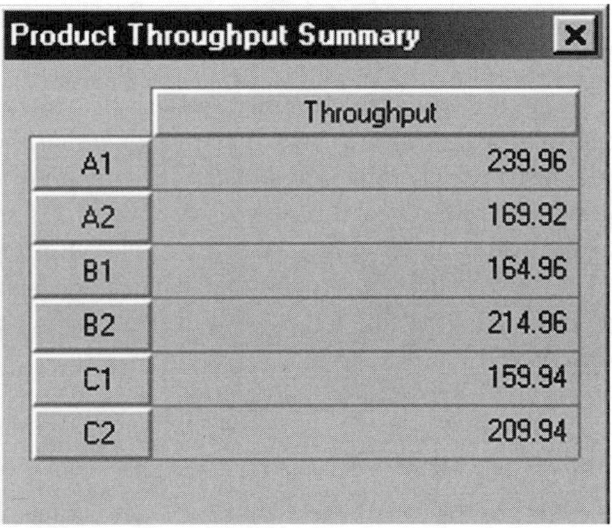

**Figure B.31   Finance View | Information | Product Throughput Summary**

**Figure B.32    Session Menu**

## Save policies

As you run this simulation multiple times, you'll find yourself changing various policies (and from this walking tour, you know that there are a lot of them among the three operating functions!). Since the simulations reload to their default policy settings each time you start over, it's nice to have a way of saving a previous policy configuration before you exit the scenario file to start again. "Save Policies" gives you the chance to do this, so you can begin the next running of the simulation with the policies in place at close-out of the previous run.

## Load policies

This is the other side of the coin. When you start a new simulation run, you can use this feature to replace the default simulation policies with the ones you saved from a previous run.

## Information

This window contains credit and asset information (Figure B.33). The first entry explains something that may have puzzled you when you first looked at the Simulation Status along the left side of the screen: negative cash flow numbers. The ADV200 Company operates with a $1,000,000 line of credit from its bank. So the –$235,448 you saw in the "Cash Flow" block in the Simulation Status means that the company is that far into its $1,000,000 credit line. It still has over $764,000 available in its credit line, but pays interest on the credit it uses. That interest shows up as "Finance Expenses" in the P&L Statement.

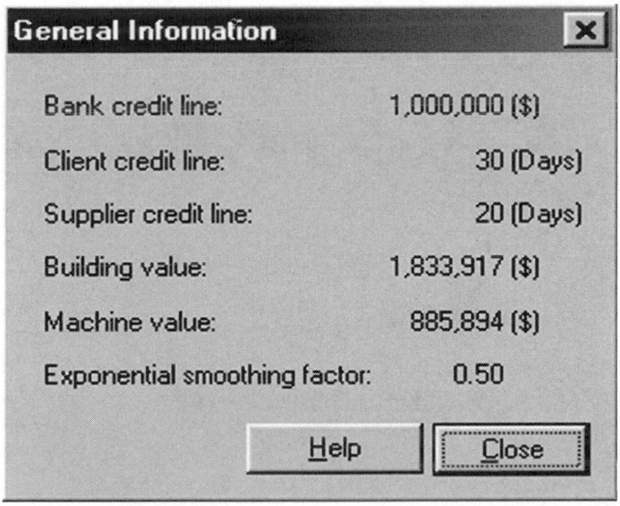

| General Information | |
| --- | --- |
| Bank credit line: | 1,000,000 ($) |
| Client credit line: | 30 (Days) |
| Supplier credit line: | 20 (Days) |
| Building value: | 1,833,917 ($) |
| Machine value: | 885,894 ($) |
| Exponential smoothing factor: | 0.50 |

| Help | Close |

**Figure B.33   Session | Information**

One reason that credit line is important to the company is the next two elements in the "General Information" window (Figure B.33): "Client Credit Line" and "Supplier Credit Line." Notice that the values for these are "30 days" and "20 days," respectively. What this means is that the company has to pay its suppliers within 20 days of raw material delivery, but it, in turn, is not paid by its customers for 30 days or more. So without a positive cash balance in the bank, the ADV200 Company really needs that line of credit to keep the business going!

This concludes the walking tour of MICSS. We recommend taking more time to familiarize yourself with each of the functional views, all the information they contain, and the policies (variables) you can change. Useful "Help" menus associated with each window explain most of what you need to know.

> Note: The MICSS is the proprietary intellectual property of MBE Simulations, Ltd. (Israel). The purchaser of this book is granted a license to use the software contained on the compact disk that accompanies this book. This license is activated when the software is registered with MBE Simulations, Ltd. Purchasers of this book may register their copies online. At that time, an access key will be issued to the purchaser that permits the software to be installed and operated an unlimited number of times. Instructions for registering the software are contained on the compact disk.

If any difficulty is encountered with the on-line automated registration procedure, send an e-mail message to:

elyakim@netvision.net.il<br>or<br>gsi@goalsys.com

The access key will be provided by return e-mail.

# Appendix C: Plant 120

I f you haven't started the MICSS program in your computer, now would be a good time to do so, and follow along as we examine Plant 120. This is a fairly simple operation, selling only two products, produced by five work centers, using three materials.

In our tour of Plant 120, let's start with its financial status. (Refer to the *Finance View.*) This is not really bad performance:

- The plant made $85,000 last year
- The plant actually earned interest ($11,430) on the money in its operating account

These are decent financial results. They were achieved by actually running the virtual company (by means of simulation) for the preceding year. So why rock the boat? Why not leave this plant alone?

For the answer to that question, let's move on to Marketing and Sales, where the problem will be apparent. (Refer to the *Marketing View.*) As you can see, this plant's reputation in the market is hurting. It only delivered product A1 when the customer expected it 75% of the time last month.* Product A2 is even worse — only 49% of its deliveries were on time. Plant 120's overall reputation is only 65%. In fact, Plant 120's on-time delivery performance was so bad that two of its most lucrative contracts were not

---

* In the MICSS, "Reputation" is based initially on the percentage of on-time deliveries, but it's corrected for large orders and the number of days delivery is late. For example, a large order that is 10 days late for delivery will degrade the numerical "Reputation" score more than a small order that is only 2 days late.

renewed by customers in December 1998. So profits for 1999 are sure to take a hit.

Plant 120 delivers to its customers strictly on long-term contract — four of them *(Marketing View | Information | Contracts List)*. If this deplorable delivery reliability doesn't improve, Plant 120 can expect to lose one or more of these contracts as well. What do you suppose will happen to the cash and profit picture then?

Let's go back to the *Marketing View.* Look at the status of the two products Plant 120 produces (A1 and A2). Both have significant firm orders (474 and 334 units, respectively) and minimal finished goods inventory on hand to assign to the next order due for delivery. Over 500 units of A1 and 400 units of A2 are on the production floor now ("WIP").

Now let's look at Plant 120's marketing policies *(Marketing View | Policies | Product Parameters)*. The quoted lead times, expressed in working days, are 44 days (almost 9 weeks) for both products. The company works 5 days a week, 8 hours per day, throughout the year. In this simulation scenario, market demand doesn't change.

It's time to visit the production floor *(Production View)*. All five work centers have one machine each. Let's see the logical layout of how the final products are made. (Refer to *Production View | Information | All Products Routing*). This shows the sequence of production tasks for all six products. Work flows from left to right.

A1 is an assembly of two parts. One part is made of raw material Y1, which goes first through Machine 1 (M1) for 6 minutes, then on to Machine 2 (M2) for 11 minutes. The second part is built from raw material Z1. It, too, passes through Machine 1 (M1) in 10 minutes and Machine 3 (M3) in 12 minutes. The two parts are then assembled, in the Assembly work center (AS), which requires 14 minutes per unit. The Packaging (PK) operation packs one unit of A1 for shipping every 9 minutes. A2 has a very similar route. Notice, however, substantially more time per unit is required to process A2 at most locations.

Every day the production scheduler plans new work orders based on the contract delivery requirements (refer to *Production View | Policies | Work Order Planning*). Current policy sets the minimum batch at 100 pieces. So, if 60 units of A2 are needed to fill a contracted delivery, the information system issues a new work order for 100 units of A2. The first 60 will be applied to the contract work order. The remaining 40 are available (finished stock) to commit to later orders. Any subsequent orders will use these 40 first. Only when a new order exceeds this number will the information system issue a new work order — for another 100.

The material release policy currently used (*Production View | Policies | Raw Material Release*) is MRP. Once a work order is created, the materials are released to the production floor as scheduled by the MRP system (provided there is enough stock in raw material inventory). The MRP lead time is 7 days, meaning that each step in the process for each product has 7 days to be completed. No release of materials can take place without an active work order, and work centers can work only on existing work orders.

To get an idea of the actual load on the work centers, take a look at the "Machine Utilization" report for the last two months (*Production View | Information | Machine Utilization*). Notice that all work centers except M3 reported a significant amount of idle time during November and December of 1998.

Let's move on to the Purchasing department (*Purchasing View*). Plant 120's purchasing tasks are especially simple. There are only three items to manage: Y1, Z1, and Z2. Y1 is in a stock-out condition, with a re-order for 619 already on the books. Z1 and Z2 each have 268 and 237 on hand, respectively, and 240 more Z1s are on order as well.

Take a look at the purchasing policy (*Purchasing View | Policies | Purchasing Policy*). The MRP system takes care of generating all purchase orders as needed to fulfill production needs. The system projects a stock-out time, based on current firm orders in the system, backs up from that date to 5 days before the supplier's quoted lead time, and submits a re-order at that time. There is no safety stock established. Red-line time and red-line level aren't used (*Purchasing View | Policies | Material Parameters*).

A general manager had better know with what kind of suppliers the company works. The *Purchasing | Actions | Suppliers* screen provides some information about Plant 120's suppliers. Notice that the current supplier (default) is "Regular." They take a long time to deliver (average of 33 work days after an order is placed — about 6.5 calendar weeks), but they charge less for each unit of raw material supplied. The "Fast" supplier is clearly much faster, but also more expensive, both in unit and shipping costs.

We started our tour of Plant 120 with the profit-and-loss statement. Now let's examine some important information provided by our Finance department (*Finance View | Information | Contract Cost Analysis*). Work your way through each of the products, in turn. Notice that contract #1, to the ABC Company, appears to be a money-loser. Unfortunately, Plant 120 can't do much about that, because the same company also awarded the plant contract #2, which *DOES* make money for the plant. So Plant 120 has accepted one apparently unprofitable contract in order to also win the second one that is more profitable. Contracts #3 and #4 are both solid moneymakers. In any case, it's not good form to cancel a signed contract! In this simulation, the most you can do is not to renew it, but it won't come up for renewal during the 6 months you'll be in charge.

We're almost finished with the tour. We didn't cover all the information and policies in this tour. Before you start to run the Plant 120 simulation, take some time to familiarize yourself first with the tutorial embedded in the MICSS software. Then review Appendix B and note the differences between it and this simulation scenario. This particular company runs for only 6 months. However, while going through that period, you *must* have full control over what's happening if delivery performance is to improve.

You can run for multiple days by specifying a stopping date in the "mm/dd/yy" box. We don't recommend running the simulation longer than 1 week at a time, for reasons that will become apparent if you try it. Once you have a feel for how the simulation works, you may be able to run the simulation for longer periods. You can pause the simulation at any time by clicking on the "STOP" button, or by pressing the "S" key, which may be quicker if your computer has an exceptionally fast processor.

## First Run Instructions

For the first run, don't change any of Plant 120's policies. Run the simulation for a week at a time. Each time the simulation pauses, take a look at the sales summary graph, machine utilization, and any other display screen you think may be useful. One particularly useful screen is *Work Order Status*. You can get to this screen two different ways. Perhaps the most useful is to do so from the Master Production Schedule (*Production View | Information | Master Production Schedule*). From this window, you can watch the delivery due dates, then highlight the work orders that are getting close to that date, click on the *WO Status* button on the MPS screen, and see where that work order lies on the production floor. Another useful screen is the Shipment List (Marketing View | Information | Shipment List). On this screen, you can see when the next shipment is due and how many units it requires. This information is not obvious when you look at the Master Production Schedule.

Observe what's going on and take action as required. In most cases, this means expedite when a work order seems to be in danger of missing its required delivery date. There are two ways to do this:

- Manually break a set-up on the machine where the potentially late order is queued and direct that machine to work on the almost-late order (*Production View | Actions | Set Unit Manually*). At the completion of the manual intervention, the machine will automatically revert to the original work order.
- Add an additional shift to increase productive time for a day or two (*Production View | Actions | Add Extra Shift*).

At the completion of the run (July 1, 2000), complete the "Plant 120 Management Report" provided (Figure C.1). After you've captured all the reporting data, you may reset the simulation (*Any View |Session | Open | PRD120*).

Remember: Your objective is to deliver on time — do everything you can to avoid late shipments!

**OBJECTIVE:** Improve Plant 120's delivery reliability to 100% by July 1, 1999 while keeping costs as low as possible.

|  | 1998 (12 months) | 1999 (6 months) |
|---|---|---|
| **PROFIT** | $85,285 | |
| **SALES** | $2,256,282 | |
| **CASH** | $610,732 | |
| **REPUTATION** | 65% | |

How well did you accomplish the objective?

What is the potential to improve performance in the next 6 months?

Policies that should be changed:

**Figure C.1   Plant 120 Management Report**

### First Run Analysis

What were your results? Were you happy with the way the 6-month period ended? Go back to Chapter 6 for an analysis of Plant 120.


## Second Run Instructions

Now it's time to see whether the future will *really* unfold as the Plant 120 future reality tree (Figures 6.10a and b) suggested that it should. The first thing to do is to change the production policies in accordance with Injections #1, 2, and 3:

- Begin by opening the *Production View*, activate the *Policies* menu, select *Work Order Planning*, and change the *Minimum Production Batch* to "1." This is equivalent to Injection #1, and will force the processing batch size to equal the amount specified in each work order.
- Also in the *Production View*, select *Policies | Machine Policy*. Change *Dispatch Policy* to "EDD," in accordance with P2, in the first conflict (Figure 6.3r). "EDD" means "earliest due date" and will ensure that each work center does not defer work on the next work order due for delivery. This will implement Injection #2.
- In *WO Acceptance* change to "Partial WO" (this is Injection #3, and it implies transferring in smaller batches).
- Remember, we're using an MRP system that was configured to release materials 44 days before the deliveries are due. If we leave that value in place, we expect that the production floor will start to become clogged with work-in-process, confounding the effects of the new production policies we've instituted. So for this run, let's reduce the contract start time from "44" to "30" (*Production View | Policies | Planning for Contracts*). Additionally, let's reduce the MRP lead time from "7 days" to "5 days" (*Production View | Policies | Raw Material Release*).

Now we have to *CHANGE THE PURCHASING POLICY* in accordance with Injections #5 and 6:

- Open the Purchasing View and select the menu *Policies | Material Parameters*

     For Y1, enter "160" in the column labeled *Red Line Level*
     For Z1 and Z2, enter "80" in the column labeled *Red Line Level*

Now when you're in danger of not having enough raw materials to release for production at the required time, the simulation will display a small red box ("flag") in the status bar beside the "Legend" icon that says "Materials." This will prompt you to stop the simulation and initiate a re-order to the "Fast" supplier.

Injection #4 (Figure 6.6) is a management policy. For the purposes of the simulation, it guides our decisions, but it shows up in the future reality tree in Injections #7 and 8. To implement these injections, periodically check Rough-Cut Capacity and Machine Utilization (*Production View | Information | Rough Cut Capacity* or *Machine Utilization*).

There are three more injections we need to consider in changing the way we manage Plant 120. These are really management policies. They guide our decisions on how to run the simulation/Plant 120, but they don't fit into any particular simulation variable.

- Injection #NB-1a tells us to enlarge batches and/or use the "Save Setups" policy (*Production View | Policies | Machine Policy*) anytime a resource's protective capacity is threatened. (Refer to Figure 6.11.)
- Injection #NB-1b tells us to treat set-ups as significant only when they exhaust protective capacity. In such a situation, Injection #NB-1a would also apply. (Refer to Figure 6.11.)
- Injection #NB-2 tells us to accept raw material cost increases as long as the change in throughput ($\Delta T$) remains positive. (Refer to Figure 6.12, Chapter 6.)

Figure C.2 summarizes the settings of MICSS policies for both the first and second runs.

Now run the simulation again for another 6 months, a week at a time. Complete the "Plant 120 Management Report" provided in Figure C.1. Don't close the simulation at the completion of the second run. See "Third Run Instructions" below, for more details.

## Second Run Analysis

Well, how did the second run work out? Considerably better, if you changed production policies to reflect drum-buffer-rope. You probably noticed that there was still some due date pressure in the first 2 or 3 weeks of the simulation run. The production line still had orders queued from the 44-day contract start time and 7-day MRP lead time. But the most problematic area

| MICSS POLICY | First Run | Second Run |
|---|---|---|
| **PRODUCTION** | | |
| *Raw Material Release* | | |
| Policy | MRP | MRP |
| Default MRP lead time | 7 days | 5 days |
| *Machine Policy* | | |
| Dispatch Policy | Save Setups | EDD |
| WO Acceptance | Complete WO | Partial WO |
| *Work Order Planning* | | |
| Frequency | Fixed Interval | Fixed Interval |
| Interval | 1 day | 1 day |
| Minimum Production Batch | 100 | 1 |
| *Red Level Policy* | | |
| Red Line Time | 0 | 0 |
| *Planning for Contracts* | | |
| Days to Start Before Shipment | 44 | 30 |
| **PURCHASING** | | |
| *Material Parameters* | | |
| Red Line Level | 0 | 160 (Y1); 80 (Z1, Z2) |

**Figure C.2   Plant 120 Quick-Reference Policy Matrix**

is the batch size. When you need only 33 units of A2, processing the whole 100 units will take so much time that the next delivery of A1 is sure to be late! This is a very important aspect of the simulation, because it demonstrates the fallacy of the large fixed batch scheme. Until the large batches already on the production floor are cleared out (delivered), manually redirecting the AS work center from one product to the other several times during the first month is required. You might even have found that some additional shifts were required during the first 2 weeks, but after that the system was "flushed" of unnecessary work-in-process, and the flow became smooth and fast. You should also have noticed the following effects:

- By July 1, on-time performance was consistently at 100%
- Reputation (the 6-month rolling average) recovered to 100% (or fairly close to it) — the objective was achieved!

- Machine utilization and rough-cut capacity indicated a significant "liberation" of hidden capacity. Instead of running at or above 100%, as Plant 120 did in the first run, these figures are now in the 80 to 90% range.
- More cash in the operating account.
- Profit was positive for the first 6-months of the year, though it will not reach last year's levels because of the long-term contracts lost in December 1998, when on-time delivery performance was so bad.

## Third Run Instructions

By now, you should have sufficient understanding of the dynamics behind Plant 120 that you're ready to try to recoup the business lost at the end of 1998. Before you close out the second run of the simulation, you should save all the policies that you changed at Plant 120. To do this, open the *Session* menu, select *Save policies,* and name the new policy file "PRD120a.plc" (*Session | Save policies | prd120a.plc*).

Now open a different simulation file: prd130.mcb (*Session | Open | prd130.mcb*). This simulation will look exactly like Plant 120. In fact it *is* Plant 120, with one significant change, but from here on we'll refer to it as "Plant 130." Besides the four existing contracts that you saw in the original Plant 120 scenario (prd120.mcb), you'll be offered the opportunity to take on new contracts as well. Be forewarned, however, you'll need to make this choice carefully. The newly liberated capacity that you realized by changing operating policies can be quickly overrun by accepting too much new work. But there is a chance to recover some of the profits lost in 1998 when contracts were not renewed.

After loading the Plant 130 scenario (prd130.mcb), be sure to reload the new production policies you saved above. Select *Session | Load Policies | prd120a.plc.* Verify that your policies have, in fact, been updated by checking the Machine Policy (*Production View | Policies | Machine Policy*). The *Dispatch Policy* should read "EDD" and *WO Acceptance* should read "Partial WO." If they do, you can be sure that the other policies have been updated as well. If they don't, the policy file you created earlier wasn't saved properly. You'll need to verify all the policy changes outlined in "Second Run Instructions," above, and update them as necessary.

Go ahead and run Plant 130 — see how well you can manage your capacity!

# Appendix D:
# The ADV200 Company

The ADV200 scenario is considerably more complex than the Plant 120 situation we used to explore production issues alone. If you haven't started the MICSS program in your computer, now would be a good time to do so, and follow along as we examine the ADV200 Company.

## Differences Between the ADV200 Company and Plant 120

The most significant difference between ADV200 and PRD120 is the type of market in which they operate. ADV200's market consists of a very large number of small customers, and there are no contracts with those customers. The ADV200 Company publishes list prices and quoted lead times (QLT) for all its products. Any customer placing an order for one or a few units of a product accepts these two terms. But the company also commits itself to ship those units at the specified price precisely when promised: the number of days indicated in the QLT after the date the order is received. (Remember that the QLT reflects working days, not calendar days.) Unlike the real world, the company can't decline to supply a customer order in this MICSS simulation. The ADV200 Company advertises the prices and QLTs and is obligated to accept all orders under these terms. This makes determination of both the price and the QLT a sensitive, critical management issue.

## Your Objective

Another difference concerns *your* role. You're not just a production manager now — you're the *general* manager. In Plant 120, your only real charter was to ship every order on time. As general manager of the ADV200 Company, the whole company is your responsibility. You're now responsible for profit and loss as well. In other words, we — as the stockholders — expect you to make money! That's not too unreasonable, is it? And you have a whole year to achieve profitability. Of course, we also expect you to maintain the ADV200 Company's sterling reputation for on-time delivery, otherwise the company has no future. So, we expect to see you maintain the "Reputation" score above 85, while making as much money as possible. And how much is possible? This is one of the questions we'll leave for you to answer! Let's take a more detailed look at the ADV200 Company.

# The ADV200 Company Profile

This company sells six different products, produced by seven different work centers, using three materials. The management team has just been terminated because of lackluster company performance. You have been appointed to run the company while the board of directors searches for a new chief executive. If you can turn the company around during the course of the board's search, there's an excellent chance that they will give the job to you permanently. All you have to do is to succeed where your predecessors failed!

In our tour of the ADV200 Company, let's start with its financial status. (Refer to the *Finance View.*) The 1997 profit and loss statement (as of 1/1/98) shows why the owners are looking for a new management team.

- The company lost $256,000 last year.
- The company finished the year over $235,000 into its line of credit.
- Interest (finance charges) on the company's credit line alone amounted to $158,000.

To be frank about it, these are lousy results. They were achieved by actually running the virtual company (by means of simulation) for the preceding year. Obviously, some of the policies and actions of the former managers weren't very good.

This is too depressing to look at any longer — let's move on to something more encouraging. (Refer to the *Marketing View.*) This company has quite a good reputation in the market. Its customers value highly the reliability the

ADV200 Company provides. Notice in the status bar on the left side of the screen that the company's reputation is 100%. As you'll recall from the MICSS guided tour (Appendix B), this means that not a single order for any of the 6 products was delivered late in the last 6 months of 1997. This is certainly an encouraging achievement to build upon.

Look at the status of the six products ADV200 produces (A1 through C2). Most have some finished goods inventory on hand, ready to assign to the next order due for delivery. Some orders are on the production floor now ("WIP").

Let's look at ADV200's marketing policies (*Marketing View | Policies | Product Parameters*). The quoted lead times, expressed in working days, are 35 (7 weeks) days for products A1 through B2 and 30 days (6 weeks) for C1 and C2. The company works 5 days a week, 8 hours per day, throughout the year. In this simulation scenario, there are only two ways to influence market demand. Changing quoted lead time (QLT) is one. Changing selling price is the other.

One important piece of information: What were last year's sales like? Let's take a look. (*Marketing View | Information | Sales Summary Graph.*) Notice that sales started out relatively strongly, trailed off in the first quarter of 1997, peaked in the summer (a seasonal phenomenon), then trailed off again toward the end of the year. You can examine the individual product sales graphs in more detail at your leisure. After running 1998 several times, you may conclude that the seasonal peak applies only to certain products and not to others. It will be up to you to determine the trend in the future.

Now let's visit the production floor (*Production View*). Notice that two of the seven work centers ("GT" and "PK") have two machines. All the rest have only one. Let's see the logical layout of how the final products are made. (Refer to *Production View | Information | All Products Routing.*) This shows the sequence of production tasks for all six products. Work flows from left to right.

A1 is an assembly of two parts. One part is made of raw material W2, which first goes through GT, where it requires 10 minutes to process a single unit. Then it goes to Machine A (MA) for 5 minutes, then on to Machine B (MB) for 15 minutes. The second part is built from raw material W3. It, too, passes through the GT, Machine C (MC), and Machine B (MB). The two parts are then assembled, in the Assembly work center (AS), which requires 13 minutes per unit. The Packaging (PK) operation packs one unit of A1 for shipping every 20 minutes. The other A and B products have comparable routes. The C1 and C2 products don't need an assembly operation. Their routing is a simple sequential line.

Every week, on Monday morning, the internal information system plans new work orders based on the new market requirements that have been received (refer to *Production View | Policies | Work Order Planning*). Current policy sets the minimum batch at 120 pieces. So, if 62 units of A2 are needed to fill a customer order, the information system issues a new work order for 120 units of A2. The first 62 will be applied to the customer order. This means 58 are available (finished stock) to commit to other orders. Any subsequent new orders will use these 58 first. Only when a new order exceeds this number will the information system issue a new work order — for another 120.

The current material release policy (*Production View | Policies | Raw Material Release*) is "immediate." Once the work order is created, the materials are released immediately to the production floor (provided there is enough stock in raw material inventory). No release of materials can take place without an active work order. Work centers can work only on existing work orders.

To get an idea of the actual load on the work centers, take a look at the "Machine Utilization" report for the last 2 months (*Production View | Information | Machine Utilization*). Notice that all work centers reported a significant amount of idle time during November and December of 1997.

Let's move on to the Purchasing department (*Purchasing View*). The ADV200 Company's purchasing tasks are especially simple. There are only three items to manage: W1, W2, and W3. As of today (January 1, 1998), there are enough W2 and W3 materials stocked to fill all existing orders. There are only 1400 units of W1, so a purchase order has been automatically issued for 2160 more units.

Take a look at the purchasing policy (*Purchasing View | Policies | Material Parameters*). When the stock of any raw material drops below the order level, an automatic purchase order is issued to the default supplier in the amount needed to raise the stock to the maximum level specified (in this case, 5000 units for all three raw materials).

A general manager had better know with what kind of suppliers the company works. The *Purchasing | Actions | Suppliers* screen provides some information about the ADV200 Company's suppliers. Notice that the current supplier (default) is "ABC." They take a long time to deliver (average of 44 work days after an order is placed — about 2 calendar months), but they charge less for each unit of raw material supplied. The "Fast" supplier is clearly much faster, but also more expensive.

We started our tour of the ADV200 company with the profit-and-loss statement. Now let's examine some important information provided by our finance department (*Finance View | Information | Product Cost Analysis*).

Work your way through each of the products, in turn. Notice that one product, B1, appears to be a money-loser.

We're almost finished with the tour. We didn't cover all the information and policies in this tour, but considering your previous experience managing Plant 120, this should be sufficient to get you started. This particular company runs for a full year. However, while going through that year you *must* have full control over what's happening and be able to respond quickly to the changes. You're free to specify how long the simulation runs before stopping to allow you to conveniently review the results and consider changes you may want to make. You may choose to run day by day, or a month at a time. You can run for multiple months by specifying a stopping date in the "mm/dd/yy" box. We don't recommend running the simulation longer than 1 month at a time, for reasons that will become apparent if you try it. You can pause the simulation at any time by clicking on the "STOP" button, or by striking the letter "S" on your keyboard.*

## First Run Instructions

For the first run, don't change any of the ADV200 Company's policies. Run the simulation for a month or two at a time. Each time the simulation pauses, take a look at the sales summary graph, the machine utilization, and any other display screen you think might be useful. At the completion of the run (January 1, 1999), reset the simulation. Then refer back to the discussion of the ADV200 Company in Chapter 10.

## Second Run Instructions

Now it's time to incorporate the policy changes developed through our analysis of the ADV200 Company (Chapter 10). We're assuming you've read that discussion before commencing this run. If you haven't done so, now would be a good time to do it.

Start with the injections (policy changes) in production. Reset the following parameters:

---

* With the speed of computer microprocessors these days, a month can easily pass by in the simulation before you can position the cursor over the "STOP" button and click it. We suggest using the "S" key for quicker reaction. Subsequently, clicking on the "Run" button will resume the simulation.

- *Production View | Machine Policy*:

    Change "Dispatch Policy" to "EDD" (earliest due date) for every work center. This will direct each work center to start on the next order due for delivery, even if it means breaking set-ups to do so. Change "WO Acceptance" to "Partial WO" for every work center. This will allow each work center to begin the next order without having to wait until all the pieces for that order are physically present at the work center.

- *Production View | Work Order Planning*:

    Change the "Planning Frequency" to "Fixed Interval" and set the interval to "1 day."

    Set the "Minimum Production Batch" to something less than "120." Use your own discretion about how small to make the batches. Be aware that if you reduce this value to "1," you may find your critical work centers spending a lot more time setting up than they should. Try different batch sizes in different simulation runs. We suggest trying a minimum batch size of "30." Then run the simulation again with a minimum batch size of "1." This experiment should demonstrate the effects of exceedingly small process batches on total setup time.

- *Production View | Red Level Policy*:

    Set the "Red Line Time" for each product to "5." This will allow the simulation to activate a red "Orders" warning flag anytime an order is not at the shipping dock (completed) within 5 days prior to its scheduled shipping date.

Now let's adjust the marketing policies. Reset the following parameters:

- *Marketing View | Policies | Product Parameters*:

    Reduce the "Quoted Lead Time" values for each product. We suggest doing this in controllable increments. Try "25" for all products. This is a significant change, and you should carefully monitor its effect on the "Total Load" carefully. If you're able to run the simulation for a couple of months under these policies without missing any deliveries, you may be able to reduce QLT more without creating so much demand that you overload your most restricted resource (CCR). But remember: a traditional seasonal peak demand begins sometime in June or July.

# Guidelines: Running the Simulation

1. Try leaving the computer display on the *Production View,* with the "View Total Load" box checked. Monitor the expansion and contraction of the planned load (red bar). Don't allow the planned load to exceed approximately 90% of the highest quoted lead time (in hours) without stopping the simulation to add some overtime.

2. Don't panic if you start seeing an order "red flag" once in a while. Pause the simulation, go to *Production View | Information | Master Production Schedule.* Red flag work orders will be highlighted in brown.

    Select each highlighted work order in turn, and click on "Show WO." This will tell you where in the production process the work order lies. Recognizing that you have 5 days until the order is late, make a subjective judgment as to whether the work order is close enough to the end of the process to be completed within the next 5 days.

    If it is, ignore the red flag and resume the simulation. The red flag will clear itself when the order reaches the shipping dock, without becoming late.

    If the order seems too far upstream in the production process to make it to the shipping dock before the delivery date, add overtime as necessary to expedite the order, and resume the simulation. Return to the "View Total Load" screen and watch to see if the added overtime results in a contraction of the red bar (to some value well below 90% of the QLT).

3. Continue pushing the quoted lead times gradually downward, until the system starts exhibiting indications of destabilization: increasing frequency of order "red flags," occasional late deliveries, excessive expediting (more than once or twice a month, or for more than a day or two at each occurrence). Run the simulation at this "ragged edge" until the end of the year, and note the effects on net profit, cash flow, and reputation. Are they better than the 1997 results, under policies reflecting "traditional management wisdom?"

Can you do better?

## Third Run Instructions

For the third run, try putting the ADV200 future reality tree - Manipulating Demand (Figures 11.9a through d) into effect. Change the same production and marketing policies you did for the second run. You might start your quoted lead times at 20 days across the board, and run the simulation for a month at a time. When you see signs of increasing pressure on the CCR (high planned load factors, occasional order red flags), see if you can manipulate market demand through selective adjustment of quoted lead time and price to relieve some of the pressure on the CCR, and still make *more money at the same time!* HINT: Liberate some capacity at the CCR by selectively raising prices on the products that deliver a lower profit margin but consume inordinate amounts of the CCR's capacity. Then "load" that newly liberated capacity with demand for more products that deliver a higher profit margin by selectively lowering the quoted lead time on those products. (Remember to use the throughput-per-constraint time rule for rank-ordering your best products, and watch for the CCR to shift to a different resource — then manage *that* resource as the constraint.)

Run the simulation for another year, using the same guidelines as in the second run. As you change the demand distribution of products across your capacity, you should make more money.

*Note*: Figure D.1 summarizes the policy changes from one run to another.

| MICSS Policies | First Run | Second Run | Third Run |
|---|---|---|---|
| **MARKETING** | | | |
| *Policies* | | | |
| Quoted Lead Time | 35 (A1-B2); 30 (C1-C2) | 30 (A1-B2); 25 (C1-C2) | 25 (ALL) |
| Price | (Default) | (Default) | |
| Safety Stock | 0 | 0 | No change to remaining values |
| Red Line Time | 0 | 5 days | |
| **PRODUCTION** | | | |
| *Raw Material Release* | | | |
| Policy | Immediate | Immediate | |
| *Machine Policy* | | | |
| Dispatch Policy | Save Setups | EDD | |
| WO Acceptance | Complete WO | Partial WO | |
| *Work Order Planning* | | | |
| Frequency | Weekly | Fixed Interval | |
| Interval | Monday | 1 day | |
| Minimum Production Batch | 120 | Your Discretion | |
| *Red Level Policy* | | | |
| Red Line TIme | 0 | 5 days | |
| **PURCHASING** | | | |
| *Material Parameters* | | | |
| Max Level | 5,000 | 5,000 | |
| Order Level | 3,000 | 3,000 | |
| Red Line Level | 80 | 80 | |

**Figure D.1   ADV200 Quick-Reference Policy Matrix**

# Bibliography

Corbett, Thomas, *Throughput Accounting: TOC's Management Accounting System*, Great Barrington, MA, The North River Press, 1998.

Covington, John W., *Tough Fabric: The Domestic Apparel and Textile Chain Regains Market Share*, Severna Park, MD, Chesapeake Consulting, 1996.

Cox, James F., III and Michael S. Spencer, *The Constraints Management Handbook*, Boca Raton, FL, St. Lucie Press, 1998.

Dettmer, H. William, *Breaking the Constraints to World-Class Performance*, Milwaukee, WI, ASQ Quality Press, 1998.

Dettmer, H. William, *Goldratt's Theory of Constraints: A Systems Approach to Continuous Improvement*, Milwaukee, WI, ASQ Quality Press, 1997.

Goldratt, Eliyahu M., *The Haystack Syndrome: Sifting Information Out of the Data Ocean*, Croton-on-Hudson, NY, The North River Press, 1990.

Goldratt, Eliyahu M., *It's Not Luck*, Great Barrington, MA, The North River Press, 1994.

Goldratt, Eliyahu M., *Critical Chain*, Great Barrington, MA, The North River Press, 1997.

Goldratt, Eliyahu M. and Robert E. Fox, *The Race*, Croton-on-Hudson, NY, The North River Press, 1986.

Kendall, Gerald I., *Securing the Future: Strategies for Exponential Growth Using the Theory of Constraints*, Boca Raton, FL, St. Lucie Press, 1998.

Leach, Lawrence P., *Critical Chain Project Management*, Boston, Artech House, 2000.

Lepore, Domenico and Oded Cohen, *Deming and Goldratt: The Theory of Constraints and the System of Profound Knowledge*, Great Barrington, MA, The North River Press, 1999.

Levinson, William A., Ed., *Leading the Way to Excellence: The Harris Mountaintop Case Study*, Milwaukee, WI, ASQ Quality Press, 1998.

Lockamy, Archie, III and James F. Cox, III, *Reengineering Performance Measurement*, Boston, MA, Irwin Publishers, 1994.

Mabin, Victoria J. and Steven J. Balderstone, *The World of the Theory of Constraints: A Review of the International Literature*, Boca Raton, FL, St. Lucie Press, 2000.

McMullen, Thomas B., Jr., *Introduction to the Theory of Constraints Management System*, Boca Raton, FL, St. Lucie Press, 1998.

Newbold, Robert C., *Project Management in the Fast Lane: Applying the Theory of Constraints*, Boca Raton, FL, St. Lucie Press, 1998.

Noreen, Eric, Debra Smith, and James T. Mackey, *The Theory of Constraints and Its Implications for Management Accounting*, Great Barrington, MA, The North River Press, 1995.

Ptak, Carol A. and Eli Schragenheim, *ERP: Tools, Techniques and Applications for Integrating the Supply Chain*, Boca Raton, FL, St. Lucie Press, 2000.

Scheinkopf, Lisa J., *Thinking for a Change: Putting the TOC Thinking Processes to Use*, Boca Raton, FL, St. Lucie Press, 1999.

Schragenheim, Eli, *Management Dilemmas: The Theory of Constraints Approach to Problem Identification and Solutions*, Boca Raton, FL, St. Lucie Press, 1999.

Smith, Debra, *The Measurement Nightmare*, Boca Raton, FL, St. Lucie Press, 2000.

Srikanth, Mokshagundam L., *Regaining Competitiveness: Putting* The Goal *to Work* (2nd rev. ed.), Wallingford, CT, Spectrum Publishing, 1995.

Srikanth, Mokshagundam L. and Scott A. Robertson, *Measurements for Effective Decision Making*, Wallingford, CT, Spectrum Publishing, 1995.

Stein, Robert E., *Reengineering the Manufacturing System: Applying the Theory of Constraints*, New York, Marcel Dekker, 1996.

Umble, Michael M. and Mokshagundam L. Srikanth, *Synchronous Manufacturing: Principles for World-Class Excellence*, Wallingford, CT, Spectrum Publishing, 1995.

# Index

## A

Accounting
  constraint, 46
  cost, 46, 217, 232
  throughput, 46
ADV200 Company, 321–329
  conflict, 188, 189
  constraint shift, 204
  current reality tree, 185, 186, 194, 195
  differences between ADV200 Company
      and Plant 120, 321–322
  effective exploitation of capacity, 198
  first run instructions, 325
  future reality tree, 192, 193, 196, 197,
      200
  problem, 184
  product prioritization, 199
  profile, 322–325
  running of simulation, 327
  second run instructions, 325–326
  third run instructions, 328
  verifying proposed solutions, 191
Airplane analogy, 27
All products routing, 290
Assemble-to-order, 63, 70
Assembly buffer, 105, 106, 108
AT&T, 212
ATE, see Automated test equipment
Automated test equipment (ATE), 35

## B

Batch size, impact of on bottom line of
      organization, 254
Batching Policy, 297
Bibliography, 331–332

Bill of materials (BOM), 139, 142, 161
BM, see Buffer management
BOM, see Bill of materials
Buffer(s)
  assembly, 105, 106, 108
  CCR, 106, 108, 132
  DBR, 133
  dynamic, 144
  financial, ultimate, 176
  holes in, 126, 127
  management (BM), 123, 125, 149, 176,
      see also DBR control mechanism
  shipping, 105, 107, 115, 162
    definition of, 163
    holes in, 128
  sizes, uniform, 152
  superfluous, 151
  time, 123, 146, 150, 175

## C

Capacity
  adding, 220
  CCR, 162, 239
  cutting, 220
  demand and, 29, 157
  effective exploitation of, 198
  elevation in, 241
  excess, 121, 214, 215, see also Excess
      capacity, managing
  hidden, 56
  infinite, 137
  non-productive, 209
  overload, short-term, 167
  planning, 69
  productive, 209
  protective, 91, 119, 210

**333**

# H

# I

# J

# K

# L

# M

# License Agreement for the use of the MICSS program

## *Manufacturing at Warp Speed* Workshops

Did you like this book? The message behind it emphasizes the need to simplify the complexity of manufacturing systems and yet guide management to superior decisions that generate more profits, while keeping the whole system under control.

While the messages in this book are desgined to keep it simple, changing well-rooted paradigms is not easy. Profound understanding of these messages is essential. We've done what we could to facilitate that understanding—as much as this medium will allow. However, for some people, other forms of learning are more appropriate.

The content of the book can be covered in the classroom in a 3-day concentrated workshop. The MICSS program is used extensively, and participants run it themselves, with guidance as needed from the instructors. The content itself is presented in PowerPoint graphics, followed up with interactive, open discussion to ensure understanding, then tested in the virtual environments of Plant 120 and ADV200.

Shorter workshops, either one or two dys in duration, are available for managers who need a more general understanding. Please, call or e-mail Goal Systems International for more information on *Manufacturing at Warp Speed* workshops. A detailed description of the workshops may be found at www.goalsys.com.

Goal Systems International Inc.
Gsi@goalsys.com
www.goalsys.com
(360) 565-8300
111 Hurricane View
Port Angeles, WA 98362